DEDICATION

Wendy, thank you for your continued patience, inspiration and encouragement to make our dreams become the reality we have been blessed with in life.

Thank you also to my family, both near and far, and those who have passed on, who without their love, strength and support I surely wouldn't have completed this work.

WAITING FOR DORIC

To Geraldine,

enjoy the read! :")

Waiting for Doric

One family's leap into country life

Shaun McKenna

First Edition. Formatting by Olivia McKenna. Cover design ©·2018 Olivia McKenna. Illustrations © 2018 Wendy McKenna. Bible scripture quotations are from the King James Version. All rights reserved. 'The Torry Coo' © 2018 Shaun McKenna. All rights reserved.

ISBN: 978-19-80665-30-4

CONTENTS

WAITING FOR DORIC

WAITING FOR DORIC

And God made the beast of the earth and his kind, and cattle after their kind, and every thing that creepeth upon the earth after his kind: and God saw that it was good.

Genesis 1:25

PROLOGUE

THE TORRY COO

A wee quine said to her Ma one day
"Foo's 'at doon 'ere oan the fairm?"
"It's a coo", said her Ma
"An' onybody will tell ye…she's nae ordinary coo".

"But Ma, fit why is she nae ordinary coo?"

"Well, she's a rowie eatin', reed heidit coo, fae 'Torry
A hairy crubbit al coo wi' a wint
Wi shooders as wide as Pittodrie
Be careful when ye fin' yersel' bent.

Wi ' laing jaggy horns on her heid
be sure ye dee fit yer telt
or ye may find one, up yer erky!
'an 'ats something ye 'll never want felt"

…ken fit a mean?

"Dad…Are we there yet?" For the umpteenth time that day, Jake uttered those words I just loved to hear. We'd already been on the road for around eleven hours at that point, but being the ever so patient man that I am, I once again replied, "we'll be there soon" and hoped to goodness that would keep him quiet for just a little longer.

On this occasion our sojourn was taking us far up to the top of the Isle of Skye, almost as far as you can go. When we reached our holiday cottage destination it had taken us all of 12 hours and heaven knows how, because I hate stopping for breaks on the way to anywhere. It had been an extremely long day and we were ready to make a hasty retreat to our beds, so we could wake refreshed and prepared for the adventures to begin the next day. Early the next morning, we were up and out on foot to explore the surrounding area, and find places we could go and investigate further during our holiday. One of the first things that the kids came across was 'Tubby', the little cairn terrier who lived up the lane from where we were staying. Almost every day from the first, the kids would walk up the lane to see Tubby and have a play with him. Further along our adventures that day, we stumbled across a graveyard. Now, this wasn't any run of the mill graveyard, but it just so happened to be the last resting place of Flora MacDonald. Flora remains one of Scotland's bravest heroines, who in 1746 helped to facilitate Bonnie Prince Charlie's escape to the Isle of Skye, just months after the battle of Culloden. It meant very little at all to the kids who were bored ridged with it, but to me it was truly exciting stuff. Putting all of that aside, what got my mind going most of all were the hills, which just happened to be right across the road from the cottage we were staying in. As we walked back late that afternoon, I was conjuring up a plan. Straight after we had cleared up the dishes after tea, my plan sprang into action. "Wend, why don't I take the boys out for a walk for a while to give you some peace? We won't be long." So, off we went. Sam (13yrs), Jake (11yrs), and myself, in search of adventure. Unbeknownst to me, we were going to find more than we'd bargained for. We crossed the road, and even today I can still clearly see the view in my mind's eye as I said to the boys, "there's three hills there" as I pointed. "One, two, three…Which one shall we climb?" Surprisingly enough, neither of them opted to choose the big hill, but guess who did? "No", I said. "let's go up that one!" Pointing to the larger hill of the three on the right. This particular hill was known as 'Suidh' a'Mhinn', all 1171 feet of it. So off we set, slowly trudging our way over the fields of purple heather towards the foot of the hill. As we began to get closer, we found that we had to skirt around to the left of a small lake at the base of some enormous cliffs, on the front side of the hill. They seemed to increasingly rise heavenward with every step we took towards them. When we reached the left side, we were all in fine fettle and keen to start the climb to the summit, and climb we did! We soon found that due to the hill being so steep we were basically climbing in an upright position on our hands and knees, until it began to plateau off some several hundred feet up. I can remember stopping the boys in their tracks to point out a golden eagle flying above us in the deep blue sky. 'Awesome' doesn't quite do it justice. To lay on our backs amongst the rough mounds of grass, just staring up at such a bird in its own wild habitat, is really something else. We saw it disappear downwards out of sight to our right towards the cliffs. I told the boys we would have a look to see where the eagle had disappeared off to, before we made our descent down the other side. By this point I had worked out that we were now only feet away from the top of those mammoth cliffs, the same ones which we had seen earlier, rising up before us. Silently, we crawled on our bellies commando style, you know? Like action man. We took it very slowly across the grassy hilltop, until we reached the cliff edge. Even before looking over the drop in front of us, I turned and said to the boys, "Don't you be telling your Mother about this, she'll murder me!" They both acknowledged with a knowing smile, and almost in unison there was a gasp from the three of us as we saw exactly where the eagle had disappeared off to. We peered down the hundreds of feet of rock face beneath us, and could see that she was now sitting aloft her nest, perched high up on the edge of a rocky outcrop. I'm not great with heights at the best of times but this was well worth getting the heebie-jeebies for. What a fantastic experience we were having! So much so that time got away from us a little bit. After we backed off and moved away from the edge, I could see from the stunning sunset in front of me that the sun was rapidly on its way down. We made our way across the hilltop, with me stopping the boys from time to time and shooting ahead to scout out the route ahead of us. But before we knew it, the sun had set and the lights had well and truly gone out! With total darkness around us, I began to panic and with my heart thumping out of my chest and sweating cobs, I had definitely felt better. I knew that as long as we continued to make our way down with the cliff on our right-hand side, we'd surely be fine. What felt like hours later, I began to barely make out a light in the distance. If my bearings were correct, these very lights could be the Church of Scotland chapel, just along the road from where we were staying. After several fields and fences later, we found that this was the case as we eventually reached a road with the chapel. I breathed a rather heavy sigh of relief, but knew in the back of my head that we had not yet reached our destination, so our adventures may not yet be over for the evening. We laughed and joked as we made our way north down the winding lane towards home, recalling our hilltop escapade as we walked, but things suddenly came to abrupt halt. You know what it's like. Whilst walking through the darkness, your eyes soon become accustomed to the lack of light and that was just how it was. Just as we began the final leg of our journey, we could hear off in the distance footsteps coming towards us. These weren't footsteps any of us had heard before, and whatever it was had more than two feet for sure. What made it worse was along with these footsteps came the sound of heavy, laboured breathing. As if these sounds weren't enough, out of the darkness several hundred yards away from us in the road appeared a very large lump. We stopped for a moment or two to try and figure out what was ahead of us, without much success. Without giving it a second thought, I pulled the boys in behind me and told them to hang back there unless I told them to run. If I shouted "Run!", they'd to leg it as fast as they could back along the road we had just travelled, towards the chapel. After taking a very large gulp of courage, we slowly, ever so slowly, crept forwards together taking just one fairy step at a time. This was until the picture started to become clearer. As the lump in front of us increased in size, so did the heavy breathing, which by this point had become more of a snorting sound as we moved towards it. We once more paused, and it was only at that moment that we realised just what we were facing through the light-starved darkness around us. The tell-tale signs were there for all to see, but we just had to stand and stare for a few moments, helping our eyes and brain to synchronise together. we could make out the rather large, pointy things sticking out the sides of its head. Now, I've loved Highland coo's for many a year, but this was neither the time nor the place to become better acquainted with a Highland bull. My heart once again started to race, which wasn't helped by this monsters repeated dragging of his front hoof, back and forth across the tarmac road. I hastily grabbed the boys, taking the scenic route up the hillside to our right to ensure we gave him a wide berth, and didn't wind him up any more than he already had. Standing from a safe vantage point behind him, we watched him disappear out of sight along the road. Our unforeseen encounter undoubtedly stoked a raging fire in my belly, making me even more determined that one day I'd turn my long sought after dream into a reality, and have Highland coo's of my own.

Wow! What a night we'd had. Back down the hillside, and around the bend. Before we knew it, there we were, back at the cottage...Phew! As we walked through the gates, I instructed the boys to quickly get themselves bathed and ready for bed, reminding them not to not utter a word to Mum about the finer details of our adventure. But I needn't have bothered. As we walked up the steps, before even reaching the top, the front door was flung open and I was welcomed home with what was at the time an unknown missile, which I quickly attempted to dodge. Unfortunately, Wendy is far too good a shot for her own good, even down the length of a hallway. Her dented hairbrush still today bears the scars of that evening. My ears will forever ring with those words, "Where on earth have you been till this time with my boys?!" A tale was told that night to satisfy her need to know, but only now will she know the full goings on from that eventful evening on the Isle of Skye.

1 CHILDHOOD TALES

On April 13th 1963, as my Granma Christie walked into the maternity ward of Forester Hill Hospital, Aberdeen, after first visiting the nursery, she exclaimed to my mother "Well I've got no doubt, out of all the babies in there, which is ma new grandson!". "How's that?" my Mother enquired, at which point she went on to say that the bright red glow which reflected onto the ceiling, sort of gave it away. I was almost born prematurely on three separate occasions in March of that year and in the end my Dad missed out on his tax rebate, as a result of my late arrival. This was because I was due to be born on March 21st, before the end of the tax year, but ultimately didn't show my face until April 13th. This was into the next tax year, something which it appears I've been blamed for ever since. Apparently, in the first instance I was going to be called Paul, but after not one, but both of my Granmas had turned their noses up at the name, my parents decided that Shaun was a much more fitting name for their little bundle of joy. I'm told that it took me seventeen months before I was walking, I would shuffle around on my behind to get from A to B and never actually crawled, en route to walking.

I'm assured I was a very happy child, one who made friends easily and for one reason or another, one who always got noticed, which I can only put down to my head full of ginger hair. I was an adventurous child, which has been apparent on many occasions throughout my life. I wasn't a sickly child at all, but did suffer from asthma from around six weeks old, which incidentally was diagnosed at the same time as my first 2 teeth appeared.

My first home was at 31 Victoria Road, Aberdeen (or Torry as it's known locally). We lived there, above a florist shop, until I was dragged kicking and screaming south of the border with my Dad's job in 1966. Dad was a plumber by trade and had joined the prison service down in England, rather than Scotland. North of the border the height restrictions meant he was just a little too short to get recruited. I was the second to be born into the family with one older brother, Kevin, a younger brother Christopher and a younger sister Marianne. All of us boys were born up in Aberdeen to Brian and Wilma McKenna (neè Christie). My sister wasn't born until after February 1967, when we moved south of the border, to a little place called Kirkham in Lancashire. My Dad was posted to the open prison there, and we lived in the staff quarters adjacent to the jail, called 'The Mede'.

Initially I wasn't overly keen on going to school, and recall my mother putting me onto the school bus with my big brother. After several attempts to stop me running back off, she had the driver close the door to block my escape route home, at which point I kicked the doors all the way to the school gate. When I got to school, my teacher, Mrs. J (who very soon turned out to be fantastic) wouldn't let me go home, and so I'm afraid once again I resorted to kicking her as well! I went to Strike Lane County Primary School in Freckleton, which I believe later became Hall Cross school. After the unnecessary upset of day one was over and done with, I loved my time at school. In fact, all my school years. Except I suppose, the summer of '78 when 'Ally's tartan army' failed miserably in the World Cup. That's really when I experienced playing hooky for the first time.

I learned to write, not with some boring ball pen or chunky crayon like most people, but with an italic fountain pen, which has helped my handwriting no end over the years. I was never one for being much of a reader really, and beyond Dandy, Beano, and Whizzer and Chips, I wasn't much interested really as I'd rather be out doing stuff, rather than just reading about it. I suppose that's why I was often caught daydreaming in class! I would sit and watch the pied wagtails and the magpies out on the school playground, intrigued by them and fascinated by the wildlife that was all around us. It's amazing that all these years later, we have pairs of pied wagtails living on the farm and I love to see them raising their young through the summer months.

As a young boy, I can always remember the picture we had on the living room wall and it's probably the same picture that so many other folks had on their walls too. The picture depicted a rugged mountainous landscape, with purple heather covered hills and the loch nestled down in the bottom of the glen. The shallows of the loch were lapping at the shores and most importantly, there were highland cows and their young calves grazing along those same shores, standing up to their ankles drinking from the crystal clear water around them. That picture has stuck with me for many years now, and I'm sure that seeing the cows and calves every day planted the seed for what was to come many, many years later.

I have so many very fond memories as a young boy with great friends at school. Like so many kids of that era, I would spend so much of my time outside, whether it was climbing trees, building dens, going conkering, and in some cases even getting into mischief! I remember like it was yesterday. Filling my pockets with plums, damsons, apples, and pears and eating so many that I ended up with a bad stomach ache. But that didn't stop me doing the same thing on countless occasions. I loved spending time with my brothers and friends searching for wildlife. We would look for birds' nests, hunt for frogs, toads and newts. On some occasions, my long suffering mother would have to put up with so much, due to our exploration of the wider world of nature. I remember dropping a big jar of young frogs on the kitchen floor (which smashed) and she wasn't overly bothered about the smashed glass, but all of those frogs was a different story! Over the years my mother had similar such frights on many occasions when she would stumble across a family of field mice, or baby birds all tucked up warm in my sock and undies drawer.

In the fields around where we lived there were many disused air raid shelters which we explored, finding old bullets, and all sorts of military paraphernalia. It was a haven for young boys. Some of my favourite haunts back then were Bluebell Wood; a tree we called 'Old Mother Lime', Quakers Wood, and Figure 8 Pond. I can still recall playing football for hours with my friends at school and on the footy field behind our house, but that field behind our house holds other, more harrowing memories.

A tale is told from my early childhood, when I was probably around ten years of age. I was playing a game of the day, which was titled, 'Cats got the measles'. I don't recall any of it. This game involved you standing in a circle with your legs crossed. You would then sing a rhyme whilst uncrossing and crossing your legs. There were various lyrics to the rhyme, but these are the words my brother tells me we would all sing:

'The cat's got the measles, the measles, the measles, the cat's got the measles, the measles got the cats.'

At the end of the rhyme, those who were standing with their legs uncrossed had to take off an item of footwear or clothing. Well, you see the thing is, on the day in question I happened to be out playing this game when my mother couldn't find me, and had been shouting me in for tea. So, off she went on the hunt, in the end finding me behind the garages, next to the footy field. When she found me, I didn't have a great deal of clothes on, but all of the 6 girls I had been playing the game with were almost fully dressed. What could I say? So, I was a bit of an exhibitionist. Maybe that's why I was cast in the school plays? Well, when I was really young and had no fear. My favourite role was in Snow White and the Seven Dwarves, when I was cast as 'Bashful' the dwarf. At the time I didn't appreciate this and only later realised how perfect the casting was for me... I was short in stature and would get embarrassed easily, therefore turning red at a moment's notice.

One of the highlights of my early childhood was getting my first proper bike. It was the Christmas of 1973, and so clear in my head, as that was the year that Slade released 'Merry Christmas Everybody'. I could hear it playing as I almost wore those tyres out riding around and around 'the block' on our new bikes. This 'block', which was just a small square of streets that was just the right size for us to play on. Thinking back, it always seemed the place for people young, and old, to ride their bikes. I remember my two brothers and myself rushing up from the living room to the front bedroom to stare out of the window. My mother wondered what all the noise was, as we rampaged up the stairs and so came to see what all the fuss was about. We had noticed that Mr. Gray, another prison officer who worked with my Dad, was out on his bike giving his little girl a ride round 'the block'. Nothing unusual about that, you would think. But as Mr. Gray had a hairstyle which was a bit of a comb over, we would fall into hysterics every time he came flying around the corner of the street outside our house. His hair would flap up into an upright position like a yacht sail. Oh, the stupid things we remember, eh!

As a family, we used to regularly go for days out and holidays to explore the world around us. If it wasn't the sand dunes at Lytham, it was out walking and playing footy with sheep doufers, in the trough of Bowland. If it wasn't watching the salmon leap up in Royal Deeside, it was a day out at Chester Zoo. What patience my folks must have had to put up with four bratty kids, in the back of an Austin 1100, along all those little 'A' roads for hours on end until we reached Granma and Granda's house up in Aberdeen. I don't think it took them too long to work out who the trouble makers were and to separate us for the journey. The most successful method to keep the peace in the back seat other than to play stupid games, was for my parents to play the right music on the 8 track stereo. I suppose that's where my love of music began, whilst learning and singing along to all those old songs that were played up and down the highways and byways that we travelled.

Some of my favourites included hits by Cilla Black, The Carpenters, and Johnny Cash to name but a few. My Dad used to like to travel through the night, setting off late in the evening so we would arrive bright and early the next day ready for our adventures to begin. I remember us stopping in a small border town in the dead of night. Once again somebody wanted a wee! The funny thing was that we noticed as we set off on our journey again, that on the opposite side of the road there was a shop called 'The Wee Shop', which made us all giggle for miles after, until us kids once again all nodded off to sleep.

I don't know why, but I was forever getting into bother when I was young. Nothing serious at all. I was just mischievous and more often than not, whether I was with my brothers, a couple of friends, or with a larger gang of kids, it was always the little ginger kid that got noticed. Just my luck! One of my favourite books I had as a small child and I still have today, which I remember buying from the school book club, is called 'M for mischief'. Some may say that it was just a sign of things yet to come.

I got my first job back when I was only around 9 or 10 years old, helping the 'Mothers' Pride' bread delivery man, Alf. He delivered to all the homes in the area, including the streets on 'The Mede' where we lived and also at the RAF camp down the lane. I would walk up to each door, knock and hand them their regular order. This order could consist of anything from cakes, a loaf of bread or barm cakes, (baps or bread cakes as they're called over here in Yorkshire). When I say cakes, I mean individual strawberry or mandarin tarts, meringues or egg custard tarts, you know the sort of thing. I would get paid a whole 35p each week and get a mixed box of cakes to go with it. Ooh! Even today when I smell freshly baked bread it brings it all back to me in a flash. One of my favourite parts of the job was going to those houses which ordered the big crusty loaves each evening. Why? Well, because they were wrapped in brown paper bags rather than being sealed in plastic bags. This allowed me to break off a corner of the loaf and scoff it as I walked up each of the footpaths. Do you know in the two years that I helped Alf, I didn't once get my ear clipped for doing it, but I suppose that's because I made it my job to never get caught.

Apart from my little job, something else that I used to love doing was spending time on my friend, John Mason's farm. If my memory serves me right, he lived down a little lane in Freckleton on the family's Dairy farm. I remember in the summer of 1973, spending most of the summer at his farm. We would just be doing kids' stuff, building dens in the haystacks, sunbathing on the new barn roof (which wasn't a great idea for a redhead!) I can clearly remember walking through the milking shed and drinking fresh milk straight from the enormous milk vats in there. I can still taste it now. Thinking back, I don't know what it was that I loved so much about being on his farm, but whatever it was, it's stuck with me all these years. It may have just been being around the livestock, or it could be that I just saw it all as one big adventure playground. Life was so different back then, which I know makes me sound like a right old codger, but it's true. As young ones we just had so much more freedom to just be kids. Looking back, it was clearly one of those moments in my life, like so many others, which has helped to shape my life and the lives of my family.

Unfortunately, I lost touch with John and my other friends from those early years. In April 1974 as a family, we moved from Lancashire over to Hull, in the East Riding of Yorkshire. My Dad being a prison officer, had been posted to Hull Jail. Although I do remember Maidstone down in Kent, being an option for us to move to as well. Nevertheless, East Yorkshire is where we ended up. In the months leading up to moving house, I had taken my 11+ exam to establish whether I would be going to Kirkham Grammar School like my brother Kevin, or whether Carr Hill Comprehensive was the place for me. As it happens, I never did find out if I had passed or failed, although I'm sure it will have had 'F' stamped all over it, but you never know.

2 ENTERING A WHOLE NEW WORLD

Moving to Hull was a completely different world for me, coming from a tiny rural setting into a city. I remember day one at my new school and, living on Sutton Park Estate, we attended Sutton Park Junior School, which was just up the road from us. I was almost 11 years old and the scars are still there from walking into school that first day, wearing those lovely grey shorts and long grey socks. You know the ones, with green hoops around the top. Nobody else would have even thought about wearing shorts to school, especially grey ones. I think somebody was having laugh at my expense, and I certainly got some comments and lots of sniggers. My mother has a lot to answer for! I can also remember not understanding half of what people were saying to me, and I couldn't quite decipher what names they were calling me either. It was like they were speaking a completely different language!

At 13, I moved to Sir Henry Cooper High School, the same school as Kevin my older brother. I was in fact the last of the family to attend the school, because my mother apparently wanted my younger siblings to get an education, as apparently that's something Kevin and I failed to get in our secondary schooling. I did enjoy my secondary education in the main, even if I wasn't the smartest kid in the class. I loved Art, P.E. and Geography. I can recall my first real attempt at working with clay in my art class, when I chose to make a ceramic highland cow. I still have a list of those people who dared to complement me on what they thought was a clay sheep!

I also really enjoyed going on Geography field trips, whether it was for just a day out or if I was lucky enough, a residential trip for the week. Going on such trips to Farndale and Langdale End proved to have a positive impact on my life. Probably because they were in farming country, and we the opportunity to go out walking a lot and we experienced many adventures in the great outdoors. Another reason the Farndale trip sticks in my mind, is because I suppose that's when I was first introduced to the Beatles. Mr. J. the

Maths teacher played 'Here Comes the Sun' and 'The Magical Mystery Tour' all week and when I hear those old songs today, it whisks me all the way back to the farm we stayed on, during that trip back in 1978.

I had many friends, both inside and outside of school and was always spending time with them either playing footy, bike riding, climbing trees or building dens. Sometimes after school, we would play footy all evening on Frog Hall Lane. We would keep going until the sky got totally pitch black, before heading off home. When I think about den building I remember that long hot summer of 1976 when with friends we made the best den ever! It was dug into the ground, in fact on the land where 'Paxdale' is now sited on Sutton Park. After digging the hole, which was rather large, we boarded it over and then covered the outside with turf. To the untrained eye it looked like just part of the surroundings. Thinking about it now, it looked like the neighbourhood where the Teletubbies lived. We would go snaffle tins of beans and loaves of bread from home and then meet in the den and scoff our stash of grub. We knew how to live, let me tell you!

At around 14 I got my first paper round, delivering the Hull Daily Mail to homes on Grizedale each evening. During my stint as a paper boy on Sutton Park, alongside my brother Kevin, I remember causing the paper shop manager a whole heap of grief. Rushing out of his cigarette smoke filled office all flustered, after hearing that his paperboys had gone on strike and were picketing outside the front of the shop! The story was that I was being paid less than other paperboys and was delivering at least as many, if not more papers than they were. But cutting a long story short, it was all sorted out and financially things were made right, obviously in my favour. For some reason, the manager didn't manage that shop for much longer at all.

Some people may tell you different, but other than a few hiccups I wasn't the worst whilst growing up. I only ever had mischievous fun. One of our money making schemes involved collecting pop bottles, knowing that if they were returned to an off licence, you would get money back on each one of them. So, on a nice dark evening we would acquire lots of these bottles from peoples' doorsteps and then do the neighbourly thing and return them to Goldfinch Wines off licence on Grandale, to then receive lots of ready cash. We would then wait half an hour, to give Reg, the manager time to stack them all in the crates out the back and then we would scale the back gate and collect a bunch of the same bottles again to repeat the process all over again. I wasn't a bad lad really, honest!

I can remember it like it was yesterday and it's crazy to think that over 36 years have gone by since 2 September 1980. To most the date means nothing, but to me that was the day my world changed. This was the day, or to be exact, the evening, that I first spoke to the girl I was destined to spend my life with, Wendy Anne Thatcher. Although it was the first time I had been introduced to her, I had been watching her from afar for probably 18 months.

I wasn't stalking her, but rather I was just a little obsessed with her, in a healthy way of course. You see back then I was the shy ginger 17 year old who struggled to talk to the girls. Although others may disagree with that. It was a whole new world for me, this girl-chasing lark, if I'm honest I didn't have a clue what I was doing.

When I think back, I suppose it wasn't all girls who I got tongue tied around, but only when I thought they were out of my league. That's when the embarrassment kicked in. I can still feel the embarrassment rising up through my body as I slowly turned a vivid crimson colour whenever I spoke to her. That's why all those years earlier, Bashful was such a fitting role for me in the school play.

Although we both lived at different ends of Yorkshire, Wendy living in York and me in Hull, we both mixed in the same circles through our church. On the night in question we had attended a youth dance in Beverley. Many of my friends would talk to Wendy without any problem, but they didn't see her the way I did. It was like that hit song back in the day. I thought that she was 'Too nice to talk to', so that night I conjured up a plan to have a friend talk to her on my behalf, and give her the heads up that I wanted to get to know her. What happened next, took me completely by surprise. She immediately marched up to me and said "I hear you want to talk", which I now know is Wendy all over. That completely threw me and if I didn't know what to say before she arrived, I certainly didn't know what to say after she sat down. Now being aware that she was training to be a hairdresser, I pulled out one of my best chat up lines. "When my hair grows, will you cut it?" Agreed, it's not one of those run-of-the-mill conventional chat up lines, but whatever the case, it worked well enough to get her interested. Before long, she had fallen under my spell… I wish! I can remember asking her for a dance and of course she said yes, clearly she must have been watching my moves herself. For the next few months we would catch up at youth activities and spoke regularly by telephone (that's if she could get her Dads lock off the house phone). Thinking back, I did have my favourite phone boxes I used to frequent, those that were on a good running route, and of course those that didn't whiff quite as bad as others.

Although we had been speaking since the September, our first proper date didn't happen until December. Just before Christmas I was staying at my friend Gary's house for a few days. Wendy and I had planned a night out whilst I was in York. The plan was that I would meet Wendy's parents Valerie and Neville, under the clock at the front of Marks and Spencers, in York City Centre at 5:00pm sharp. I left my friend's house in Holgate, giving myself plenty of time to get there. I can remember rushing through the crowds on Coney Street, fretting that I was going to be late. I was always one for making a good first impression. As I turned the corner to walk across Parliament Street, it was almost 5pm and I was sweating cobs. It's just as well that I had 'borrowed' lashings of my brother Kevin's expensive Aramis aftershave to ensure that I smelled the part, if nothing else. In reality I may have overdone it on the smelly stuff stakes, but never mind.

As planned, Wendy's parents were there on time and so before long we were on our way to their home. If seeing Wendy wasn't exciting enough, there was a second reason to be excited too. I'd never had a ride in an electric green Lada before, what a treat! Wendy had been at work that day, which was why I was meeting her back at her parents' house. When we arrived at their home, Wendy had just got in from work and was already well on with getting ready for our first date. I can remember sitting nervously on the green velour sofa, the one with the orange cushions. As I awaited her appearance, I remember being serenaded by Donna Summer's 'On the Radio' from the bedroom. Wendy had the record player turned up loud! I was just starting to get a little fidgety when the lounge door opened. I thought "great, we're ready to go!" But no, that wasn't the case. It was then, just for a moment that I thought that I had been transported onto the set of 'Sale of the Century'. Wendy's mother walked in with her hostess trolley, with its squeaky wheels laden down with more salad than I'd ever seen in my life. Val later told Wendy that she thought I didn't eat enough to fill a sparrow, although I didn't think I did too badly.

After wading through what seemed like half a well-stocked Sainsbury's produce aisle, we got off to the pictures. We went to see the latest blockbuster, 'Flash Gordon' and all went very well. I can't remember too much about the night, other than that Wendy paid us into the Odeon. At the time, I was still attending sixth form and was only earning money from writing out the morning paper rounds as well as my own regular evening round on Stornaway Square, six days a week. What I'm really saying, is that I wasn't overloaded with cash around that time and Wendy did most of the paying out. She was making good money hairdressing, and got lots of tips from many of the lovely old dears she looked after in the salon. Any money I did have was spent on bus or train fares over the next few years, travelling between Hull and York, which continued for most of the way through our courting days. I have tried to make amends over the past thirty whatever years though.

I stayed on in the sixth form at school and alongside undertaking my Art A-level, I re-sat my Maths O level and took Metalwork. I had been awarded a grade D in my Maths exam and those people in the know felt that I could have done better. In the end I actually re-took the exam not once, but twice, achieving an E and a U (Ungraded) in my final attempt. That was when I thought it best to leave the Maths alone and never venture into the world of accountancy. On leaving school I was successful in gaining a place on a YTS (Youth Training Scheme), with Hull City Council. I worked with a number of other young people and over time we painted murals, including one which was along the bank of Barmston Drain, on Northumberland Avenue in Hull. We also spent time travelling around the handicapped day centres, working with people to create mosaic pictures. These were all pieced together to form one enormous mosaic, which may still be viewed today on the wall of the first floor in the Central library, in Hull City Centre.

On 7th July 1984, Wendy and I were married at our church in York. Afterwards, we had an evening bash at an unusual venue in Hull, but one which is steeped in local history, 'The Welly Club' on Wellington Lane. So began our life together, living in our 2 up 2 down in Sutton-on-Hull. Our introduction to married life didn't get off to the best of starts, thankfully not through any of our doing. Only a few nights before the big day, a gentleman (after having had a few too many shandies), decided to park his purple Ford Cortina in the front wall of our treasured little terraced house on Leads Road. So for the few nights leading up to our wedding day I slept in the front room of the house, until the insurance company could get the work carried out. I do recall just nodding off to sleep, on one of those evenings when two old ladies, on their way back from 'The Ship' in the village, stood outside the front of the house and started discussing what they thought had happened to the house front. Whilst peering in through the gaps in the makeshift boarding they must have got the shock of their lives when they saw that cocoon like sleeping bag move, and they realised there was someone inside. They soon scuttled off down the road.

The work to put our home right was completed whilst we were away on our honeymoon. It was at this point that I whisked Wendy away for the trip of a lifetime. Well, ok. So it wasn't, but it was certainly memorable! My Grandma, straight after our wedding, flew out to Canada on holiday. This meant that her home in Edinburgh was empty, and it was cheap too. So guess where we went to party for a couple of weeks? What I hadn't thought about in preparing for our honeymoon, was what it would be like staying in sheltered accommodation. Every day we were stopped by many of the pension-aged residents for a chat, and we were even invited to go and play Beetle or Bingo in the Day Room. It wasn't surprising that we had a busy schedule planned, so weren't able to take up any of the offers, but were grateful for them all the same.

The funniest moment of our stay in Edinburgh was during our first night at my Granma's place. We had been out seeing the sights, and got back to where we were staying. After Wendy's bath she got tucked up in bed to watch the TV. It was then my turn for a bath and whilst I was in there it had got a bit steamy, so I turned the fan on to clear the steam. The problem was that the cord I pulled wasn't controlling any sort of fan at all, but was actually the emergency cord. Unbeknown to me, by pulling the cord, contact was made with the warden on duty, who looked after the sheltered accommodation. So as you can imagine, Wendy got the shock of her life when the voice of the warden started booming out of the speaker in the wall. "Are y'all right hen? Hiv ya fallen?" We assured the warden that nobody was in trouble and her assistance was not required. You can take it as read that the cord wasn't pulled again, and we've had a lot of laughs about that incident ever since. Wendy has said from that day to this, that all too often I have put her in situations like that over the years. I can't understand at all what she means, although for one reason or another, I have tended to court calamity with increased regularly throughout my life.

At the time we got married, I was selling cars at Crystal, the Ford dealer on Holderness Road in Hull, which was my introduction to the world of sales. I did in fact go on to thrive in this world for the next 19 years or so. My time selling cars was a little short-lived, as myself and a couple of other staff were unexpectedly (and harshly I might add) made redundant, just a couple of months after our big day. On leaving, the Sales Controller told me that he thought I was just too nice to be selling cars, but I still put it down to the economic climate at the time. One of the best bits of business I did whilst at Crystal, was getting my Dad fitted up with a new set of wheels. As part of the deal he needed to trade in his pride and joy, an automatic, purple Austin Allegro. In return he was able to drive away in a sandy beige Ford Capri. My thinking was that if 'The Professionals' drove a Capri, then that was good enough for me Dad. The only improvement on that would have been for Dad to drive away in a 'Gran Torino', like the car on 'Starsky and Hutch'. Apart from the deal he got, it was a car that suited him so much more to be driving around in. The Allegro did have a lot of history behind it. One of its best features being a dodgy door handle, which meant that we often had to do a 'Dukes of Hazard' style entrance to get into the driver's seat. This was always good fun, even if we got a few raised eyebrows in the process. I'll tell you what though, if I tried from now till next Christmas, I wouldn't be able to get in the window that way now.

After having the first of a number of miscarriages, Wendy was once again pregnant and like most of them it wasn't plain sailing at all. It was around that time that I really started to appreciate how important my role as a husband was, and how I should be far more supportive. I suppose my understanding increased after an incident in the Gateway supermarket at Bransholme Centre, as it was called then. As we wandered around the store doing our shopping, Wendy got a little dizzy and light-headed. I told her she would be fine, but she insisted that she was going to fall over. "Don't be daft, just hang on to the shelf, you'll be fine". Well, before I knew it down she went, all over the floor of the condiments aisle. I couldn't believe it. She was festooned in Oxos and other such stock cubes, amidst a pool of water. Well, I thought it was water! The staff were scurrying around her like bees round a honey pot and they like us, thought that due to being late on in her pregnancy, her waters had broken. So an ambulance was called, and after a little trip to the hospital with full flashing lights along the way, it was established that her waters were all intact and baby was fine. So, if her waters were all in one piece this could only mean one thing, and that was that she had in fact had a little accident in the condiments aisle. I told her not to worry about it and it was all fine, but she wouldn't have it. From then on in we shopped in Asda or Aldi for the rest of our years in Hull.

The summer of 1985 was when our whole world was turned upside down, when the first of our children, Holly Louise was born. After a few false starts, she was born in July almost 6 weeks early, weighing in at only 4lbs 5oz. Due to her being premature, she spent some weeks in the Special Care Unit at the Hedon Road Maternity Hospital, which was where all but one of our children were born.

We visited her every day, with Wendy staying overnight on many occasions. It had really paid off getting my Dad into a nicer car a few months earlier, as Wendy and I needed to make frequent visits to the hospital to see our little bundle of joy, and guess which car we cadged in order to get there? We could even listen to Lionel Ritchie on the tape player too, now that was a bonus. This parenting lark took a little time for us to get used to, with our complete lack of experience being reflected on a regular basis. Just one example of this was when Wendy and her mother were going out shopping for the day. I was out grafting in whatever job I had at the time while they were standing at the bus stop awaiting the number 10 bus to town. After only ten minutes chatting on, did they realise between them that our newborn was still perched between the cushions on the sofa in our front room. Luckily, the bus stop was across the road from our little terraced house, so only moments later it was all sorted out.

Over the next fourteen years we had our other five children. Next was Sam, well Samuel Jason actually. He was born in September 1987 and was our biggest bairn, weighing in at 8lbs 7oz. For almost 3 weeks he was without a name, as we just couldn't decide. When it came down to it, he was nearly a Barney, but my choices never won the day with any of the kids. Sam had a right head of hair and every bit of it was bright ginger. As it happens, it's turned out that Sam, other than me, is the only other one in the family to have ginger hair.

Next to arrive was Jake Lucas. He was due to be born on the Tuesday, but labour slipped over into a Wednesday in November 1989. Jake and Sam, being the only boys in the family, tended to stick together from very early on. Sam was always keen to look after his little brother, but in reality, Jake didn't need a lot of looking after by his siblings. He could always stick up for himself as well as his brothers and sisters. This protective nature has been known to spill over in his teenage years. One example of this being when one lunchtime, he marched into the brimming full staff room at their secondary school, to highlight to a particular PE teacher exactly the error of her ways.

She had unwittingly given a detention to his little sister and that was just not on at all.

A couple of years went by, and in February 1992 Olivia Emily Grace was the next to join the clan. I recall that Wendy went into labour at home during Emmerdale, and after driving with some haste down to the hospital, found that the labour wards had all been refurbished since we were last in there. Whilst going through all that pain and discomfort, Wendy was able to listen to music to help things along. I can remember that the two songs which played during the final stages of the birth were, 'I'd really love to see you tonight' by England Dan and John Ford Coley, and 'I'm doing fine now, without you baby' by The Pasadenas. It's funny how I can still remember them all these years later.

Next to turn up was Evie Catherine Mary, and she was born in November 1994. That evening my parents called and said they were bringing a bucket load of KFC over for tea. I can still see it in front of me now. Feeling uncomfortable, Wendy was sitting cross-legged on the bed. We were just about to start to tuck into the grub when pop, her waters went! Within minutes, we were once again tearing down that little lane to the maternity hospital. I've always loved a nice bucket of KFC too!

Naomi, is the baby of our family. Unlike with the other kids, who were a couple of years apart, there is a five year gap between her and Evie. Naomi was born in June 1999 and I can remember it like it was yesterday. Only weeks before she was born, I took Sam and Jake with some friends over to Manchester to see our team, Manchester United. They were parading through the centre of Manchester, after winning the treble that year. I had fears as Wendy's due date got nearer and United kept winning things, that we weren't going to make that trip. Thankfully, it all worked out in the end. From day one, all of her big brothers and sisters spoiled Naomi, taking turns to look after her. I'm sure that all the confidence she now shows is in no small part due to the influence of her siblings.

During our younger days, I tested out a number of jobs with various companies. All sales jobs, because I thought that was where my skills lay. These jobs included selling photocopiers, computers, drinks machines, and cable TV. None of which was ever going to be my long-term career, but I definitely learned a great deal along the way, and in some cases I just stumbled over the lessons I was learning. I do recall arranging to meet with my boss Paul, whilst working for Rediffusion. I was out selling Sky TV in its infancy, knocking door to door to members of the public, in their homes. One of the stipulations to get the job was that I was required to have my own transport. Well, that's fine. There's no problem with that, I thought. Some months after starting with the company, my boss arranged to meet me out on the job. He wanted to work with me for the morning to see how I was getting on. I waited for ages in the cold for him Just freezing my doo-daas off. He just didn't show up, so I just got on with my job. In fact he had shown up, but just couldn't find me. As a result of not getting hold of me, he then drove across Hull to my home. It was before the days of the mobile phone and he wanted to see if there had been a problem. He spoke to Wendy and was informed that yes, Shaun had set out that morning to meet him at the agreed place at 10:00am, and that was all she could tell him. "What kind of car does he drive, and what colour is it?" My boss enquired. "Well, it's red and a bit rusty", was her first response. "Well, what kind of car?" He repeated. Wendy replied, "Well it's between a bike and a car, I suppose. If it had four wheels, it would be a car. But as it's got two, I suppose we'd have to call it a bike". "What do you mean? So he doesn't have a car?" My boss exclaimed. "Well, he goes to work on my fold up bike every day and just uses that to get about!" Nobody ever mentioned to me that I needed a car, just transport. I was able to get to wherever I needed to around Hull, even in my suit, tie and neatly pressed white shirt. I'd just perch my briefcase on the handle bars and off I went. It wasn't long before I left that chapter of my employment and set off in search of bigger and better things.

7th April 1986 was when I got my first big break in the world of work and heck, I was so excited. That was when I started working as a sales representative for 'Cow & Gate' babyfoods. Initially I covered a territory across Yorkshire, selling babyfood to chemists. Over the next fifteen years, in one way or another, I covered most of the north of England and Scotland. I can still remember the excitement as I was driving home with my first real company car, a dark blue Vauxhall Astra. I previously had what 'Crystal' termed company cars a couple of years earlier, but I would never have any one of those cars for more than a few days. In fact, because I wouldn't want to put much petrol into them as they would disappear elsewhere so quickly, I did run out of petrol 14 times in the 7 months I was in the job. The most embarrassing of those instances was whilst waiting for people to cross the road at the zebra crossing, outside the 'Hull Daily Mail' offices on Jameson Street in Hull. What a nightmare that was! Anyway, after 15 years selling baby food with the company it was time for a change. If I'm honest, I was getting fed up of trekking down to the head office in Wiltshire so often. It had started to become a bind, and it meant that I was staying away from home too often, especially with a growing young family. Thankfully it wasn't long before I found the right move, which was into a Regional Manager's position with a pharmaceutical Company, 'Pharmacia'. My role was again a field based position, regularly making trips down to the UK Head Office, in Milton Keynes (I'd never seen so many roundabouts in my life). As a company, they were enormous and trading all over the world. It was my job to run a sales team which again covered the north of England and Scotland. Still now I know my way around our nation, and that's mostly due to all those pharmacies I came across over the many years that I was on the road. It has definitely come in handy many times since.

In 1996, it was time for a move and with work I wasn't in a position where I was tied to any particular town, so we moved from Hull to York. Although we had thought about it previously, financially we were never in a position to do much about that thought, other than think it. It was certainly a struggle initially, but in time it proved to have been the right move for us to take.

During the first twenty plus years we were married, we didn't have a great deal of money at all. Not that it was ever a problem, with Wendy keeping a tight hold of those purse strings. We never missed a mortgage payment, and never spent beyond our means. In fact, it took 22 years before we went on our first foreign holiday. We decided to take the kids to Tunisia, all inclusive. In hindsight, although it was an experience which we laugh about now, it was a bit of a nightmare. We chose more wisely the next time, that was for sure.

Up to the point of us venturing out on our first foreign excursion, we had always taken our family to stay in a cottage or lodge, out in the countryside somewhere. I suppose that's where we felt most comfortable. We visited Cornwall, Wales, The Lakes, and The Dales, but more often than not we would find ourselves up in the highlands of Scotland. We once stumbled across the advertising of cottages in the back few pages of 'The Scots Magazine' or 'The Dalesman'. It was either fate or just plain good luck that we did come across those pages, because for a decade and more we tapped into the hidden gems advertised within them. What was always comforting about booking through these magazine pages was that if Mrs. McGregor was fully booked up for the week, then she would put us in touch with her friend Mrs. McGroogy down the road, who also had holiday accommodation. It happened like that so many times over the years. It's funny, because more often than not we would find ourselves out in the middle of nowhere, with not a lot to do except walk and very few places to spend money. This just so happened to be the way we liked it.

We would always make it a habit during our days out adventuring to find a village bakery near to wherever we were staying, so that we could drop in and buy everyone a 'fine piece' (a cake or at least something nice to eat). We always had a great time. Building dams in streams, climbing hills and trees, searching for wildlife and fossils, exploring countless rock pools, getting soaked to the skin, and in some cases even getting the odd midge bite or two. I think it's worthwhile noting at this point, that recently whilst looking through old photos, over the many years we dragged the kids all over the British Isles there was one little pair of red wellies, that made most of those trips with us. They were handed down all the way from Holly to Naomi and there's a fourteen year gap between them. Now that's value for money! Cheesy as it may sound, more than anything, our holidays were a chance for us to spend good quality time together. This is something even now in hindsight, I wish we had done so much more of. When I look back at what we got up to back then, when the kids were young, it reminds me just how much some of them would moan about what we were doing. Whether it was walking those supposed endless miles, or just spending time in the great outdoors in all the inclement weather that Britain chose to throw our way. But you know, here's the surprising thing. Now that they've all grown up, it appears that we get a completely different picture altogether. They all love to get out there on their own adventures now, either with each other or with their own families. Who'd have thought, eh?

In 2002, I had been working for Pharmacia for over two years and life was sweet. I was working for a great company, was really well paid, worked with some lovely people, and things were going so well. Then it came like a bolt out of the blue. The company was merging with Pfizer, who again were a major international drug company. How was that going to impact on me and my family? In a nutshell, operations were moving south from Milton Keynes into Hampshire and if I was staying with the company, that's where I would need to move. Cutting a long story short, we decided to just take the redundancy package on offer and go to seek our fortune elsewhere. It was obviously an uncertain time for the family and even though the package I walked away with was very good, I was still out of work and needed employment quickly!

As it happened a friend of mine, Kent, had heard that I was on the hunt and contacted me to ask what my plans were. He was senior management working for a training provider. He worked with unemployed people, with a view to placing them into full-time employment, and this was all on behalf of the government. The business he worked for was creating a National Sales Manager role, and enquired as to whether I would be interested in having a chat about such an opportunity. Cutting to the chase, I started with the company a few weeks later. As it happened, my time in the business was short as only 7 months later myself, Kent, and his brother-in-law James, all jumped ship, in order to set up a new company. After much discussion we called the business 'Inspire 2 Independence', but from almost day one we referred to it as i2i. Whilst we were still setting the new business up, another of Kent's brothers-in-law, Matthew, also joined us. Wendy and I had never even thought about setting up our own business ahead of this opportunity, but when you are taking risks with others around you, it definitely softens the blow. The new business set out to work in the same field as our previous employer, that of the welfare to work industry. But as we had no office, no contracts, and no cashflow, we needed to find work quickly. At the time, people had concerns that we were doing the wrong thing in setting up, that we were very senior management heavy, with 4 owner Directors and no staff. But we were motivated, keen, and determined to forge our own path in business.

When I think back to the summer of 2004, in the sweatbox we called an office at the Innovation Centre at York University, we would brainstorm daily, seeking ideas as to how and where we could tap into any available funding to set the ball rolling, and achieve our first contract as i2i. As luck happens, we were awarded our first contract across in Stockport, Greater Manchester, late in 2004. I know it wasn't on our doorstep, but hey you can't have everything, can you? After all the initial set-up of the contract, myself, Kent, and James travelled across the M62 most days to our office. It was in the middle of town, opposite the Stockport job centre. We'd deliver the programs to those unemployed people, who were being referred onto our program. For someone who had never delivered such courses before, working with individuals who had been out of work for long periods of time and in the main were not overly keen to either attend our courses each day, or be bothered about getting a job at all. It was quite an eye opener I can tell you. But there were always those who had been through a tough time and needed support, guidance, and lots of encouragement to help them to draw closer to fulfilling their own potential.

One such man we'll call Albert. Now, Albert's life in the previous few years had been quite a rollercoaster, and had been thrown into turmoil as he had got in with the wrong crowd. He subsequently got involved with drugs, and as a result was arrested, lost his job, and been put on remand until his trial. This went on for a couple of years until ultimately his case was thrown out of court. In the meantime, his life had been ruined. Soon after his release from Strangeways prison, his wife had become very ill and so he had been caring for her 24/7 until her untimely death, shortly before we met him.

The story doesn't end there though, as only days before he started on our program, one of Albert's daughters had been involved in a car accident, With no seatbelt being worn, she went through the car windscreen and was now in hospital in intensive care. When we first met Albert, his life was all over the place. He was very keen to get into work and establish some stability at home for his daughters, but due to having a criminal record, he saw no working future for himself. To see how that man's life changed after being given the right support and guidance, really made a mark on me. It confirmed to me that the decision to move into this industry, and in fact to set up the business, had been the right move after all.

Over almost the next ten years, many lives were changed for the good through the efforts of the business and the fantastic staff we employed. Things went from strength to strength, up to a point where we had 14 offices across the north of England, a central head office based in York, and 358 staff working hard. So, why after almost a decade was it time to make a move on to pastures new?

3 YOU MUST BE MAD

If we go back a little bit into spring 2011, Wendy's health wasn't at all where it should have been. She had visited the doctor on a number of occasions, but things didn't appear to be getting any better at all. After once again feeling quite unwell, she had made another appointment and visited the local doctor's surgery, after which she explained that the doctor was running yet more blood tests and was to wait for the results. After only couple of days, Wendy got a call requesting her to go to the surgery. We thought nothing of it, as this had happened before, and so on attending the appointment, I sat and waited for her outside. A little while later, she came out of the surgery and headed straight for the exit and out to the car. What we hadn't been made aware of, is that as part of the blood tests which were carried out, a CA125 test was carried out. Now I wouldn't know a CA125 from any other test, but it is used to look for the early signs of ovarian cancer in high-risk patients. The GP had told Wendy that she believed that she did in fact have cancer, and she would be called into hospital within 24 to 48 hours. We won't go into the gory details, but over a number of weeks Wendy was in and out of hospital. After surgery, she went through lengthy outpatient treatment with the end result being that she was given the all clear. Her consultant said she should go on and live her life to the full.

All that which had been experienced during the spring of 2012, as you may well expect, did have a lasting impact on Wendy, myself, and the rest of our family. I believe that may well have been the starting point that set both of our minds considering our long-term future, and how we saw it panning out in the coming years. Were we really making the most of life, and doing what we could to make our dreams come true? What sacrifices were we willing to make in order to fully appreciate the good health we both now had? Had we put ourselves into a position where we were just chasing money, which would never bring us real happiness or fulfilment?

We would often speak about what we wanted to do with our lives as we got older, but why would it have to be when we were older? I often felt that there would come a time when there would be a shift and it would be Wendy's time to shine, and for her to work her magic and live some of those dreams she had. For many years she had spoken at length about opening a teashop, or a little shop selling vintage clothes, gifts, and home-made crafts. You know the sort of thing I'm talking about, with lots of bunting draped around the place and looking so very quaint. If I'm honest, I felt bad that I was not able to get things sorted, so that she could chase that dream much earlier. But maybe now was her time. Wendy was and is a fantastic Mother to our six children, but as we were fast heading towards 30 years of marriage, maybe it was long enough for her to wait to go in search of her dreams?

Throughout those years, she and I had spoken about many dreams. These were so often scuppered, due to financial constraints or just bad timing. But now things were different, and as a family we found ourselves in a very blessed position. Yes, we had worked hard and had taken many risks to get to where we were, and many folk had commented that they would love to be in our position of owning a business. Life had changed for us, and we found ourselves in a position which opened up so many avenues which had never been available to us in the past. In spring 2012 we were lucky enough to travel to Melbourne, Australia for 5 weeks and to spend time with my brother Kevin, his wife Chantal, and their 3 boys, who treated us like royalty. Later that same year we were able to fly to America and tour down the Pacific Highway, between San Francisco and Long Beach for more than a month, which was beautiful too. But whilst in America, a further seed was planted. We witnessed much of what money could buy, with people and their expensive cars, boats, and the many other trappings which the world sees as part and parcel of a successful life. We also witnessed those who had nothing but the clothes on their backs. I took a photograph as a reminder to me of an unfortunate soul who was sleeping rough immediately outside the hotel we were staying in. It got me thinking, was what we had in our life really making us happy? If we could, how would we change things moving forward and just how could we simplify things?

We regularly spoke late into the night about all sorts of things, including buying a home with some land to grow our own vegetables. As mad as it would seem, we also laughed about getting some livestock and working towards becoming more self-sufficient. We wanted to create a small business where Wendy could sell homemade items, both food and other things, and for me to set up a photography gallery and arrange guided walks around the Wolds. I suppose the real stumbling block to all of that becoming a reality was that business at i2i was going so well, and building on the success which had been generated over the previous ten years. It would always be difficult to move away from that, and if we were to move on, what would we do financially to support ourselves and our family? In reality, the only obstacle to change was ourselves, and being brave enough to take that leap when the time was right.

In early summer 2013 myself, along with the other three owners of i2i, arranged to meet up for a walk on the Yorkshire Wolds. I took them to one of our regular haunts at Wayrhamdale, and after walking for a few miles we sat on the side of one of the beautiful valleys to discuss the future plans for the business. After much discussion, we all committed to plough on and to take things to an even higher level over the coming years.

Some weeks after this, Wendy and I were out wandering on those same Wolds. As I recall it, we were walking around 9 miles so not so long at all really. Starting in Thixendale, we followed the Yorkshire Wolds Way route until we reached the deserted medieval village of Wharram Percy. After stopping for lunch, we then took a right turn off the Wolds Way route, continuing along the Wold tops towards Burdale, and latterly looping back round into Thixendale. What was so significant about the walk on that day was that as we walked and talked along field after field, across the tops and without thinking, between us we had eliminated all excuses or obstacles we could think of which could possibly stop us from taking that leap to move out into the country to live our dream. That's when things started to get really scary. I was unsure as to how my business partners, who were not only business colleagues, but our friends whom I had known for many years outside of work, were going to react to the news that I was planning to leave the business.

It didn't take long to find out how they were going to react, as a few days later when we were all in the office, I sat them down and explained our situation to them. They had been aware that our long-term plan was to move out into the country, and for Wendy to have some other business interests. But it was clearly a bombshell. What made the situation a whole lot more uncomfortable, was the fact that only weeks earlier I had committed my future to the business plans we had discussed. Cutting to the chase, the news was taken very well. Over the coming weeks all the nitty gritty was sorted out, which would enable me to leave knowing that all was left in very capable hands after my departure. They obviously thought we were crackers and told me so on a regular basis. They thought that somewhere along the way we had lost our minds. "You must be mad!" Was uttered many times during those weeks after breaking the news. Why would we leave a thriving, very well-paid business (in fact a business which has been a massive part of your life for the last decade), to take a running jump into the unknown, to do all that we had spoken of? Almost every day in the weeks following my decision to leave, I was encouraged by the rascals I worked with to stay. That continued all the way through until my final day with the company. Financially, we believed that we were where we needed to be to do what we wanted to do, and we had learned over the previous couple of years that money clearly wasn't everything. We believed that if we didn't take hold of this wonderful opportunity we had in front of us and learn to make the most of the skills and resources we had to hand, we would forever regret the missed opportunity. That wasn't a place I ever wanted to be, whatever the outcome of our adventure in the long run.

Oh, but hang on. There was a problem…We can't move anywhere if we haven't sold our house! At the time, we lived in a beautifully renovated old schoolhouse in Strensall, York. We had been trying to sell our house for over a year, and so the pressure was on to find a buyer. Have you ever had one of those times when you're a little unsure as to whether you are making the right decision or not, and then one by one things start falling into place? As sure as I'm sitting here, that's exactly what started to happen. All of a sudden we started to get viewings on our home. These were people who didn't have a purchase chain and were cash buyers. It was a crazy time! In the end we accepted the full valuation offer from a gentleman and his family who were moving back to the village from abroad. Suddenly everything started to come together.

With everything suddenly on the move we thought it might be wise to get ourselves out there, and start looking at a few houses. Up to that point we had been looking at properties north of York, in areas like Hovingham and Helmsley, but nothing had ticked enough boxes or hadn't felt right. I can remember that I had shown Wendy the details of a lovely property in East Yorkshire, and at the time I wasn't too sure exactly where it was located on the map. We decided against it in the end, because as nice as it was, Wendy was keen not to just go for a big posh house in the country. The property I showed her had lovely manicured lawns around it, which had put her off. With the pressure mounting, I arranged for us to view a property out near Everingham, again in East Riding. After looking around the property, we felt that it didn't have sufficient land attached to it for us to develop things the way we wanted to. So, now what?

There we were on a chilly Thursday afternoon in October, with nowhere left to go. That's when, from down the side of my driver's seat I pulled out the details of that property at 'Long Meadow Farm'. We had previously disregarded the property because it had those beautifully manicured lawns. I was sure it was somewhere in this same area, so we had a wander. Lo and behold, we found it! After craning our necks driving past a couple of times, we were intrigued to have a bit more of a look, so I called the agent who initially said that we wouldn't be able to view at such short notice. I pressed the point a little and she agreed to call the vendor. A few moments later she called back and said that the owner would show us around in an hour. We made a hasty exit to Pocklington, a few miles down the road and waited for the clock to strike 4, when we could return for a proper skeg.

4pm came around quickly, and we were welcomed by the lady owner. As it was now getting dark, she showed us around the land outside and explained the full extent of the plot, which reached up to 40 acres. We then viewed inside the house itself, but in total we couldn't have been on site longer than around 25 minutes, and most of that time was outside. Although we were offered opportunities to return for further viewings, we never returned until the day we moved in. How mad is that?!

What's also funny is that the two oldest of our three girls who were still living at home, didn't see the house, other than pictures, until the day we moved in. If I'm honest, I was keen from the start and Wendy didn't need much persuading at all. She could see the potential, which was very apparent on the site. Within days, we had our offer accepted and an agreement for us to purchase only 8 acres and not the full 40, as had been advertised. Yet more wheels were now turning towards our fast approaching leap into the unknown, and things were getting really exciting now.

With so much happening, I took Wendy away to the Lakes for a long weekend. It was one of our treats and we would normally try to visit in the spring, and again in September or October. We liked to marvel at the autumn colours, which are in such abundance up there. Whilst we were sitting in the hotel lounge one evening, we decided that we should come up with a business name for our new venture and so we started brainstorming ideas. We can't have come up with many earth-shattering suggestions at the time, because other than 'The Ginger Cow Company', I can't remember any of our other ideas. Both Wendy and I have loved Highland Cattle for many years. I suppose coming across so many as we dragged the kids around the Highlands for years, must've had an influence. I am both a Scot and ginger, so that also assisted us in making the decision to go down the Ginger Cow route. We slept on the name for a couple of nights and subsequently we both felt that it fitted with our future plans, as well as being a name which was memorable. If things went the way we hoped they would, we would hopefully get a few Highlands ourselves too.

Our trip to the Lakes was memorable for another reason also. Up to this point we had two border terriers in the family, Scout and Elsa. But for the women-folk I live with, that wasn't enough and I was regularly hounded that we should add another one to the clan. I'd consistently said no, but in a moment of weakness as I sat in the hotel lounge on our first night away, I took it upon myself to trawl the interweb to maybe find a new addition to the family. I must at this point explain that I wasn't being totally anti-social sitting on the internet. Wendy had gone to get herself ready as we were going out for a meal, and of course I would take all of two minutes to get myself sorted. With the wonders of the web, I found just what I was looking for.

After having a great couple of days away, we took a little detour via Durham to pick up our new puppy. Needless to say, when we arrived home and the squeals of delight had subsided, I found myself in an unusual place, in the good books! Well, at least for a few days anyway! The new little lady was named 'Boo', which wasn't my choice. But then again, it's rarely going to be my choice, is it?

Time was moving on and things were being wound down at work, ahead of my impending departure. Lots of decisions were being made regarding who would be taking care of those business areas for which I had been responsible, like HR, physical resources, IT, phones, along with our fourteen offices plus Head Office. The biggest decision I found myself making, was whether I should take with me my limited edition Range Rover Sport. With its red leather seats, and its own heated steering wheel and TV, was I moving on to an even nicer set of wheels instead? I obviously plumped for the nicer set of wheels, and a much more fitting vehicle too, under the circumstances. A lovely fifteen year old Landrover Defender, only just been run in with 130,000 miles on the clock! I can still see it now, with me driving back along the M1 from West Yorkshire, after picking it up. Windows down, and the country tunes blaring out. This was a much more fitting jalopy for a soon to-be-country lad, than the car with all the bells and whistles I was leaving behind. Besides, I was going to be far too busy to be sitting in the car watching TV, and if I needed a heated steering wheel to keep my hands warm then I was surely going to struggle in the new life we were about to embark on.

Not long before the big move came along, I had made arrangements to surprise Wendy. I arranged for her to speak to one of her heroines. For more than a year up to that point, Wendy had been watching a TV programme online, which she had stumbled across one evening. The show was called, 'Christine's Garden' and featured horticulturalist Christine Walkden. With all the goings on during the last year, Wendy would often seek something to help her to relax and to take her mind off any worries or concerns she had. Well, 'Christine's Garden' did the trick, every single time. We tried to buy the DVD everywhere, but unfortunately it never made it to DVD, and so the programme had to be watched via YouTube. In the process it would often use up much of our internet package as a result, but it was more than worth it. Anyway, I had a thought that I would contact Christine and see if we could arrange for her to have a chat with Wendy. Maybe Christine would even give her some pointers ahead of our leap into the unknown, especially in the 'grow your own' field. It was a Thursday night, and we were all sitting around the dinner table as we did as a family most evenings, when at 7pm sharp the phone rang.

I answered it, obviously knowing who was going to be at the other end of the phone and as the caller requested to speak to Wendy, I quickly handed the phone over to her. It had worked a treat! It was a complete joy to watch the look on Wendy's face change from a confused 'who am I talking to' face, to an excited 'can't believe I'm talking to her' face, as she realised just who she was talking to. They were on the phone for over an hour, and got on like a house on fire. It was really interesting to find that there were in fact many similarities in their lives, which further inspired Wendy and boosted her up no end. I was extremely grateful for Christine making time to speak to Wend, and for all her kind words of encouragement.

4 TAKING THE LEAP

Very quickly the day came when I was to bid a fond farewell to office life, and all the hustle and bustle of business. Would I miss it? It was certainly going to be strange. But a new and exciting chapter was about to unfold in not only my life, but the lives of my family around me. I would be lying if I didn't say that it was just a little bit scary. For the next two weeks we were doing all the packing, and tying up loose ends ahead of the big move. But before we knew it, flamin' noras, the removal trucks were stacked up to the gunnels. They were ready for off, and there was no turning back.

It was all hands to the pump. Wendy, myself, the 3 girls and our married kids too, all unloading trucks, squeezing furniture through doorways, and emptying boxes for many hours. It wasn't long before Wendy started to get us sorted and the house looking a little more organised. Very quickly we realised that spending only 25 minutes looking at the place all those weeks ago, maybe wasn't long enough. We couldn't fit half the furniture into the farm house, so into the barn it all went. Most of it has come in handy though, when kids have since left home and we've been able to offload it onto them. I remember waking up on that mid-February morning and staring in every direction, out of all the windows upstairs, just drinking in the views which were now ours. In fact, for several weeks I was getting into bother for just aimlessly wandering around the place in a daze. It was just so beautiful, and I suppose I couldn't quite grasp the reality that we were here for good. It wasn't just a holiday trip this time.

Each new day that arrived gave us further opportunities to investigate our new surroundings. I was so often in awe, as I came across something else which I hadn't noticed in the previous weeks. The whole place was awash with wild birds, including various members of the Tit family, Chaffinches, Thrushes, Yellowhammers, Robins, Starlings, Jays, Pied wagtails, Blackbirds, Woodies, and of course the mighty Wrens who live here in abundance. We also have tawny owls living on the land, and when we arrived we had 35 rooks' nests in our little grove of trees too. When we have had visitors come to see us they have commented on the noise that the rooks make, but we soon got used to it, and don't notice it at all now. The numbers have increased over time, all the way up to 46 nests built last year.

Soon after moving in, there were a couple of priority jobs which needed to be attended to around the place. We needed to find a fencing company to fence our land off with stock fencing, which we had agreed to have completed as part of the terms and conditions of purchase. After doing a little homework and seeking opinions of others, I had a number of companies come and quote for the job, with a decision being made to go with Rob Matthews, from Scackleton. It just so happens, Rob had a wood yard just up the road from where we had just flitted from. We arranged for the work to commence in the spring when the weather was a little kinder. Well, we hoped it would be anyway. Another of the first tasks was to get the house decorated inside. We again spoke to a number of companies and plumped in the end for Alan, a local decorator who clearly knew what he was doing. When it came to costs, he was never going to attempt to take out my eyes either. It wasn't long before the place was starting to look and feel like home. It's amazing what a lick of paint can do to change your outlook.

One of the chores I had to come to grips with quickly was our lovely heating system. Now, in our early years of married life we had solid fuel heating with an old rayburn fire, so I was used to shifting buckets of coal. But nothing could prepare us for the 'Bosky' boiler, which we now had in situ to heat up both our central heating and water. Can I at this moment explain that when I say central heating, I would use that term very loosely in this instance. Most of the radiators didn't work and those that did, were useless at best. So alongside the antiquated shower, I wasn't winning any brownie points with the women folk I was living with. To put things in perspective, we now had one loo and one bathroom for myself, Wendy and our three daughters, Olivia (21), Evie (19), and Naomi (14). Bearing in mind we had just left a beautiful home with four loos and 3 bathrooms, with underfloor heating throughout and all mod cons thrown in too. It was fast appearing like it wasn't the smartest move I'd ever made. As you can imagine, it wasn't too long before we had the bathroom refitted. Some weeks before the new bathroom suite was fitted, I caught our Evie outside one teatime. It seemed that she had resorted to taking a shower in her undies with the hosepipe at the front of the house, with the whole world going by. Things must have been bad!

We started to settle down out in the country and get to grips with life away from the hustle and bustle of town, which really suited us down to the ground. When the odd occasion drags us into York or Beverley, it does feel quite claustrophobic with all the buildings around, and the busy roads you have to contend with. I know it's not overly busy, but compared to where we now lived, it was becoming more and more like a different world to us. But that was a good thing. In fact, it was a great thing.

Even before we left, Wendy had been growing all sorts of veggies from seeds, which were now thriving seedlings. All were carefully transported from the many window sills where they were residing in Strensall, and could now be parked in our two new greenhouses, waiting for warmer weather to arrive. In the meantime we could transform the vegetable patch we had acquired, extending it considerably through replanting dozens of roses around the property. This enabled us to create new vegetable beds in places where the roses had once stood. We were excited to have such a wonderful space to be growing things, also giving Wendy the potential to be jarring, bottling, and selling all manner of treats in the months to come.

Ahead of our move we had been put in touch, through a friend, with a journalist, Lucy Oates. Lucy was keen to write an article for the Yorkshire Post, about our plans to move from the city to the country, and all that it would entail. Things progressed and the article was soon in print. Lucy had then been in touch to come back to see us, now that we had moved in and wanted to run a follow-up story detailing the progress we had made, and how we were finding things after the leap. We arranged the visit and it was great to catch up with her. We excitedly went through all that we had accomplished thus far, and detailed some of our plans moving forward. It's really funny how things work out. With us now being in print for a second time, people started to notice. When Wendy was in the local Sainsbury's, she had the checkout operators on a couple of occasions mention the stories from the paper and even when I went to make an appointment at the doctors' surgery, I was recognised from the picture in the paper. Although it may just have been that I was wearing the same furry green jacket that I was wearing in the paper that she recognised.

That reminds me, I loved that furry green jacket. For months on end I hardly took the thing off my back and Wendy threatened me with all sorts, if I didn't get rid of the thing. I used to hide it, in various places to try and stay one step ahead of her, so she couldn't torch it as she had suggested. In time, our daughter Holly and her husband Tom bought me a new one very similar, but not a vivid electric green colour. I wasn't camouflaged in the outdoors like I had been, but I got a lot less earache for wearing it as a result. The smelly old jacket eventually got torched, just to keep the peace, but I've got photos of us both which I can look back on with fond memories and I can think about the many good times we had together.

It was early spring in 2014 when things started to get really exciting for me. That was because we started to look at our plan for animals to come and live at Long Meadow Farm. Of course we had brought some animals with us, our three border terriers and our five chickens. These included Wendy's three jubilee hens that she got for her birthday in 2012. At the time it had been the Queen's jubilee, so they were named Queenie, Diana and Katie. The remaining two chickens were Rita (the 'evil one') and Zac the rooster. Very soon after we moved in we met our new neighbours across the road, Matthew and Sarah Green. With their son and daughter, they lived down the drive opposite our place. Matthew was in the egg business and so had many thousands of hens on site, beside where he lived. During one of the first conversations I had with him, I cheekily mentioned that I would have to come and talk to him nicely about cadging some hens off him. We had hardly finished talking and the phone rang and it was Matthew asking if I wanted some of his hens. Well, "that's a result!" I thought. He explained that he was clearing one of his sheds, and the resident hens were off to chicken pie land (my words not his), and would I like to come the next day and pick some up? I got organised the next morning, took my quad and trailer over the road to pick up our new chooks. I soon drove away with almost 30 hens and several bags of feed too, all for nowt! This was the first of many times when Matthew and Sarah have helped us out.

Sarah even took Naomi to school, as she's an art teacher at Pocklington School where Naomi attended. We had originally planned to take Naomi into York each day so she could continue to attend Huntington School, and then pick her up at the end of each day. But when we really thought about things, and worked out the time and money it would cost, it was really not feasible. We looked into all the schools locally, not that there are many, but in the end we bit the bullet. We arranged to take Naomi to Pocklington for a meeting with the Headmaster and a tour of the facilities. After completing the entrance test with flying colours, she started attending Pocklington after the Easter break. We had never considered sending any of our kids to a private school, but circumstances and finances were juggled to make it happen for Naomi. I thought that we may get a few sarky comments from her older brothers and sisters on the subject, but we only got positive comments and support from all of them.

Anyway, back to the hens. We parked our new residents inside one of the stables and waited for their new home to arrive, which it duly did. With our Jake's help I got it built and water tight, even if there were a few hiccups, and a whole lot of tantrums in between. So the des res was complete, and the hens were all set to move in. But we had a little job to do before we could move them. We needed to clip their wings. This just consisted of clipping some of the primary flight feathers on their wings. We didn't want them to fly out of the large enclosure they would be living in, and wander into the clutches of Mr.Fox. We decided to keep our pet chickens separate from these new ones, as the pet hens were tame and we were unsure how everyone would get on if we had them all living together. They all soon settled in, with both sets of chickens thriving and all started laying some beautiful eggs.

It wasn't long until we twigged that we were going to have far more eggs available to us than we would be able to cope with. After some discussion and a trip to the local farm shop to buy egg boxes, Wendy started selling them outside our gate, on a little fold up table. It was the sort of table that always reminded me of my Granma's little card table. The one we used when she taught us to play 'Whist' or 'Beetle', all those years ago. It wasn't long before Wendy was doing a roaring trade in eggs, all at just £1 for half a dozen, free-range, farm eggs. That's a right bargain. They were so different to the eggs we used to buy prior to having our own hens. The yolks so bright yellow, you would hardly need to show them a pan of boiling water and they'd be poached!

Before we could bring livestock onto the farm we needed to register our farm with Defra and the Animal Health Unit. Then we could get ourselves a CPH, or Holding number. This would entitle us to keep livestock, but it meant that everything was registered and above board. So shortly after gaining our holding number, and after our hens had settled in, we had our first sheep arrive. We had done a lot of homework with regards to the livestock and sheep particularly, as some folk had advised us to steer clear of them. "They just drop dead on ya, for any number of reasons" we were so often told. But I'm not one for listening to too many people's advice, and we went on to make our own decisions. We considered a number of sheep breeds ahead of buying, but there were a couple of factors which won us over. We were looking for a smaller breed, which were more manageable when handling them. We looked at which breeds were hardy and could cope with the wonderful weather we have in the UK.

Another factor I had to consider was that I'm a proud Scot, and so any breed that hailed from over that side of the border was going to win brownie points with me from the start. After much deliberation, we went for Shetland sheep and Hebridean sheep with both fitting our requirements. I was later to experience many times that these being small sheep also meant that they were very fast runners too, but more about those experiences later.

The first sheep to arrive were three ewe lambs and a tup, all Shetlands. We had hand-chosen these, and they were delivered to us as we hadn't a trailer or facilities to pick them up at the time. I learned later that all sorts of animals are quite at home riding in the back of a landy. From the beginning, we have endeavoured to give those animals who would be living with us for any length of time, a name. I trawled the internet seeking out gaelic names for all the sheep as they arrived. I soon found that as I couldn't pronounce many of them, they were subsequently changed to names which more readily suited their characters. As I never got much of a look-in with naming our kids, I saw it as only right that I should have the biggest say in naming our farm animals, and so I started with Kehna, Coco, Baa Baa and Torradon the tup.

Almost before we could draw breath, we took two further deliveries of sheep. The first was a further two Shetlands, whom we named 'Badger' and 'Useless Mother' (I'll explain later), and then half a dozen hebrideans which we bought from Pete Fletcher down in South Yorkshire. This was the first of many dealings we would be having with Pete over the next few years. Out of the six hebrideans, there was only one that was at all endearing who we named 'Cloud'. If you could pick her up and sit her in the sky, she would fit in very well. She looked just like a threatening black cloud out there in the field.

In our early days at Long Meadow farm, we were keen not to jump into things until we had done countless amounts of research. We didn't want to get caught out and make hasty decisions, that would later come and bite us in the bum. We went to see a few smallholdings, so we could see how others dealt with life and we spoke to various farmers who clearly had far more experience than we would ever have. We wanted to get things right first time. As much as we could do anyway. It was during a visit to a smallholding in the nearby village of Everingham, that we were able to make contact with a local pig breeder. An ex-policeman had moved out to the country, and like ourselves had radically changed his lifestyle in order to raise livestock on his farm. After meeting the pig breeder and discussing rearing pigs, we arranged to take delivery of 3 male Pietrain/middle whites, who arrived on my birthday in 2014. The pigs had a lovely new home. A spacious grassy paddock with lots of room to run about, a nice sturdy, straw-filled shelter, with plenty of shade from the chestnut and walnut trees which surrounded them. Like most other things we were now experiencing, this was all new to us and the pigs were intriguing. They loved to play, and were constantly running around the place in a little gang, looking for mischief and mayhem. We had heard that most pigs love to dig, but never imagined that they could clear a 30 foot patch of grass in their field before bedtime. But that's just what they did! From day one in our life of rearing pigs, we have always had an electric fence around them in order to keep them safely inside. We needed to ensure they didn't get out and cause trouble around the farm, or worse still on the roads or elsewhere. Because we were always planning to raise the pigs until they were large enough to take a trip to our freezer, we didn't give them serious names, and so any pigs destined for a plate have always been named 'Piggy McDoodle'.

Things didn't start off ever so well on day one with the porkers. Late in the evening, I took my usual wander around the growing menagerie, just to check all was well and everybody was bedded down for the night. The hens had all taken themselves to bed, the ewes were all snuggled down and happily chewing away, Torrodon had found a field corner to cosy up in and off I went to check on our latest arrivals. I walked around the perimeter of the field, but there was no sign. As I hadn't brought out my torch with me, I climbed over the gate and went for a closer look around the field. Still no sign. I started to panic. Where had they gone? There was no sight nor sound of them anywhere. I ran back to the house and grabbed the torch and ran frantically around the place, searching for the missing porkers. My adrenalin was pumping. Where the flamin' devil were they? I had visions of them galloping across the fields in search of food, or maybe they were homing pigs and were heading back to the farm they came from. There were no signs of an escape, so I trundled back to the pig pen for a second time. I had already checked inside their bed and there was no sign of them, but thought I'd check again just in case. As I walked through the doorway of the shelter, I stopped and listened. There was only silence. I waded through the piles of straw, which was almost waist high. I could hear snoring! I carefully lifted a pile of straw off the top of the heap in front of me and there we have it, these little piggies hadn't been to market and definitely hadn't had roast beef. They had actually stayed at home and were sleeping soundly, all tucked up in their bed. I covered them back up again and took myself off to have a sit down. After all that excitement, my blood pressure needed a breather!

As days went by, we were trying to allow our pet hens to roam free around the farm. As with all of the animals, we were keen to give them the best life we could within the bounds of safety, and as long as it was practical. It wasn't long before Zac the rooster started to cause us a few problems around the place. I'm sure that he was just frustrated, as his ladies could come and go around the place, yet he was hemmed in due to his size. He wasn't able to squeeze his large muscular frame through the fence rails like the ladies could, and so would strut about getting more and more angry as a result. If ever he was in one of those moods, it was best to steer clear. I would always let Wendy and the girls know that he was having a strop, so they could leave him well alone. Although he never caused me any grief, I do recall on one occasion when he was really misbehaving. I needed to get close enough to him in order that I could clip his wings to stop him from catching enough air to get up onto the top of the paddock fence. That would've been all I needed, him getting out and causing trouble around the farmyard. I took precautionary measures and dressed up accordingly to protect myself with two hoodies, a woolly hat, my chainsaw helmet with the visor down, and protective gloves. You can never be too careful can you? As it happens, he behaved himself impeccably, and I just got all hot and sweaty for ten minutes under all that gear. Things were going well on the farm. Although it was still very early days, we felt that we were starting to get to grips with the animals, the slower pace of life, and spending most of our time outdoors.

As each new day arrived we were being subject to so many experiences that we had never come across before. Some of them were taking us right out of our comfort zone. Much of what we were doing was uncharted territory, and it would have been so easy for us to shy away from so many of these tasks. But that was never on our agenda! Why ever would we have leapt like we did, if we were not going to grab these opportunities to learn with both hands? We spent lots of time observing the animals and their behaviour, trying to have them become more familiar with us as a result. Whilst watching the sheep one day, I noticed that Kehna had a bit of a mucky backside and had dags as a result. After doing a little reading, trawling the internet and talking to Matthew, my ex-sheepfarming neighbour, we worked out that it was the long lush grass that was causing the issue. We established that there was only one way of sorting this little problem out, and that meant Wendy and I had to get very hands on with a certain sheep's rear end! We arrived at the field armed up to the ears with scissors, a small pair of shears, iodine, a bucket of warm water, (I wouldn't want my bum doused in cold water!), a scrubbing brush, and gloves. Oh, and some cake to tempt the ewe! Now, when I say cake I obviously don't mean the Victoria sponge type of cake. It is in fact just concentrated feed, and that was all news to me.

This was the first of many, many occasions when we have had to gather our sheep up, after chasing them around the field for far too long. I knew that there must be an easier way to catch them, even without a trained dog. Eventually, with the help of the bucket of grub, I was able to catch her and sit her down on her backside, ensuring that Wendy had full access to the mucky end. As I held the sheep, Wendy set to and started to give Kehna a brisk wash and brush up. Before long, it was all sorted and she looked as good as new. The sheep that is, because it certainly wasn't Wendy! She had been speckled from her knees upwards with unmentionables. All the same, she enjoyed getting down and dirty with a sheep and we learned lots and have laughed about it many times since. If truth be told, that's when Wendy had the brain wave that we should be filming all of our experiences. Wendy started to hound a variety of television companies and programme makers, like 'Countryfile', Channel 4 and Channel 5, with the idea that we should be having our new life unfold for viewers across the nation. No luck so far, but it hasn't deterred her efforts.

Zac the rooster's unruly behaviour had been going on for far too long, and so during one of my many wanderings around the farm, I came up with an idea. An idea which on the face of it, could solve two problems in one. The other problem was that Torrodon the tup wasn't overjoyed that he couldn't spend his days in the company of his ladies next door, and so was taking his frustrations out on the fence posts. In hindsight, it may not have been our best idea. What we decided to do in our wisdom, was to move the two feisty fellas in together. So Torrodon could live in the same paddock as the hens, but would live in the field shelter behind the stable rather than in the chicken shed. From the very first minute he arrived in 'Chicken Town', he appeared to be making an impact. Our 'I'm not scared of anything' rooster had just had the wind taken right out of his sails, and was visibly scared witless. I'll tell you what though, it was a joy to see! It was working beautifully. I slept soundly that night, feeling proud of myself that we were able to tackle these obstacles which were being thrown our way, and to me that was progress, or so I thought.

The next morning I awoke early, probably around 6 o'clock, with all the joys of spring. The dawn chorus were in full voice and life was sweet. I can remember it like it was yesterday. It was a Sunday morning, after breakfast and I was all kitted out in my Sunday Best. I was just going to nip around the farm to check that all was well, before heading off to church. One by one I checked that everyone was hunky dory, but I soon established that our friend Torrodon had taken the rooster problems into his own hands. He had decided that when we told him the day before that he was moving in with the chickens, sharing a paddock wasn't ever going to be enough for him. What befell my eyes that morning is an image which is as clear today as it was back then. Somehow, and I still can't fathom how, he had squeezed his fully grown, sheepskin-rug covered body inside the smallest of our hen houses, through a door we surely borrowed from Alice's adventures in Wonderland! How on earth do I get him out? He was laid on the floor of the chicken house, with just his head poking out of the very small, sliding front door. He even had the nerve to throw me that 'Don't blame me' look, which only made things worse. Before I attempted to extract him from the shed, I grabbed my phone and quickly took a picture, so I could show everyone. Just a simple explanation was never going to do this tale justice. After a great deal of pushing, shoving, jumping up and down, and a fair amount of cursing, (all in my suit and tie) I managed to get the little devil out of there! As a result of the morning's fiasco, we thought it was probably best to shift him back pretty sharpish to his old paddock, which we did that afternoon. We'd just have to cope with Zac's mood swings, as best we could. There was a brief lull in the poultry problems for all of six days, until the next Saturday evening. That's when my next trauma occurred.

The farmyard was all settling down for the night as usual ,and just before heading out to the Chinese takeaway I said to Wendy that I would make sure all was well around the farm. All was well, except when I checked that the pet hens were all snuggled down for the night. I could see that Rita had taken herself off to bed, but our Jubilee hens Queenie, Diana, and Kate were nowhere to be seen. This was unusual, and had never happened before. They always returned home at dusk. Wendy said, "You go to the takeaway and I'm sure they'll be in when you get back." I got back from the Chinese takeaway, after a wrong order, only to find that all three of chickens were still missing from their beds! I searched for hours, marching up and down the fields with the smallest torch in the world. I was freezing my rear off, but to no avail! I kept calling for them, but still no response. But I did keep finding what I believed were clues. I kept coming across lots of small downy feathers....

"Blast!" I thought. That was it. The fox must have had them. Undeterred though, I continued on following these feathers, and all the while I was hoping for a good result. As time ticked on and it was fast heading towards midnight, I called a halt to the search for the night, with high hopes that a new day would bring me better news.

I couldn't sleep and got up at five to continue the search. That's when I spotted Katie in the garden! Then, from out of nowhere, Queenie showed up. As if by magic, just as we were leaving for church, Diana appeared too. Where they had been we'll never know, but we had been thinking the worst all night. As you can imagine, it was yours truly getting it right in the neck for not protecting our flock, like a proper farmer would! Just for the record, I did later establish where the downy feathers were coming from. It appears that an unnamed daughter had borrowed my expensive duck down coat and whilst wearing it, a hole had somehow appeared in the arm. Funnily enough, it was the same duck down coat I had been out searching in. Of course, as it was a breezy night, I was losing my feathers by the dozen along the way. It's good to know that at least they weren't the result of some fox-fest on the farm.

As the weeks progressed we were learning so much, and making many contacts within the farming community locally. I had been on the search for IBC's for several weeks, and eventually through one of these contacts, I was able to track some down. If you'd asked me a few months ago what an IBC was, I wouldn't have had a clue what you were talking about. But of course with all this education I've been getting, I know that they are large 1000 litre tanks which are used to store liquids, and once emptied and cleaned out they can be used to store fresh water for the animals. I arranged for the tanks to be delivered and then organised an extra pair of hands to come and give me a hand, roping in one of our sons, Sam. We cracked on and secured two of them separately onto the top of piles of old pallets I had acquired, and got them all ready to go into the fields later in the summer, when the highland cattle arrived. The third tank had been earmarked for our porky friends. We were able to carry the beast of a thing into the pig pen and then lovingly jet-washed it and cleaned it out, before perching it carefully on top of some building blocks. The water trough was then sited underneath the tank tap and we were almost ready for action. All that was left was to fill it with water. We left the hose running for an hour and a half while we busied ourselves with other things, and came back to switch the hose off and test it out. I couldn't wait. This was going to save me such a lot of time compared to shifting water by hose and bucket. Our excitement very quickly turned to despair. The flaming tank had a leak! For weeks after I hunted for a cap to shut off the IBC connection. Could I find one on the net? Could I flamin' Noras!!

Towards the end of April, Rob Matthews and his team started the work on our fencing. One of the first things he needed from us was an understanding of where we wanted the fences to be sited. After a great deal of thought and discussion, (and far too many pretty pictures), we came up with a plan. In the finished plan we thought that we would have sufficient paddock space for all the animals. It was organised and manageable in its layout, and it would look good too. Whilst visiting other farms and smallholdings over several months, we had heard too many stories of goats turning up on the village green, or people getting calls to say, "Your sheep are on the 1079 again".

We decided therefore from the start that we were going to get the fencing done right first time, rather than cut corners or go cheap and patch up what was already in place. We settled on post and rail fencing almost everywhere, with 5 rails throughout. In between the two proposed cattle fields, we even double-railed the fence, just to make sure we had no mishaps along the way. Whilst the fencing was being put in, which was getting up towards 1000 metres in the first phase, we had separate pens and races built. One for the sheep and one for the cattle. That has undoubtedly proved time and again, to be one of the best decisions we've made since moving in. It was worth taking advice from those in the know, and has made life so much easier many times since. As almost every one of the metres of fencing was sited, they were watched by Elsa, one of the dogs. Two of the dogs, including Elsa, were out most of the day roaming around the place, always close enough to hear my whistle. All the while we knew that Elsa would be in the middle of a field watching the fence grow, as the weeks went by. Scout was always too lazy to go too far, and the third of our borders, Boo, is a little monkey. She would be off after rabbits, the minute you turned your back. She was indoors, unless we could keep a sharp eye on her.

Already, we were finding that we were getting away from the farm less and less, and that our life was developing around all that was going on at Long Meadow Farm. It just so happened that there was the Rare Breeds Sale going on at Murton Auction Centre the very next Saturday. We thought we would mosey on down for a look. When I say 'for a look', I knew full well that with three women in tow, it was highly likely that we would be doing more than just having a look.

We wandered around, checking out the cattle, the sheep, and the pigs. That's when we came across the goats. We had spoken about goats many times, so when the Pygmy Goats were spotted, that was it. It wasn't long before my ears were ringing, and so I relented and agreed to enter the auction for two of these beautiful Pygmy goats. I had been to a number of auctions previously, but never had I been bidding in guineas. I didn't know one end of a guinea from the other, and so I didn't even know how much I was agreeing to pay for the goats. Even if I did win the auction, I could see some of the more seasoned old farmers around me laughing, as I clearly didn't have a clue what I was doing. Anyway, all went well and the two goats we wanted, we got.

Now we just needed to get them home, which took a little sweet-talking to the lady in the white coat, at the back door of the auction. Apparently, it's not the done thing to transport livestock in the back of a Landrover Defender. Well, not the type with four seats in the back. After I switched the charm on we were ready for off, and whilst Wendy sat in the front, Evie and Naomi sat in the back and looked after the newest members of our farm family.

The goats soon settled into their new home in one of our stables. We extended the fenced area outside the stable, so they would have more space. On completion of the new gates and fencing, we let out Stacey and Nessa, as we called them. It was taking a little while, as they were still a little nervous and so we left them in peace to come out in their own time. Within ten minutes they had escaped! They had somehow slithered through the gap between the bottom two rails, (which happens to be only six inches) and they were now running around the front chicken paddock. Another chance for me to get some exercise around the farm, I thought. That'll be great fun! But after 15 minutes of trying, my thoughts had somewhat changed. Just as I was about to take drastic action, I heard the reinforcements arriving. Scout and Elsa came hurtling around the corner of the barn, into the paddock and promptly rounded them up and back through the paddock into their stable. Phew! Who would have thought Border Terriers could round up animals like that? Must be all that training they've had!

Needless to say, our goat security measures were quickly reviewed and the necessary action taken to ensure this didn't happen a second time. The upgraded security measures consisted of a length of wire, run between each of the gaps in the fencing. Once the work was completed, I planned my day around jobs that could be done within sight of the goat house, just in case they got any funny ideas. Other than a few sideward glances and sticking their heads through the gap in the gate, things passed off without any incidents. That is until the electrician arrived. I had been hanging around for him all day and within 60 seconds of me leaving my sentry post by the goat house to walk into the barn, I saw one of the goats run past the barn door, closely followed by Scout and Elsa. Once again the dogs saved the day, and the goat was returned safely back into her home. It was time to rethink security, once again!

With every day that dawned, there was new stuff to be learned. Whether we were ready to learn or not, the lessons just kept on coming. Now, being a 'Ginner' and not ever appreciating the harm the sun can do, when Wendy mentioned that the pigs, (who are also fair skinned) were getting sunburnt, I hadn't even given it a thought. It's just as well that Wendy had not only noticed, but had devised a method of getting them covered in suntan lotion. I was promptly provided with a spray bottle, full of sun lotion and instructions to go and get them lathered up to protect them from those harmful sun's rays. Surprisingly, all went well and they are now much better protected. One thing that I have learned over recent weeks, is that pigs are smart in so many areas, but not all. They have some beautiful and very large chestnut trees in and around their paddock and they can often be seen taking turns piggy-backing, so they can reach higher up to forage on the leaves and chestnuts which are higher up the branches. Yet on the other hand, there are times when they don't use their brains or common sense to find shade from the sun under those same trees, but prefer to park themselves in the middle of the field to roast. Well, maybe not roast as we don't get that much sun, but they certainly grill a little.

Having never worked on a farm, or had any experience at all with most of what we were coming across each day, I think that we haven't been doing too badly at all so far. There are always things that have been a little more taxing to do than others, and one of those jobs came up when we needed to worm the sheep. We had taken lots of advice and after visiting the local farm shop to get the supplies I needed, we were all set for the job. The only thing was that we couldn't get this 'Drench Gun' to work. "It must be broken", I said. I searched the internet, but still couldn't fathom it. Every time I pulled that trigger, nothing came out the other end of the gun. Maybe I hadn't put it together correctly? So I took it apart, and with Wendy overseeing proceedings, we checked we hadn't lost or misplaced any parts and set about piecing it all together properly.

I'm afraid that at this point, I let myself down and performed the first of many 'Rumpelstiltskin' dances I have performed on the farm. For those not in the know, that's when I jump up and down and generally 'lose it'. This is all whilst steam appears from my ears, I spout gibberish, and turn a deeper and deeper shade of crimson. This often, but not always, occurs following the unsuccessful completion of a task, generally after a great deal of frustration has been endured. In my past life, examples of this behaviour have been witnessed on a number of occasions on the football field. To be honest though, I just put it down to having ginger hair, or as my teacher as a 9 year old would call me, 'tête rouge'. So, where do we go from here? The sheep need to be wormed, we've got all the bits, we just don't have the know-how to get this wretched drench gun to work! Who can I ask? Of course, we once again roped in Matthew our neighbour over the road. "I'll be there in a moment", he said. And sure enough he was.

We stood out of the drizzle just inside the back of the barn, with the drench gun in my right hand and the worming medication in my left, both items connected by a tube. I explained in detail the problem we were having. He just said, "Lift up that hand", as he pointed to my left hand holding the medication bottle. I promptly lifted it up, at which point he said, "Try it now!" I did, and miraculously it worked perfectly. "It works by gravity", he said. He wasn't even laughing when he told me. Did I feel like a clown, or what! "Do you want a hand and we can just worm them now?", he said.

Well, the thing was that I hadn't got to the farm supply store to get some field gates, so we could pen them in and make life easier for ourselves. Within a few minutes we were on the way to another of his farms to pick up some field gates, which he said I could borrow till I got sorted out. (That reminds me, it's now nearly 3 years on and I'm still using them). It wasn't long until we were back at the farm. I had given Wendy a shout and we had all the sheep in the pen, ready to get the job done. Matthew grabbed the first sheep and said, "I'll do this first one, just to show you and then it's all yours". He explained the gap between their side teeth was where the gun nozzle needed putting through. I had to be careful not to put it too far down their throat, or I could damage them in the process. We got them wormed, everything cleaned up and packed away before it got dark. I was buzzin', as they say. On a very small scale, this really felt like proper farming. Progress was being made and I was loving it.

It was only a couple of days later, when we had additional worming activities to attend to. But this time, these were neither expected nor planned for. Ahead of bringing our first weaner pigs onto the farm, they get wormed at the breeders, soon after they are born. But it appeared that one little porker had done a runner and been missed out, or just needed a further dose. I was out, as always bright and early, and went to feed the 3 little pigs. This is when I noticed, as I walked across their paddock, that there appeared to be some foreign object stuck to the back end of one of them. After I got closer and made further investigations, I could see that it was in fact a long worm hanging out of his rear end! I called them over, turned the prime suspect around, so I could get a better look, then promptly took hold of the worm end and dragged it out in one go. It didn't snap, so there were no bits left inside to cause trouble later. Who would have thought I'd be doing that a few months ago?

I popped out to Gate Helmsley, to the farm supplies store and soon returned with the necessary medication I required to worm all 3 of the pigs. At the time I felt it wise to take care of all three of them whilst I was at it, but that was before I thought about the job in hand. In order to worm the pigs, any medication wasn't given orally, like with a drench gun. Oh no, it was never going to be that simple was it? With pigs, they needed to be injected into their neck. Now I'm not that smart at all, but I knew from the beginning that these pigs 'aint going to hang around for long when that needle hits their neck. We soon had a plan. No ordinary plan, but one that was built around all those cowboy films that I had watched over the years. I was going to use a lasso.

Now it was obviously going to be easier if I had an extra pair of hands to help me out, and so I roped in another son, Jake, to give his old Dad a hand.

As Jake is a diabetic, he is used to dealing with needles daily. So I got him to do the injecting part, whilst I lassoed each pig and then hung on for dear life trying to keep them stationary, until each one had been sorted.

Although it had only been a matter of weeks, the eggs Wendy was selling at the front gate were selling out quickly each day, and we really couldn't keep up with the demand. That's when we arranged to purchase a further 15 hens to add to our flock. We thought that this would be sufficient, and we didn't want to go overboard with numbers. I returned with our new hens, which were unlike all those we had already. All of our laying hens were hybrids, like 'Gingernut Rangers', and were all the same colour. But now we would have white Ambers, black Marans, a couple of Speckledy grey hens and a Blue Maran too. All of which were lovely birds. Initially, they were kept in a separate paddock away from the other hens just until they had settled in, and then we opened the gate and they mingled beautifully. That was until the clock struck 9pm and it was bedtime. The new hens didn't fancy bunking up with their new friends and just wanted to go back to their own beds, next door! That was never going to happen, so then I had to chase them all around the field like a mad man, catching each of them and individually placing them all inside their new home. Thankfully, that was an activity I only had to take care of for a few nights and they've been settled ever since.

With all the success of selling our eggs, Wendy soon started to branch out into other areas. Before long, she was selling jars of chilli jam alongside our homegrown strawberry and raspberry jams too. Things were going so well that for Mothers' Day that year, the kids all pitched in together and made her a little vintage cart, which was a step up from the little card table. It had more space on the top, and she could create lovely displays. Once decorated with copious amounts of bunting and suchlike, it was looking the real deal. As sales were continuing on an upward trend, it was decided that we would buy a small shed which could be sited inside the front drive, beside the barn. That's when things were soon taken to another level, because she was able to sell a whole range of homemade craft items and vintage gifts, that she had lovingly sought out over a number of years. To be selling such things had always been part of the plan and although this was only at an embryonic stage, this part of her dream was now coming to fruition. She was selling many items that had been made in the main by Wendy and Holly, our eldest daughter. Cushions, children's clothes, bunting and quilts.

5 IS IT TIME YET?

As each day dawned, I was still in that frame of mind that everything was so new to me. It was an adventure we were part of, and I so badly didn't want it to end. I was now on a roll and wanted to be trying everything, getting involved in so many things that to others would just be plain boring. But this is what I had wanted for so long. Mending fences, building shelters, cutting down trees, clearing overgrown woodland, digging ditches, and getting to know so much more about the animals we had brought in to live with us.

It was a late May morning and as I do so many mornings, I looked over to my right as I walked through the yard. The sun, which had just risen, was casting shadows through the white poplars across the front paddocks. I was on my way, on what appeared to be just another normal day. The sort of day we were becoming accustomed to, taking care of chores and loving every moment of it. I let Queenie and the gang out, then Zac was out puffing out his chest, drinking in the crisp morning air. It was the turn of those hens in Chickenville, where all our laying hens live. As I opened their door and stood clipping the door back onto the side of the shed, that's when things all changed around here. I could see something out of the corner of my eye…Was I really seeing what I thought I was seeing? Over in the next field with some of the sheep, there was a little white flash in the corner. As I walked closer I could see that it was in fact a lamb! A LAMB! How on earth could this have happened? We never bought ewes in lamb, or did we? Very quickly I worked out that one of the two sheep we bought from a breeder, must have been pregnant. She must have been in with the tup last December! This wasn't part of the plan. We weren't even organised. We weren't due to have lambs until April 2015, but the script had somehow been rewritten for us!

I quickly grabbed my mobile phone, which more often than not resides in my pocket, and called Wendy. As she answered, I took a big breath,

"There's a lamb in the field". "What?", "I said, there's a lamb in the field!" "Where's it come from?" she said with a puzzled tone to her voice.

I started to laugh and just said "Well, I'm just guessing, but I'm thinking, from its Mother!" I'll tell you what, I'd never seen our lass move so fast. She was down that field quick smart. The ewe which had just given birth was attending to her little ewe lamb, who was the tiniest of things. We later worked out that she was as small as she was because her mother would only have been seven months old when she got pregnant…Good grief!

After, thinking things over in my head and trying to work out what had gone on, I thought to myself, "We bought two sheep from the same place, could it be that in fact the other sheep was expecting too?" I quickly scanned my eyes across the field, to see where the second ewe was in the field. Immediately I thought, either she has eaten all the pies or she too is 'with child', or lamb, in this case. Moments later, the decision was taken to move mother and baby and expectant mother down to the stables, so we could keep an eye on them with the nights still being a bit chilly. We then scrambled 'Team McKenna' and operation 'Safe Haven' was underway. It took all five of us, to round them up and escort them through the paddocks, down to the stables. It was a little bit hairy, and we could have taken an easier route by putting them all in the trailer. But, as you know, we know nowt and so didn't want to be manhandling them and inadvertently do any damage. In the meantime we had prepped the stable, ready for their arrival.

Initially, Mother and baby were doing great. The little one was feeding well and they were both getting some well-earned rest. Overnight we took turns on a rota to keep an eye on Mother and baby, as well as the expectant mother. She has been showing what we thought were the early signs of labour. By the next morning there was no progress on that score. Oooh! I'll tell you what. It was just like 'Lambing Live'! Well sort of. Just without anyone knowing quite what they should be doing. Over the next 24 hours, we had a busy old time of it. We've since come to know that it wasn't busy in the slightest. When we let the new mother out into the paddock, the lamb who had just been born, was for some reason rejected by her mother. After giving it a go ourselves and then after taking advice, we tried any number of ways to try and get them back together, but without success. It was a nightmare! What a flamin' failure, I thought. The first lamb we have, and Mum decides to turn silly devil on us. It was sad, but we just had to crack on and feed the lamb ourselves. We firstly used goats milk, which we got from our nearest supermarket. Then we got some Lamblac, which is replacement ewe's milk. It was decided that the new lamb was to be called 'Pip', and the ewe was called 'Useless Mother' (for obvious reasons). With a rota now going full steam, we all took turns feeding and checking on her in the stable through the night and during the day. She was beginning to thrive and all this attention was doing the trick. In the meantime, the second pregnant ewe had her lamb.

A ram lamb and thankfully she was and has always been a great mother. As she has a black and white striped head, we named her 'Badger' and her lamb we called 'Rambo', obviously because he was a ram and we just thought it was a good fit. We never had any problems with these two and Badger was doing a super job.

People have often asked about how the three girls at home have coped and adjusted to life out in the country. Well, Olivia and Evie continued for a time to be commuting into York for their work. Although the travelling was a bit of a bind, they soon appreciated why we did what we did when they could come home to the peace and quiet which country life offers. Naomi, as has been said, moved schools and was settling in well. Although, the expectation levels from her new school are considerably higher than any of us had experienced before. Thinking back to that time, I think that I was surprised at how well the three of them settled into their new life, the efforts they each made to help out around the place and to play their part in this adventure. Having said all that, the moment the Quad bike arrived, surprisingly enough, it did seem to create an even more positive vibe around the place. One thing that definitely changed for the girls and Wendy too, was the change in our mode of transport out on the farm. Leaving behind the Range Rover Sport and bringing in the old Landy to take its place didn't go down ever so well in some quarters. But the thing is, we have had far more laughs in the Landy than I can ever remember in the last car, or even the ones before that. Well, who else gets to ride in the back of a smelly old Landrover, over the Wolds to church in Beverley each Sunday? We really were like the 'Beverley Hillbillies'. It doesn't matter if you are dressed up to the nines in your 'Sunday Best' and who cares if you smell of sheep when you get there? It's all part of the fun I say. In fact, we made the whole ride even more enjoyable. Not only could you spend the journey jiggling about, whilst unusually facing sideways throughout the trip, but we took a packed lunch with us for yet more enjoyment on the return trip. When we passed people on the road, or when other vehicles got up close behind us, with those four bouncing around in the back and soft lad playing chauffeur up front, we were bound to get a few funny looks, weren't we? But it's those things that memories are made of.

As part of our adventure, it was always our longer- term plan for Wendy to be opening a farm shop/teashop, and to look at the possibility of us bringing camping pods onto our farm for people to come and stay. With this in mind we arranged for a planning consultant to come and see us, with a view to us starting the process to ultimately get the necessary permissions for us to roll out our business development plans over the next couple of years. All that we discussed with the consultant didn't appear to be anything too ambitious. We were quite buoyed at the thought that things might actually happen the way we were hoping. But let's not get too ahead of ourselves shall we. Over several months we waded through paperwork, all the while submitting a variety of documents and paying ridiculous amounts of money to progress our applications, with a hope that things were going to be accepted and luck was going to work in our favour. We then just needed to sit back and let the process unfold, and we'd see how things turned out.

After doing some asking around and making a few calls, I tracked down someone who could take care of shearing our flock of sheep. As much as it would be a great thing to do for myself, I thought at the time that it was a step too far. It made me think back to one of our family holidays when the kids were younger. Wendy and I took them all, and my parents, to a tiny 450 acre island off the Mull of Kintyre, called Sanda. There was nobody else on the island but us, lots of sheep, seals, and the peregrine falcons who nested there. Whilst we were on the island the owner brought a couple of New Zealand lads and their dogs over to round up and shear all of the island's sheep. I can remember us sitting with the kids for what seemed like hours, watching them shear countless numbers of them and the memory of that graft has stuck with me. I know it's not a good excuse, but with my dodgy shoulders, it would kill me off!

I had arranged for this young lad, Mark Dale, who must have been around 20, to come around teatime to take care of my little flock. So, as arranged he turned up and as he jumped out of his van he said "I hope you don't mind, but I've brought my sister along, she's just finished her GCSE's and wanted to get out". It wasn't a problem at all and I showed them where our sheep were. I had gathered them all up in the pen outside the stables, and shifted the goats indoors, while the sheep all got their hair cut. Mark got all his equipment set up inside the other stable and was soon ready to go. I just turned my back to talk to Wendy and when I turned back around, Mark's young sister Jenny, had flipped one of the sheep onto its back and was dragging the ewe into the stable to get sheared. I couldn't believe it, that had completely taken me by surprise. I thought oh, heck I'm going to have to get stuck in here. If that young lass is doing that, then I need to be showing willing myself. So, that's exactly what I did, and between us it was all done and dusted in no more than an hour…oooh, but I did get a sweat on!

In conversation, Mark had mentioned that he was a big marmalade fan and so Wendy gave them some of her Seville Orange Marmalade and jam to take away with them, as well as payment for the job too. We have used Mark every year since and it never ceases to amaze me, the skill that's required to get that job done right. We did look into ways that we could use the fleeces, especially with them being Shetland sheep. I always had a Shetland wool sweater or cardigan as a kid and thought there must be somebody out there that could use it. We did give several bin liners full to one lady who was going to spin it and then make Wendy something with the wool in return, but we're still waiting for that lady in Fridaythorpe to come up with the goods.

Now over the many years since I first became a Dad, I've had all sorts of wild and wonderful presents given to me by the kids on Fathers' Day, but this year I got a surprise and a half, and a gift which was not expected at all. We had been out somewhere, I can't quite remember where, but anyway Olivia and Evie pulled onto the drive just a few minutes after us. They came rushing into the house and calmly said, "Oh, Dad, your present is in the boot, if you want to go and get it". I wondered, what the devil was going on, but went with it, taking the car keys from them as I walked out of the door. I turned, a little perplexed, noticing that all three of the girls and Wendy were lined up watching me, as I reached the boot of the car. I opened the boot up and got the shock of my life, as I was greeted with two beautiful Muscovy ducks, a pair in fact. They were all snuggled down inside a dog carrier and were now keen to get out and stretch their legs after their journey. The girls had been arranging this surprise for some weeks and I was flabbergasted to say the least. The ducks were promptly named 'George and Mildred' and I took them to live inside a pen within the barn, until they had settled in for a few days and were able to get their bearings. Even then it was only by chance that they escaped out of the barn one day, when we decided that they could roam a little. We were concerned that they would fly away, never to return and darken our door once more. As it happens, they didn't fly away, but often took themselves for a flight around the neighbouring fields, but always returned to the farmyard.

Unlike many duck breeds, the Muscovies were not keen to settle in a proper house, whatever shape and size it was and believe me we tried a few. Instead they would roost on top of the stables, the barn or the fence in the yard. I regularly tried to escort them into a house, but to no avail, it just wasn't going to happen. After everything had been going so well for quite a number of weeks with the ducks, it all changed when Mildred disappeared one day. It was late into the evening, getting dark and once again this clown was out looking for some unruly farm animal. She showed up the next morning, but repeated the same trick the next evening and unfortunately only a pile of white feathers with black tips were found in the long grass beside our top field. We presumed after a further 48 hours that she must have been taken by a fox, and at that moment we decided to increase our security for the ducks and the hens. She was never to return and so we very soon picked up 'Mildred number 2', so that George wasn't on his own. After losing Mildred we then shut the ducks away each night in the barn, which always took some effort, but it was worth it.

It wasn't too long before, the disappearing duck act reared its head once more, and for the life of me I could not fathom where she had gone. There wasn't any sign of her and then suddenly, from out of nowhere, she turned up, but as quick as she appeared, she was gone again, without a trace. This went on over several days and then after I clambered onto the top of the hay stack at one side of the barn, I could see where she was hiding. It was only then that we worked it all out. She was sitting on eggs! A couple of times each day, she would come out, stretch her legs, have something to eat, take a trip to the loo and finish her trip out by having a quick bath. After doing a little research on t'internet, we discovered that unlike hens, Mother Duck needs moisture for the eggs to hatch, which is why she would always go for a bath before returning to her nest.

It wasn't many weeks later that our duck family increased in size, when Mildred appeared out in the farmyard with 8 of the cutest bundles of fluff you have ever seen. It was so funny to see her tending to her new babies and the look on the face of the proud Dad as he waddled along behind them was just a picture.

Sourcing our farm residents was continuing throughout the spring into the summer months, and once the fencing had been completed for our new paddocks, it was I felt, a good time to talk to Pete Fletcher, from whom I had bought some sheep some months before. In passing, I had established that not only did he breed sheep, but amongst other things, Highland Cattle were a big favourite of his. Now Peter looked after the Rare Breeds Centre at Graves Park in Sheffield, so he obviously knew what he was doing, as I have found out many times, since I first met him. I gave him a call and arranged to drive down and have a look at his herd or fold as Highlands are called. To say that I was excited, as I drove down the M18 towards Sheffield, was an understatement to say the least and I was only going to choose some Heilan' Coos, that day. It would be a further 6 or 7 weeks until they would turn up at our place and so much needed to be done before we were ready for them to arrive. As I walked through the fields of cattle, with all shapes and sizes around me, I was in my element, like as they say, 'a kid in a sweet shop!'

Although Heilan' Coo's come in a number of colours including black, brindle and dun, I was only interested in the red ones, as they are known, but to me they are clearly ginger. So after discussing what our plans were with Pete, and taking advice from him, I settled on 4 heifers. One heifer, Monica, with her 8 month old calf, who we called Morag, with Lyndsey a two year old and Flora, who was just a yearling. We agreed that we would leave the cattle where they were until we were all organised at our end, and it would also give more time for the bull to take care of things that come naturally with Monica, in the meantime. I can remember as I was driving home, thinking, how on earth was I going to contain the excitement up until their arrival at our place? I'll tell you how, just focus on the work that needed doing and time would pass by before I knew it.

The biggest job I needed to get sorted before the coos arrived was to get the contents of all of these fields, cut, turned, baled and into our barn ahead of their arrival. Now that was never something that I could deal with myself and so needed to pull in the professionals to take care of most of that little task. I didn't have the machinery or the know-how to get it done, but there was someone I could talk to nicely, to help me out.

Within only a couple of days of moving into Long Meadow Farm, we were introduced to the Layton Family, from Bielby, a neighbouring village, who farmed the land either side of us. I first met Malcolm, one of the sons, as he was cutting the hedge alongside our front field, when he commented that I had the look of the Scottish pop sensations of the 90's 'The Proclaimers'. It must have been the ginger hair and glasses. It wasn't long before we had met Malcolm's brother Adrian, and his son Jordan, after which we were introduced to Gordon and Angela their parents. The Laytons are part of a farming family, who had worked the land in this part of East Yorkshire for many years and have amassed much experience over this time, which I have tapped into on countless occasions since our first meeting. Their help and advice has helped us out of many a scrape, since we jumped in with both feet.

So with all this experience and know-how, they were the obvious choice to turn to, to help get my hay turned around. At the time, I thought that it would all get sorted very quickly, but Gordon had other ideas. I had no idea that we needed to wait until the grass had grown so high and that we needed to await a certain date, after the Great Yorkshire Show had been and gone, before we could cut it, and we needed a run of dry weather or the lot would be lost. He talked to me about a hole above the Azores needing to close up as well, but I really didn't have a clue what he was talking about.

He must be a very patient man, because, I swear I was on that phone, what seemed like every ten minutes, asking, "Is it time yet?" Eventually, one Thursday evening in July our home telephone rang and Wendy answered it. "Is tha' lad there"…. It was Gordon on the other end of the phone and the lad he was after, just happened to be this 51 year old! He was calling to give us the thumbs up, the weather was right and all was going our way, and so on a glorious sunny Saturday in July, the time came when Adrian came over with all the gear and cut the hay in the five fields and then he left! What's going on I thought, I once again spoke to Gordon, who explained that after a couple of days Jordan his grandson would be back to turn the hay and then again a couple of days after that. Only then would they be over to bale it all and we could then shift the bales into the barn, away from any potential showers which could damage our precious stock. This hay was going to be feeding our animals throughout the next winter and beyond, so we needed to look after it and treat it carefully. I'll tell you what, there was so much to learn in this farming lark!

I know that so often I waffle on about when was a kid, but so much of what I did as a kid was, I'm sure, preparing me for the adventure we now found ourselves on. Back in those days, I spent so many hours building dens! Lots of these dens were made from bales of hay or straw. Without even giving it a second thought, we used to wreck so many of them whilst messing about, either in the fields or in my friend's barn. Now some 40 odd years later, I can honestly say that I never appreciated what work goes into preparing, drilling, fertilising, growing, spraying, cutting, turning, baling, and then shifting each bale of hay. My goodness, if I didn't know what hard work was before, I do now!

So, we had been watching the weather, and the time had come to get the hay turned once more so it could be baled. Before long the Laytons were over and we were stacking the bales in the fields, as they were appearing from the back end of the baler. I was in my element, it was great to see all this proper farming going on and it was at our place. I expected in my own mind that we would maybe get 80 to 100 bales out in total, out of our fields, but I soon saw that my estimate was way off. With this in mind, I remember stopping and thinking, I could do with some extra hands to get this lot shifted, so I sent out a pleading message to my kids, saying that I needed any available hands to come and give me a hand, to get the hay shifted into the barn. As the afternoon turned into early evening, the Laytons left and I stood and counted the bales. The 80 to 100, which I was thinking we would end up with, had somehow turned into 213! I thought I'd best crack on and get the job started.

I hooked up the quad and trailer and as I drove through the gate to head up the field, I could see Evie and Olivia heading down the lane, home from work. I wasn't sure if I could tempt either one of them to come and give their old Dad a hand, but as it happened, hurriedly Evie had ran through the front door, up the stairs, changed and was out in the field to help in minutes. She did a great job, she's always been a grafter, our Evie! After one field, I was seriously jiggered and thought I'd leave the rest until tomorrow, and that's when Jake turned up with his gang. Amy with Noah and Isla, two of our grandkids, went to visit with Nanna, while Jake and I carried on and it was for sure the right decision to do that. The very next morning the heavens opened and all the hay that was still in the 2nd field would have been ruined and lost!

In the interests of time Jake suggested that we pile the trailer even higher with the bales and also put more on the quad, so we could make less trips to the barn and get the job completed sooner. Needless to say, that's what we did and the job was soon done. I couldn't believe how willingly they had stepped up to the plate and how hard they had both worked. They had certainly grafted and I will be grateful for their help for a very long time.

After quite some weeks of reasonable behaviour from Zac the rooster, things started to come to a head in the farmyard. Wendy had walked into the front paddock to see Pip the lamb, when Zac had launched an unprovoked attack on her. Not once, but twice he went at her. She came out of there with scratches on both of her legs, from both his claws and his beak and that was through her clothes. I didn't know anything about it, not even hearing her scream, as I was in the house. The first I knew about it was when she came rushing through the door shouting..."Get your gun!" I managed to calm Wendy down, knowing that he was on borrowed time and if such an attack recurred then I wouldn't have any choice other than to get rid of him, one way or another. As a result of that attack we grounded him for a few days, to give him time to settle down and think about what he'd done, but only days later, unfortunately that behaviour once again reared its ugly head.

I was attending to some things in the vegetable patch when I heard a commotion, and turned to see Wendy running full pelt through the garden with Zac attached to the top of her back, by his claws. He was pecking her behind her head as she ran. I grabbed the sweeping brush and with one swipe I whipped him off her back and he ran back towards his pen. I immediately made the decision that today was the day he was going. We couldn't afford to have this rooster running amok in the farmyard. With our grandkids visiting regularly and hopefully members of the public visiting in the future too, this could not be left to continue. Later that very same day, he attacked Olivia too, as she got out of her car after work, so as beautiful as he was, enough was definitely enough. Once the family were all safely in the house, I took care of things and our rowdy rooster was laid to rest under some wonderful oak trees. I hated doing it, but I had no other alternative. We had experienced trying to rehome roosters before, when Wendy had previously hatched hens' eggs and we ended up with 7 out of the eight eggs turning out to be roosters. Most of them went to auction, but for a couple of quid, it's really not worth the effort and that was after trying to give them away. As it happens, my actions hadn't gone down ever so well with one particular member of the family. Naomi, wasn't happy with me at all and after the earlier events, had posted a picture of me with Zac over social media, telling the world that I was indeed a murderer and had callously killed this innocent bird. Oh dear!

Anyway onto a lighter note, Wendy's produce sales were increasing considerably and as a result, her range of products had been increased, beyond the Strawberry, Raspberry and Chilli jams. She was now up to selling not just the usuals, but now things had been taken to a whole new level with Lemon Curd, Plum jam, Mint and Apple jelly, Crabapple jelly, Meadow Sweet Cordial, Elderflower Cordial and Tomato Chutney. We have been told stories of her chilli jam being bought to be sent to Guernsey, Tenerife and the USA, so you never know where things may end up. We had a really lovely note left on the produce stand one day, it just said, "Best Strawberry Jam we have had for years, Thank You!" It's always nice to get a pat on the back, especially when it's out of the blue and not expected at all, but it goes to show, that our lass was doing a grand job.

With Wendy now dipping her toes into the world of preserve production, it was now high time we ticked something else off our bucket list. Locally we saw advertised the 'Bishop Wilton Show', on roadside signs and so as a result we did some digging and I made a phone call to ask a few questions. As we had hoped, we hadn't missed the deadline for entries and so we thought, in for a penny, in for a pound and we sought to enter a number of the classes on the day. It was the first time we had ever entered such a show and it was all very exciting, although, like so many things, we really didn't have clue what we were doing. But what the heck, who cares? We didn't. Excitedly we arrived at the show ground, clutching our range of entries and soon found the correct tent to register our items. Wendy was entering 3 classes, Lemon Curd, Flapjack and the Wonky or most interesting egg class, I entered photos in 5 subject classes, with Naomi in one class also, and Sam one of our sons and his wife Leslie, had entered their home grown peas.

We filled out the necessary paperwork and then sited each of our items on the appropriate tables, before we took a sneaky little look around the competition. Oh my goodness, what had we done. These were professionals we were dealing with and boy, oh boy, did it show. That's when Wendy was approached by a lady, as she was carefully placing her jar of lemon curd on the table, beside the other entries. The mysterious lady was asking far too many questions for someone who was just interested and after talking for a few moments, Wendy twigged that the lady was not only a member of the WI, but was also one of the judges, which then set Wendy into a right tizzy. Everything that she could flap about with regards to her entry, she did. Is it the right consistency? Is it the right colour? Have I produced the right amount? Have I let it sit for long enough? But at the end of the day, it didn't matter a jot, we were only doing it for a laugh, heck, we were newbies! We made our way around the showground, dodging the showers, looking at the various stalls and exhibits until it was time for the judging to be completed. With much anticipation we hurriedly marched back across the rainswept field, after they announced the judging was complete and the tent was now open. I could hardly contain myself as we moved from entry to entry, looking to see how we had fared in our first run out, in the very competitive world of local craft and produce shows.

So, how did we do? Well, even though everybody loves Wendy's lemon curd and she sold bucket loads of the stuff and even though she had bought the best possible ingredients, she was placed last, but she put that down to the fact that she was competing with members of the WI, who had obviously done it all before. Wendy's wonky egg did much better and was placed 2nd, as was her 4 squares of flapjack and that was a marvelous achievement, bearing in mind, she only got the recipe off the internet the night before. Sam and Leslie, who had entered their homegrown peas, had actually won the class, and they had grown peas for the first time in their life. As for our photos, Naomi was awarded 1st place for the picture she took of herself and

Torrodon the tup having a cuddle, and I was awarded one 1st place and two 2nd's out of my five entries. We didn't think that was bad at all for starters, but had to hang around all afternoon before we could pick up our winnings.

I hadn't realised, but there was actually real hard cash involved here, it's not just messing about, oh no, it's deadly serious stuff! Our overly high hopes were soon dashed though, as we stood at the cashing out table awaiting receipt of our winnings. I can still remember gently rocking from side to side, moving from one foot to the other, with this fixed grin of anticipation on my face. I have since tried to wipe much of the memory of the next few moments from my mind as the cash was handed over and the realisation became evident that we weren't going to be dining out on our winnings that night. As a result, I have struggled to recall exactly what the vast amounts of winning cash were, but I do remember that Wendy received a whole 36p for her 2nd placed flapjack. In all seriousness, we didn't ever really consider the rewards on offer, but we just wanted to take part, become more involved in community activities and above all else, have some fun as a family.

As we were getting busier and busier every day, and there was just so much to do around the farm, I was regularly getting an ear bashing from Mrs. M, who was keen for me get some help around the place. Now in the main, I will give most things a go, but it's just that there's only so many hours in a day, and with only two hands, this can limit you when it comes to certain jobs. With this in mind, we roped in our Sam, who was on holiday from University and was looking for some extra cash, so he used to travel over several days a week from Brandsby, to help us out. It was great being able to get so much more done in a day, with the three of us going at it. It's funny, but that grass just won't stop growing and we were finding that if you miss cutting it, even for a couple of days, it can really set you back. We have a ride-on mower, but still, we have so much of it that needs cutting, for the summer months, it's a constant job keeping on top of it. So, between Sam and I we had regular grass cutting days, to make sure it all looked neat and tidy. With it now being summertime, the gardens were an absolute picture, with such an abundance of flowers, which were appearing from beneath the earth every day, it just looked beautiful. Being really sad, like I am, I would take a picture of each new species of flower as it appeared. In some cases, I wanted to have a record of where they all were, for the end of the year, when we were clearing the flower beds and in the spring too when we would be preparing the soil. Also, I needed a record of where certain plants were sited because I had made a pig's ear of something and had to try and put it right. When we moved in to the farm, it was very early in the year and the numerous flower beds were obviously not looking their best. What didn't help, was that in most of the beds there was chicken wire and other wire constructions, which were now littering the place with dead plants tangled up within them, and thus needing clearing out. In my wisdom, I thought I'd just clear out the lot and do you know it made such a difference, at the time, but in reality, I had messed up big time! It was only when spring came along, that I understood why all of these wire constructions were sited where they were. Surprise, surprise, they were supporting the taller plants and flowers in each of the flower beds and of course this idiot had shifted the lot!

Even with all the mess-ups I was making, life was continuing to settle down and our learning was increasing day-by-day. Normally this learning was coming through the continuing errors I was making. In all the reading I had done ahead of bringing sheep onto the farm, I don't ever recall anywhere where it said that they were devious, scheming escape artists, but as it happens, one sultry July evening, I was about to find out firsthand that they were in fact, just that.

On that evening, as it was almost dark, as usual I went to do my rounds, checking the animals and putting to bed those who needed to be locked up. Without thinking, I set off without my torch, which I have gone on to do on far too many occasions and so have then had to rely on the widgy little torch on my phone. Everything was going so well. Piggy McDoodle and friends were all sleeping soundly, Nessa and Stacey, the pygmy goats were bedded down, Queenie, and the jubilee hens were all comfy. George, thankfully didn't need chasing into the barn that night and was already settled on top of the hay stack, with Mildred on her nest as usual. All of our laying hens were present and correct and Torridon was just having a bite to eat for supper before he went off for some kip. Everyone was doing just fine and life was good, or so I thought!

As I walked out of 'Henville' that sense of peace and harmony suddenly all changed. As I shut the gate behind me, I could hear a chomping noise in the darkness ahead of me. I took out my trusty phone, turned on the torch and to my surprise 'Kehna' the sheep had, it seemed decided that the grass was greener on the other side of the fence, after all! I asked her to follow me, which she promptly did, all the way through one paddock and into where the other sheep were all snuggled down for the night. How on earth had she got out? I thought. I proceeded to search for gaps around the whole field. The fencing was all intact, these paddocks had brand new post and rail, so that wasn't the problem. Oh well, she must have squeezed through the rails and promptly justified doing nothing about it that night, but would await daylight when I could take a better look at the situation. So I walked out of the gate, gently closing it behind me, so as to not awaken some of the sheep who were already sleeping and as I did so, I turned to check the gate had shut properly.

To my surprise, the sheep and when I say sheep, I mean all of them, were being led from the front by Kehna, all in a long line and one by one they were ducking under the gate, which I had just closed and out they were coming from their paddock. In the spring a small trench had been dug at the front of the paddock, right under the gate, to aid drainage, and it just so happened that it was just big enough for these sheep to get through. I shouted for reinforcements, but as usual, nobody heard my anguished cries, which I know is a big surprise! I quickly ran to the barn, unlocked it, grabbed a bucket of feed and locked it all up again, ran back outside and minutes later they were all through into the next paddock and hopefully staying put. Well, that was it for Saturday night.

Sunday night soon came around and once again I was taking my wander around the residents, slightly earlier this time, so it was a little lighter. Again, when I came to the sheep I noticed that two of them, Kehna, again and one of her friends were munching away in the vacant cow field. Well, as you can imagine, I wasn't best pleased! I grabbed some food and got them back to where they should be. That's when I then noticed that they had once again made their escape under a gate, just a different gate. When the fencing was getting sorted in the spring, Rob's large 4x4 had left tyre tracks in the mud, which had since dried out and once again created a ready-made escape route for these woolly renegades. I parked the two offenders back into their paddock and yet again, with great haste I ran to the barn and grabbed 4 fence posts, lobbing them up onto my shoulders, and back out I went to the fields. My plan was that I would use these posts to temporarily block the gaps and cut off the escape route. I scanned the paddocks as I walked ever nearer and Hallelujah, the sheep were all where I'd left them.

The only thing is, as I may have mentioned before, these are no ordinary sheep and somehow they know what your intentions are before you do! So as I speeded up along one side of the fence, towards the offending gate, Kehna on the other hand was speeding up down the other. I'm sure her intentions were to get to the gap before I did, to make her break for freedom once more. So with 4 fence posts on my shoulders I ran as fast as I could, which as you can imagine, carrying that lot, wasn't ever so fast, and as I reached the gate I literally launched all of the posts off my shoulders, to try and deter any escape. As it happened, I did successfully beat her in the race for the gate. Phew! I have since sorted the gaps out, so other than tunneling out, these sheep are going nowhere, or are they?

It was a beautiful sunny morning, I arose very early, as I couldn't sleep most of the night, and quickly got my chores out of the way. Late in the morning, around about 11.30am, I could hear the distant squeak, which I have since come to recognise as Pete's cattle trailer, as it came trundling down our lane. Today was the day! The day when we at 'The Ginger Cow Company' had our namesakes and mascots arrive on the farm for the very first time. I hurriedly opened all of the necessary gates and one-by-one Pete manoeuvred his truck and trailer through each one in turn, until he was finally inside the field they were initially going to be calling home. He climbed out of his truck and we had a brief chat, as you do, about his journey and so on and then it was time for the girls to get out and stretch their legs in this field of lush green grass. I really couldn't believe that the time had arrived. I just stood in awe, watching these beautiful beasts slowly make their way down the ramp into the long grass, which was awaiting them. This was only ever supposed to be a dream and if I'm honest, never did I ever think that this moment would become a reality.

Above all else, even with the farm, even with the thoughts of rearing livestock, never did I ever imagine that Wendy would tolerate my harebrained idea of us actually owning real Highland Cattle, and yet, here they were! With owning the highlanders element now ticked off my bucket list, I could, in time turn my attention to the final part of my highland cattle quest and that was to breed our own calves, but that was for the future. But one way or another, you can be sure, I was going to make that part of my dream a reality too!

After chatting with Pete for a while, he was off again, back down the road to South Yorkshire. I stood, leaning on the fence, just staring at these beautiful cows and my only thought was, now what? I wanted to start straight way to build a trust with the four of them and there was no time like the present. By this time, I had been joined by Wendy, but it would be a little while until I would get her into the field with them, but all in good time. I walked across the field towards each one of them in turn and in turn each of them either walked or galloped away from me. Maybe this relationship building was going to take a little longer than I thought. Pete gave me a call the next day to check on the girls and I have been on the phone to him regularly ever since. It wasn't long before I was able to start sussing each of them out, with each having their own individual characters.

Visitors have asked so many times, about the cattle and the sheep too, for that matter, how can you tell them apart? My response is always the same, "Can't you tell your kids apart?" With spending so much time with them, I have got to know them so much more and besides, they all look different. Just because they are all big and ginger with pointy things on their heads, doesn't mean they are all the same. Monica is the largest and I understand that she is quite large for a highland cow. She has the largest horns, of the four of them, and they remind me of the bicycle handlebars I had when I was 15, the ones I had saved up my pocket money to buy. With her being an old girl, she rarely does anything energetic and she's the one who loves a cuddle. Lyndsey is the stockiest of them all, including her horns, which are small. She has the thickest coat, and at certain times in the year, she has very fair, almost blonde streaks in her fringe or 'Dossan' to give its official name. Flora has a fairer red or ginger coat, which is the closest colour match to mine as a boy. She has a fine pair of horns and is generally the most feisty, and to me looks the most stereotypical Highlander we have. Then last, but not least, is Morag, whose registered name is actually the same as her mother's 'Monica'. Rather than cause confusion, we named her Morag to make it easy. She has a darker ginger coat, with horns that look like they will end up like her mothers in time. Her temperament is often very similar to that of a typical hormonal teenage girl, you know the type, with a good old strop now and again and I've dealt with a fair few of them over the last 30 years.

Although it took a little while before I managed to get Wendy very hands on with the cattle, she was continually surprising me with all that she was keen to get involved in. One of those such occasions was when Marigold, one of our laying hens had a problem with her rear, a prolapse in fact. We worked out how best to deal with the situation after she had googled it, to get a few answers, and then I held Marigold, whilst Wendy cleaned up her back end and then daubed on copious amounts of 'Anusol', which she had bought in for the job. Marigold, like a number of poorly hens since, then spent a couple of weeks in our hospital wing, which just happens to be where the goats live. They all seem to get on and before long she was back with the rest of her gang, out in the field.

A few weeks after the cattle arrived, we had our obligatory visit from Defra to check us out and to ensure that we were dealing with our livestock in an appropriate manner. Following the visit we needed to arrange for our local vet to undertake the routine TB test which happens regularly to all cattle herds in the UK. To enable the test to take place, I had to get the cattle into our pen and then down the race, so that they were confined enough for the test to take place. That was when I appreciated that I had definitely made the right decision in getting the pen and race installed, and a proper Highland crush gate made and installed. I had heard too many horror stories of people new to farming, cutting corners and leaving Defra officials or vets to deal with animals without the necessary support, and that was never going to be me. It was an agonising 72 hours after the TB test, before we got the result, which thankfully was all clear. Although we believed that all was well, it was a relief to get an official thumbs up to confirm that it was actually the case.

The summer was coming to an end and the nights were drawing in, so the hens and ducks were heading off to their beds earlier and earlier each day, which was a welcome sight. I would find throughout the long light summer evenings, that if I went into the house and parked myself for a few minutes, then the inevitable happened and within seconds, I was snoozing! Rather than let that happen each day, I would find jobs to do outside which would keep me busy until the hens went to bed and I could then go and lock them up, before I headed in myself. Nodding off early never puts me in a good mood, and I was reminded of this fact on more than a few occasions by the women folk I lived with, so I thought it probably best just to stay out of the way until the hens bedded down.

October was now here and for some weeks I had been putting off taking our pigs to the abattoir. This wasn't anything to do with concerns about them ending up in the freezer, but was more about the daunting task of reversing the cattle trailer into position at the pig pen gate. Then there was the small task of getting the porkers into that trailer on the Monday morning, and then towing this trailer down the 10 miles of narrow lanes to Bubwith. On Sunday afternoon, with the help of my Dad and two friends, Matthew and Aaron Smith, I managed to reverse the trailer up to the entrance of the pig pen. We did some jiggery pokery with the electric fence and set everything up for Monday morning. The pigs were to be delivered around 12:30pm to their final destination. They had all been given a tattoo, which has their herd number on it and thankfully that happened without any incidents. The next morning, Dad, Matthew and I commenced trying to move the porkers at around 11:30am. As you would expect, just when we could do without it, the heavens opened and it started to rain. Very quickly we were up to our ears in mud, with the pigs, who are much smarter than I gave them credit for, not playing fair at all!

My idea of enticing these beauties into the trailer with food was failing miserably. After an hour we had secured one of them in the trailer, but the 2 remaining pigs were turning into a much greater challenge than we had anticipated and were eating bucket loads of food in the process. With just brute force and a field gate, we managed, after trying a number of methods, to push them forward into a very small space at the bottom of the trailer ramp. At that point they decided they had done more than enough for the day, were going no further and promptly laid down to catch forty winks. Whilst all this was going on I didn't notice that Dad had disappeared a couple of times, and later found out that due to my stress levels going through the roof, he didn't want to be laughing in front of me and so disappeared into the house so he could laugh openly, which I didn't think was nice of him at all!

Things were going nowhere fast and so I decided to talk to the abattoir and let them know we were struggling and were already 25 minutes past the arranged delivery time. They said not to worry about the time, as any time up to 5pm would be fine, but he did suggest, through his stifled sniggering that we should maybe try dragging them into the trailer. Bearing in mind that they should have left us a couple of months before this time and were as a result, enormous, like twice the size of most others who make the same journey, we were never going to drag them anywhere! I came off the phone and Wendy suggested that I should maybe tempt them with something tasty. "Like what"? I said. She headed into the pantry, with a mission on her mind. What could she come up with to save the day? After literally seconds she appeared with what she said may be the answer to our prayers, her freshly made Ginger Cake! She took out a very large and very sharp knife and started to slice the cake into pieces. "Come on Wend! they're not bothered about it being sliced, just sling it here", but she insisted. I took a pile of the cake, which she had neatly sliced up and ran out the door and over to the pig pen. I waved it under the noses of the two snoozing piggies and literally seconds later, they were in the trailer, with the tailgate shut!

Who would have believed it, that the Ginger Cow Company had been rescued by Wendy's Ginger Cake? There was a very big cheer, a sigh of relief and we delivered the pigs to their final destination. I thought we coped admirably with the lanes without a problem and was able to back the trailer in without wrecking the joint, so that was good. Mind you, I had visited the place half a dozen times, prior to the big day, just to check the turning circle and to see what space there was, so I would have been surprised if I'd had too much trouble. Returning to an empty paddock was a weird feeling and as much as we fancied getting more pigs straight away, we decided to wait until spring.

6 DAD…I'M DRYING MY HAIR

I was busying away, cleaning out the pig trough, when I could hear a banging coming from somewhere up the field. I didn't think much about it and just carried on with what I was doing, but the racket continued for a little longer, after which there was a pause for a few minutes and then silence. At that moment I did consider going to investigate, but just left it to get on with what I was doing. After a further few minutes there was an almighty crack and then silence once more. Now I was interested and went to have a look at what or who was responsible for making the noise. As I walked up 'The Green Mile', as we call it, which is the grass strip which runs between our paddocks, I could see immediately who was making all the noise, but I couldn't at that point establish, exactly what he was doing, to make the noise. Then it all became clear. The only fencing that we hadn't replaced, was around the paddocks behind the stables, one of which was now home to 'Torrodon' the tup. In his wisdom, our ever-so -friendly tup, Torrodon, had taken it upon himself to start some fence remodelling. I quickly ran back to the barn, grabbed his halter and when I got back to his paddock, I called him over, haltered him which he doesn't like at all and then tied him to a fence post whilst I carried out the repairs. Once I got the fence sorted I did have to give him a bit of a talking to and before you ask, yes he did sulk. I had hoped at that point, that he had seen the error of his ways and so he wouldn't take his temper out on the fence or gates any more. For reasons known only by himself, Torrodon then set out, it seems, to single-handedly wreck the fencing around him, completely. His behaviour was getting worse by the week and it seemed that every time we went to visit 'Monica' and the girls, if we didn't go and make a fuss of him too, he would take his temper out on the new £260 gate with his head and needless to say, his horns were doing damage, big damage. Anyway, just a few nights later, as I took the dogs for a walk he started again, battering the gate! You could hear it for miles. I was not a happy bunny as he was doing real damage to it. I ran around to give him a good telling off him and explained in no uncertain terms that thrashing my new gate with his horns was not to happen and was to stop immediately. The very next morning I took a trip to the farm store to buy two electric set ups, which I could site on his gate and any other paddock or field I put him in and hopefully that would deter him.

I was quite hopeful, that things would settle down now and he would start to behave himself, but alas, that isn't quite how things would turn out. A couple of evenings later, as I did my rounds, checking that everyone was where they ought to be, I noticed that once again, our 'Torrodon' had been up to his old tricks. He had been taking out his frustrations on yet another fence post! As it was pitch black and I didn't have tools with me to mend the fence, I quickly ran back to the barn, gathered up the tools and the bits I needed and rushed back up the field, to put right the damage. Now at this point I must say that things shortly started to go a little fuzzy, but this is what I can remember. Bearing in mind I was to doing all this under torch light, I bent down and laid the torch on the grass to try and light up the target area as best I could. I took hold of the damaged fence post, which was laying forward towards me at an angle, almost completely resting on the grass in front of me and started to push it back into its correct upright position. That's when our friend Torrodon, decided this wasn't what he wanted me to be doing at all and with my head now only inches away from the post, he decided to back himself up, so he could get a better run up and then he launched himself at the other side of the post, hitting it full tilt, with his head! Of course I had no clue that he was about to do that and so was only aware of it as the post hit my head and launched me flying backwards onto my rear in the long grass.

I can remember laying there, looking up into the sky and I was literally seeing two sets of stars. The beautiful ones above me in the heavens, and then there were those which were going round and round my head, like on one of the old Tom and Jerry cartoons. I immediately checked that my teeth were all intact, just to get my priorities right, and then I cracked on to get the job finished before I went back indoors. That night I went to bed with a whopper of a thumping head, a stiff jaw and just a touch of whiplash, but all was well and the fence was sorted and secure.

It was now late October and we were getting ourselves organised ahead of putting our unruly tup in with the ewes. As usual, I had taken advice and done plenty of reading, so November 4th or thereabouts was earmarked for the big day. Funnily enough we had friends over on that big day, as Kent Mayall, one of my old business partners and his wife Nicola had come over for a visit. I told him to wear some old clothes, as he may get roped in to a job that I needed a hand with, although he didn't have a clue what the job was at all. Soon after they arrived, Wendy and I took them up the field to where Torrodon lives. Along with us I took a block of red chalk and a harness. Firstly I was to attach the block of chalk into the front of the harness and then with Kent's help we needed to get the harness onto the tup. I gave Kent instruction to straddle over the back of the tup and then hang onto his curly horns, until I told him to let go. Now whilst Kent was hanging on for dear life, I just had to work out what all these buckles and fastenings were for, and which strap fitted with which buckle. It was a job and a half, but eventually after a whole lot of sweating and a great deal of trial and error, we worked it out and got all those buckles nicely tightened up. Our tup was now all ready for action. But before Kent could let go of him, we needed to get him into the quad trailer and then we could take him down to the paddock where his ladies were I'm sure, eagerly awaiting his arrival. We drove into the ewe field and opened the back of the trailer and to say he didn't hang about is an understatement, to say the least. Now at this point we stood back to see out of interest how he would behave and had no idea of the antics and behaviour which was about to unfold. We didn't know anything about all these facial expressions that he used, the curling of his top lip, the tongue darting from side to side like he was an overexcited snake waiting for breakfast and then there was him nonchalantly sidling up to each of the ewes and tapping them on their side with his foot. He was clearly just testing the water with them to see if any of them were in the mood for romancing, but of course this was all new to us! Well, enough was enough and before long we just walked away and left them in peace, for nature to take its course.

Whilst the ewes were in with the tup, we still had Pip, our bottle fed lamb who was going to be left alone for a number of weeks. We were keen that we didn't want her to get lonely in the meantime, so we asked around to see if anyone had a ewe lamb around the same sort of age which they were willing to let go, so we could bring it in to keep Pip company. We managed to locate a chocolate brown Southdown x Jacobs ewe lamb, from Holme on Spalding Moor, which is only 10 minutes away and the bonus was she was beautiful. We called her 'Wispa', after the chocolate bar and the two of them got on great, which was a relief, because Pip moaned enough as it was. After she had earlier been put back in with the ewes, after spending so much of her time with Wendy, Pip would start bleating every time she caught sight of her across the farm, so hopefully Wispa would help her settle down a little more. Things were going really well and both Pip and Wispa were inseparable, so that was a job well done.

Things continued to go well with Torrodon, and he appeared at long last to be behaving himself through into the new year, but then one cold dark night that sense of positivity we were starting to feel, was once again dashed. Why do these things happen at the most inconvenient times? You know, when it's pitch dark, it's cold and that comfy seat is calling you. As usual, I was again making a hasty run around all of the residents, checking, locking and bolting as I went, but this time I took a short cut from the pony stable through to the big hen house. All was well, and the hens were all tucked up in their beds. I walked out the gate from the hen paddock to the green mile, and that's when I got the shock of my life. For a moment, let me just pause and set the scene for you. As I looked out in front of me, there are two fields, the one on the left hand side, is home to the cows and the one on the right hand side, is home to the sheep.

As I strained my eyes, to see through the darkness, I could just make out the silhouette of a sheep, but this sheep was in the left hand field and not the right! I walked forward, a little confused, at which point I could see that in fact the left hand field was full of sheep, so where were my cows? I looked over to my right and to my surprise, the field on my right now appeared for some reason to be home to the cows. "How on earth has this happened? Someone is having a laugh here!" I was immediately thinking, who has been in and switched them around? But for the life of me I couldn't think of anyone who would have both the know-how and the inclination to do such a thing. I wandered through the field which was occupied by the sheep, and headed for the gate at the far side. I had a plan, to get the sheep out of there, and then move the cows back into where they belonged, but when I reached the gate at the far end, the story began to unfold, and it was only then when I started to understand just what had been happening. What I found when I reached the gate, was that the 'drive in catch', which keeps the gate closed was now several meters away from the gate post, where it had started from and the gate was blowing in the breeze. I picked up the catch whilst immediately realising how this had happened, and who in fact had caused such a switch to occur. Torrodon!

I shook my head, Flamin' Noras, that sheep's going to be the death of me, I swear. I had noticed that for some days whilst Torrodon has been in with the ewes, he has been taking a lot of notice of the ginger beauties next door and was regularly up at the fence, getting up close and personal with them, well as much as he could. Well, surprise, surprise, that wasn't ever going to be enough for him and obviously decided to take matters into his own hands, or hooves. He had hit the gate with such a whack that it sent the catch far into the field, forcing the gate wide open and he then led the ewes into the neighbouring field, which gave him the chance get even closer to the Highland cattle. They were apparently not interested in the woollyback's advances and they soon took a hike into the next door field, to get some peace.

I quickly popped the catch back into the gate post where it belonged, and then set about switching everyone back to their own fields, which wasn't a great deal of fun in the dark, with only a mobile phone torch for company.

Eventually, I got them all shifted and then called the house on my phone, to ask Naomi to quickly nip into the barn, grab my lump hammer and run it out to me in the field, so that I could get the catch walloped back into the post, so he couldn't do it again. But who'd have thought it, "I'm drying my hair Dad!" So, my hopes were dashed, she couldn't help and the other 3 women folk indoors, were also otherwise engaged too. (I sometimes don't know why I bother!)

So, finding myself in that situation, the only thing that I could do, was to try and force the catch in far enough that it would stay put and then I ran 'like the wind', well as fast as my little legs would take me anyway. I ran into the barn, grabbed my lump hammer (well, if I'm honest, it's actually my Dad's hammer that I nicked about 25 years ago) and then ran back to the field to sort out the offending gate. Lo and behold, when I got back to the gate, he'd gone and done it again. After a momentary loss of control and a short Rumpelstiltskin performance, I once again moved the animals back to their home fields and then with all the force I could muster, I put that catch back into the gate post. Let's just say, it 'aint ever comin' outta there again! To further ensure that the situation didn't reoccur, I went back to the barn and returned with a ruddy great big padlock and chain, which was wrapped around both the gate post and gate. Torrodon was going nowhere. Well, in actual fact he was, because only a few weeks later, I completely lost patience with him and sent him packing. Enough was enough, as beautiful as he was, he had damaged one too many gates and so off he went, to do what he does almost as well as he deals with gates and fences. He went to fuss over people in a petting farm.

Apart from dealing with an unruly tup, things were now getting very busy around the farm, well busy for us anyway. Wendy had progressed from her little cart at the gate and was now selling from her 'Shop in a Shed'. She was able to stock many more items and as a result she contacted the local council who visited her, to check things out and ensure that her hygiene practices were up to scratch. Having lived with her for thirty odd years and knowing just how fussy she can be, it was no surprise when she was awarded a grade 5, by the council, for her food hygiene. As much as she already knew that what she was doing was correct, it's nice to get that confirmation from those people who are setting the standards. On the back of the success with the shed sales, Wendy had the brainwave that she was going to start putting together and selling hampers with her home-made produce, in the lead up to Christmas. Although people were making all the right noises ahead of time, we weren't sure how popular they would be. We need not have feared, as sales went extremely well. Over the coming weeks we had orders for over 50 hampers, and that was going to take a whole bucket load of work on Wendy's part. All the different chutneys, jams and marmalades had to be freshly made, as did the granola and shortbread. The Christmas cake could be made in advance, so it tasted just right at Christmas, when those lucky enough to receive the hampers as gifts, would be opening them up.

The shed sales continued to do really well into the winter time, but that was when we had a visit from a couple of blokes in stripy sweaters. I was sitting at the kitchen table one afternoon when I saw a van come to a halt outside the gate, after a few moments, first one bloke, then a second walked through our gate and into the 'Shop in a Shed'. I continued watching and seconds later they both walked briskly back across the drive, out of the gate and into their van. There was something not quite right with them, I thought and so I looked out of the front kitchen window and quickly jotted down the car registration, the make, model and colour of the vehicle and then took myself out to the shed to check things out. Lo and behold the money jar had disappeared. I quickly called the local police station in Pocklington, but after trying to get through for an hour and a half I gave up trying and jumped in the car and went in person. I spoke to a very nice lady officer, who explained that they would get an officer out to visit us as soon as they could manage. I thanked her and returned home to await the officer's visit. I'm really glad that no ones life depended on that police officers visit, as it actually took them a good six weeks to turn up. I appreciate that it was only £30 or so that had been taken, from our honesty jar, but I had all the evidence required, including a photograph of the culprits' footprints. That was because the week before, myself and my Dad had roped in a further 3 people and we had shifted 42 tons of dusty stones onto our new front drive, which was an ideal surface to ensure that footprints would then be left on our shed floor. Anyway, we learned our lesson and have subsequently taken the necessary precautions to ensure we don't have a repeat performance from the thieving bandits.

So much of what we have been getting up to since moving out of town, has been based around a certain date or season, and this week we had another such time-bound task. We had noticed some months before, very soon after the cattle had arrived, that they could do with more shade in their fields. As a breed they can cope with anything, rain, hail, snow, ice and wind as well, but when the sun comes out, they run for cover. As a result we had purchased four trees from a local nursery. We bought two lime trees and two chestnuts, so that one of each could be planted in each of the two cow fields. We had taken advice and understood that in time they would give wide shade cover and offer just what we and the coos were after. Well the time had come for the trees to be delivered and although we had been promised that the trees could be brought into the fields and then dropped into the holes we had already prepared. As it happens, the pond life that turned up to deliver the trees didn't have a flamin' clue what they were doing and so we had to bring our fencer Rob in to save the day. Thankfully in the end, with Rob and his lads' help, the trees were in the ground and fenced off from the coos, before dark. The very next day, I did have to communicate my disappointment to the tree nursery regarding their standard of service and the quality of employee they provided for our job and needless to say, we shall never darken their door again.

Our first Christmas out of town, thankfully came and went without incident, which is quite a change for us. A very family-orientated season, giving us a chance to spend quality time with all of the kids, the grandchildren and parents too. Before we knew it the New Year was upon u, and it was time for our visiting billy goat to arrive and join the farm. The unnamed billy came trip-trapping onto the farm just after New Year, and first impressions were good. He was a striking looking character with a multi-coloured coat, a fine specimen of a beard and a wonky horn! Initially we didn't think that the wonky horn would impact on his romantic activities with Stacey and Nessa and things were all looking good, with him and Stacey, almost from the off. With Nessa, it was a completely different story. They just didn't get on at all.

Nessa is a slightly larger goat than Billy was and as a result would constantly spend her time putting him in his place. Over the next few weeks, it was the same story repeating itself each day. After a couple of months, I arranged to take him back to his home and let nature take its course with Stacey and Nessa. Although at that point in time, we were quite hopeful that Stacey was pregnant, but didn't think that we had any chance at all with Nessa, but still hoping that we would be proved wrong in time. That very slim hope that we were hanging onto was dashed the very next day, in the cruelest of manners. I was in the goat pen early the next morning, just sitting talking to the pair of them, when Nessa decided to take a wee. I noticed something unusual, something that I hadn't witnessed before, as Nessa was weeing from a completely different part of her body, to that of any normal female goat. At that moment, a lightbulb must have appeared above my head, because it was at that enlightening moment, I realised that Nessa was in fact, a bloke! When we bought her at the auction, almost a year before, we hadn't bought two females after all, as one of them was in fact a wether, a castrated male goat. Obviously if he had still got all his bits, I would have recognised that our goat was a male, but as the necessary bits were missing and we had understood that we had bought two females, we merrily went on our way believing that was the case. It's no wonder that Nessa and the visiting Billy didn't get along, it was now no surprise at all. Following our enlightening revelation, Nessa was renamed and we decided that alongside Stacey, we would have our very own 'Gavin' on the farm.

Early in 2015, I received a very welcome, but unexpected email from Lucy Oates, the journalist who had previously written articles about us in the 'Yorkshire Post' the previous year. She mentioned that Ben Barnett, the editor of 'Country Week' from the Yorkshire Post was going to be contacting me to discuss an opportunity for us to write a column each week in the paper.

Within a couple of days, he did indeed get in touch and put the opportunity to me. They needed Wendy and I to decide between us, which one of us was going to be the face of the column, as we obviously couldn't both take it on. Very quickly I was encouraged by Wendy to take the job on myself, and so that's exactly what I blummin' well did. Although I was somewhat apprehensive to say the least, as I had never undertaken anything remotely like this before, I did see it as a massive opportunity and was really excited to give it my best shot. In the first instance I needed to get my first offering to Ben, by the next Wednesday, which gave me around a week to get it all sorted. After lots of chopping and changing and reading and re reading, I eventually got the content where I was happy and the word count where it needed to be and with heightened excitement I hit the send button and off it went. Well, as I write today, that was three years ago and my 'Living the Dream' column, is still printed each Saturday. What's quite amusing is that there's my mother, who thought I'd left school without much of an education at all, and there I was writing in a major newspaper. Who'd have ever thought it eh?

As winter rolls on into early spring, I made the time to get lots of jobs sorted around the farm. If I left these much longer, these smaller jobs would get shelved, because the grass will have started to grow with earnest, and then we are on that relentless grass cutting highway all the way through until the end of September. The jobs I'm talking about are such things as felling smaller trees and cutting back tree branches, all of which I cut up for logs for the stoves. We prune many of the shrubs around the gardens, repaint the stables and shelters, cut the hedges and prepare the vegetable patch for the introduction of this year's new produce. One of the other jobs I needed to get out of the way was to arrange for the vet to come and check Monica out, to see if she was in calf. We had left her with the bull an extended amount of time the previous summer, to ensure she had more chance of getting pregnant and so we were quite hopeful that things would work out. I called our vets and arranged for Angus Mitchell, one of the practice partners to come out and check her out. From the very start, you could just tell by that look in Monica's eye that it was going to be one of those days. Last summer, when we had the pen, race and crush gate fitted, it was for these moments in particular, that we needed to have them in place. The cattle had been through them many times, so they have all become very accustomed to the surroundings, but this week, things were going to be different!

Ahead of Angus arriving, I had walked Monica into the pen. I was trying to make things easy and it meant that I just had to walk her through the race entrance, which she had done numerous times. I could give her some feed to occupy her and then close the gate around her neck to immobilise her, so the vet could work safely behind her. Easy, done it many times, or so I thought, why would today be any different? Well, my goodness, it was. From the moment I brought the vet across the field, her mood changed. She gave me a look as though to say, "Last time you let that fella near me, I ended up with a bald patch and a jab with a whoppin' great big needle, so not on your nelly". You see, that was Angus who had called some months back when the cows were all tested for TB and it appears that cows have really good memories. Almost immediately she tried to impale me on her horns, not once but several times, thankfully I'm quick on my feet and so was able to sidestep any attempt she made to swipe me with her head. No matter what I tried, nothing was working. Whether I pushed or pulled, prodded her with my stick, spoke to her nicely, ranted like a lunatic or tempted her with food, it appeared that on that day, nothing was going to get her down that race.

After 25 frustrating minutes we were getting nowhere, the vet was a busy man, and all the while it was costing me money. So we decided to call it a day and rescheduled for the next week. As we walked back over the field to the farmyard, we got around 200 metres away and turned to see what she was up to and lo and behold she was exactly where we had wanted her all along. The little monkey thought she was smarter than we were! With a quick change of plan, I got Angus to hide behind a laurel bush whilst I quietly meandered back over on my own, to where she was. When I reached her, she just looked at me with that smug look on her face as if to say, "You took your time, didn't you?" I quickly slid the bar in behind her, so she couldn't suddenly go into reverse and then I locked the gate around her neck, all the time thinking to myself, "Why couldn't you have done this half an hour ago?" Anyway, after all the shenanigans she had put us through, Angus could now get on with what he had come to do, to establish if our Monica was actually in calf, or not. He quickly donned his slinky full arm length marigold glove, lifted up her tail and got on with the job. So, after all that messing about, surprise, surprise, the big news was, that she wasn't even in calf! Never mind, that I was humiliated by her in front of the vet, never mind that I'd wasted countless hours weighing up if she was or wasn't pregnant, but now we didn't even have a little bundle of gingerness to look forward to in the next April either. I can't believe the hours I stood leaning on the fence watching those cows grow, when all the time, they had just been eating too much dinner. Hopefully next time, we'll be successful.

The jobs kept coming and the next task to tackle was our first attempt at draining some of the water which was standing in our front fields. They are lower lying fields and historically will have been drained via field drains, out into the dyke which runs along the roadside on the lane. Over time these will almost certainly have silted up, due to the very sandy soil we have in these parts and so we needed to take another route to clear the water. I had brought in a man and his digger to clear the ditch along the back side of our place and whilst he was around, I got him to extend a small ditch which ran alongside the front of the fields. He completed the job, all except for a twenty foot stretch of ground which he couldn't reach, which ran behind our compost heap. I said, "Oh, no worries, I'll do that by hand". Well that was a smart move, wasn't it! I grabbed my spade and shovel from the barn and set to shifting all that earth, in order to connect up the two stretches of ditch. Very quickly I changed the plan and I decided to tackle it over several days rather than aiming to complete it in record time, and do my back in, in the process. Thankfully it wasn't long before it was sorted, my back was still in good nick and we were ready for those April showers, should they arrive over the coming weeks, but let's say I won't be entering any ditch digging competitions any time soon! This was our first venture into the world of field drainage and it certainly wasn't going to be our last.

On the farm we have lots of beautiful trees around the place, and behind the house we have a have a small wooded area of around 300 mainly silver birch trees which we refer to as 'The Forest', although it clearly isn't. Within that area, the forest floor is awash with some fantastic flowers which begin to emerge soon after Christmas has passed us by. First it's the snowdrops, carpeting the floor, then it's the daffodils, which come in so many shapes, sizes and colours alongside primulas and primroses. As spring continues through into slightly warmer weather in May we will have countless bluebells emerging from the soil, which I have to say are my favourites. Probably because, as a young boy, I spent much of my time climbing trees in an area we called 'Bluebell Wood' and it was blanketed in them, and so when I see bluebells, it reminds me of those many tree-climbing adventures I had as a kid. The challenge which we experience is that we watch these spring flowers flourish, thrive and come to full bloom and before we know it, they begin to disappear. Slowly, but surely, we watch them gradually disappear under a sea of nettles and the ever expanding wall of brambles, which is trying its utmost to take a full hold of everything within the forest. We have thought about spraying the whole area, but are keen not to upset things too much, or to kill off the flowers we love, whilst in the process of trying to rid ourselves of the pesky nettles and brambles. We have thought about embracing the nettles by using them practically in both food and drink recipes, but as yet we haven't yet taken that plunge! In time, we are determined to come up with a plan to create harmony in there, one way or another.

Just when I thought that things were settling down with our animals on the farm, Nessa, sorry I mean Gavin, decided to throw a spanner in the works and was able to somehow figure out how he could escape from their enclosure and take a walk on the wild side once more. As chairman of the GEC (Goat Entertainment Committee), it appears to be my responsibility to come up with ways for the goats to entertain themselves. Most of the time, they are content with using the various toys I have made or bought for them, which includes a large tractor tyre, a lovely pink slide, a range of balls, with a Disney princess ball, being their favourite. The toy which has continued to keep them entertained the longest, is a set of steps which I constructed with a platform on the top, which allows them to stand and survey all that is going on around the farmyard. What I hadn't foreseen is that Gavin is smarter than your average goat.

Picture the scene, there I was just minding my own business, watching some finches on the feeders and I caught a flash of black and white, out of the corner of my eye. I did a double take and as I looked over a second time I noticed 'Gavin', running around the farmyard causing havoc and generally disturbing the peace and tranquility we are lucky enough to have, on a day-to-day basis. I shouted, "No!" in fact I bellowed to Wendy to grab her shoes and ran over to the scene of the disturbance, and Wendy immediately ran to shut the main gate at the front of the farm. We had Gavin contained and very quickly we were able to usher him back to where he should be. It was only then after surveying the scene we established how this breakout had occurred. The set of steps which had so lovingly been built for their endless entertainment, had been pushed from the middle of their pen all the way over to beside the fence at the front. Gavin had then only to trip trap his way up the steps, onto the plateau at the top and over the 4 foot fence to freedom he went. We are still uncertain as to whether it was a one-goat-job or whether Stacey had assisted in the attempt, but their escape effort was foiled before Stacey had managed to make her break for freedom too.

As you would expect, I regularly move the steps across to the far side of the enclosure so they couldn't try again, but that was clearly never going to be good enough as Gavin, as he managed to escape, via the same route, less than 48 hours later. What we did notice, which put our minds at rest, was that each time he had escaped, he wasn't out to run amok and disappear, but in fact all he wanted was to get back into the pen with his pal. It was all a game to him, well thanks for letting us know Gav', could've saved us a whole lot of running around pal!

Just before we moved out to Long Meadow Farm, our solicitor contacted us regarding a ditch which ran through the centre of the garden at our new property and then out along the back of our fields as it stretches out behind us. The question he was asking was, were we ok with taking on the upkeep of the ditch as it was situated on the left of our property and therefore should be our responsibility. We were all ready to take the leap and so obviously without even taking a breath I said, "absolutely, not a problem". Well, on the face of it, there wasn't any problem, but what I hadn't considered was the work it would take to keep it clear and free flowing. So, here's the thing, in practical terms, there are really two ways we can clear the ditch out and ensure it's always free flowing. One is to bring in a man with a digger and incur the additional expense but as I may have mentioned previously I am really quite tight, being a Scot now residing in Yorkshire. Or alternatively we can grab the necessary tools, take a deep breath and crack on with the job!

Actually, it wasn't immediately that I got on with the job, but awaited the reinforcements arriving a couple of days later. It's normal practice around here that I give my Dad a shout if I have a job that needs doing, and before long we set to and started to spring clean the ditch. Along the full length of the ditch it is over hung by dozens of trees, including many oaks, sycamores, maples, chestnuts, willow, fir and pines, to name but a few and they all look beautiful. But along with that beauty comes the down side of countless leaves which fall throughout the autumn and winter and it appears that most of these leaves find their way into the ditch. I donned the biggest wellies I could find, jumped into the ditch, armed with my leaf rake and soon began hurling piles of muddy leaves into the wheelbarrow. My Dad's job was to manouevre the wheelbarrow along the bank side as I continued to hurl the leaves towards it. He would then, once filled, empty it at regular intervals onto our compost heap. After two and a half hours we had cleared around a fifth of the distance and my Dad looked like he had been following a muck spreader across several fields, or had contracted a deadly disease last seen in the middle ages. I on the other hand was just plain jiggered and couldn't be bothered, to keep going. The old fella could have gone on all day, but like so many times before, he had to witness those same old tantrums, as I threw in the towel. The rest could wait for another day! I just wasn't used to all this proper graft, but I was getting more used to it each week and funnily enough, I was still finding trouble staying awake, if I parked myself in a chair any time after 5 o'clock.

I soon arranged for a man with his digger to come and complete the job, which he did pretty sharpish. On the other hand, I just had to not get too hung up about the cost and the digger tracks across my lawn and start considering the wildlife, like the fish, frogs, toads and newts in the ditch, who could now see where they were going for a change.

7 LAMBING TALES

Spring was now in full bloom and the whole place was awash with flowers, the trees were leafed up and the birds were diligently attending to their nest building duties. Although we were never sure when it would happen, we knew that shortly we too would be dealing with young ones, as lambing was about to begin. The only experience we had with lambing was our brief involvement after the event late last spring, when the two lambs were unexpectedly born on the farm. This year, was to be our first chance to deal with homegrown lambs and so we had done lots of homework and discussed the dos and don'ts with many people, as we were keen to get it right first time. Now, I appreciate that we aren't commercial farmers and we don't have to deal with hundreds of sheep strewn across never-ending hillsides, but all the same this was just as important to get it right with each of our 11 ewes. This was, and always will be an important part of our adventure, bringing new life into the world, into our little world and we were excited and looking forward to savouring every single moment of the journey.

Because I record most things in my phone, I remember that it was a Thursday when our eagerly awaited lambing first began. We were watching the ewes on and off most of the day, for the tell-tale signs, which we had read so much about, and early in the evening we noticed that one of the Hebridean ewes was restless and just couldn't keep still. She was up, she was down, she must've been dizzy with going round in circles like she was, and then she was continually digging her hoof into the ground. From our research we believed that she was now in the early stages of labour and just as it was getting dark we brought her into the field pen, so we could keep a better eye on her. At regular intervals we would wrap up warm and head out into the chilly night winds, to go and check on her and the other 10 ewes, to see if any progress was being made. In, out, in, out, it did feel like I was doing a bit of a hokey cokey, but at around 12:15am her waters broke and so I decided to go back in for a brew and then head back out an hour later, to check on things once more. Well, there's nothing like being thrown in at the deep end. I got across the field and what welcomed me did momentarily send fear and trepidation through me, but I quickly got a grip and got on with the job in hand. The ewe who was indeed in labour had her lamb with its head and right leg on its way out, but was now stuck and wasn't moving anywhere fast. Believe it or not, what flashed through my head at that moment was, what on earth would Adam do on 'Countryfile'!

Thankfully, because I have Mrs. Organised alongside me, Wendy had prepared for most eventualities and so I got my rubber gloves on and gave the ewe a bit of a sweep and immediately tried to work the lamb's left leg into position, to enable it to be born, but that just wasn't happening! I then tried to slightly put the lamb into reverse in order to make room to turn the lamb, but that wasn't going to happen any time soon as things had progressed past the point of no return. There was not a chance that the lamb's leg was moving for me and so I carefully, but with a whole lot of effort, eased the lamb out. I couldn't believe it, the lamb was out! I immediately gave it a rub, checked its airways were clear and from that point on let Mum take over. Under torchlight and the stars, she had given birth to a beautiful ewe lamb. For a few minutes I just stood in wonder as nature took its course and the mother's maternal instinct kicked in, as she licked her clean and very quickly had her feeding. I gave Wendy a call, who as you'd expect, woke the house up, and before long we had a party out in the field. Our first homegrown lamb had arrived. I don't mind saying that it was at times a little scary, very daunting, it was certainly emotional and it was definitely an experience I won't ever forget. The rest of the gang soon headed back in to bed, and after checking the other ewes I took the opportunity to just sit for a few minutes and ponder. It made me immediately think about our own kids and our grandchildren and sitting out there under the never-ending expanse of stars in the crystal clear skies above me, I once again realised just how blessed I am having the family that I have around me.

The lambing continued for the next few weeks, and it seemed like every couple of days another lamb or two would be born. We didn't have a clue about the timing of the births other than awaiting those signs which tell us that they are on their way. After the excitement of the first night the births were generally much easier, but no less exciting, but we were just bystanders in the main, but needed to be on hand to deal with any situations which may arise. The next traumatic birth which needed intervention was with 'Cloud'. After giving birth to her ram lamb without any trouble, she was having twins and so had her ewe lamb soon after, but several hours had elapsed and she still wasn't bonding with this second lamb and she hadn't managed to begin feeding. Rightly or wrongly, that's when we intervened. Once again, in the middle of a field, as the early evening daylight was disappearing fast, out came the phone and onto the internet we went. After some hasty research, we made a plan. I held the mother, and lined up the teat for the young 'un and Wendy, my able assistant, directed the new lamb to make contact and latch on. Wendy then turned the ewes head so she could sniff her lambs back end and commence the bonding process. It worked like a dream and before long the ewe was licking her lamb clean as she continued to feed. There was a really sweet moment which happened after all the struggles of getting the bonding underway. The ewe raised up her head and gave Wendy a look which simply said, "Thank You!"

We continued checking the sheep every couple hours or so throughout the day and night, and the births soon jumped from 3 to 8, which was great news. Things were going well. As the contractions continued, Wendy thought that it would be a good idea to have some relaxing music playing out in the field, which may just assist in keeping the ewes calm and assist them with their deliveries. I know it may seem just a bit crackers, to be playing some of the gentler sounds of the 70's and 80's, in our field labour ward, but it does appear to help and I'm always one for having music playing and giving things a go anyway. So as our first lambing adventure came to a close after 24 days, our final numbers ended up at 14 from our 11 ewes, with 8 males and 6 females. Our final lamb was born on Sunday morning in a driving hail storm. I was soaked to the skin, but that was nothing compared to the bedraggled looking urchin that clambered to its feet in front of me. Although we expected the birth to be some weeks away, 'Kehna' the mother was showing very few signs of even being pregnant at all, so we presumed therefore that she'd come into season some weeks after all of her friends, but, once again, we were wrong.

I am such a procrastinator and am forever putting off jobs that I maybe don't fancy, so I can do them 'another day', but some of those jobs just can't wait. Wendy and I had been preparing for such a job for some time but soon after lambing commenced, we needed to crack on and tackle this particular issue without delay. We had, even up to the night before, been taking advice on how to get it right and had even had offers of help, but we wanted to rise to the challenge and castrate our own ram lambs. We had first to gather all the sheep up and whittle out the ram lambs from their mothers. No matter which way we tried, we could bring all the ewes together into the large pen, but the lambs would always find a way out and would soon disappear under or through the post and rail fencing as they were so small, and weren't interested in the least in the treats we were tempting their mothers with. Inside the larger pen, we had to make a smaller enclosure with field gates, in order that we could single out those we wanted and then one by one we picked the ram lambs off and were then able to take care of the necessary task.

The advice we had been given the night before, turned out to be good sound advice and saved a whole lot of guess work and time. The advice centred around helping the lamb to relax instead of tensing up, which certainly wouldn't help matters, if you know what I mean. Wendy would take hold of each of the ram lambs in turn and holding them under their chest behind their front legs, she would swing them gently between her legs until they became relaxed. I would then, with the help of a special tool, stretch a very small and tight rubber band wide enough to be put around the rams little doo-dahs and then the band would be released. We achieved what we had set out to do and the end result was we left the field with all the ram lambs laid down feeling sorry for themselves nursing their bruised pride and maybe a couple of other things too. We repeated the same process as reach of the ram lambs were born over the few weeks we were lambing, as this little job needs taking care of within a few days of birth and under no circumstances can it be left until later. After around three weeks their doo-dahs drop off and the lambs are none the wiser.

I don't know about you, but often I can see something, hear something or smell something and I'm immediately whisked back to a time, normally when I was a kid or when I was in my youth, and it brings back so many memories. On one such occasion I was just minding my own business, whilst in the process of encouraging the local mole population to vacate the farm and I heard a sound that instantly transported me back to that really hot summer of 1976. That's almost 41 years ago, but nevertheless the sound immediately stopped me in my tracks. I looked up, as I have done so many times previously, straining my eyes across the vivid blue sky, looking out towards the Wolds in the distance, in order to find the source of that sound. After a few minutes of scanning the skies above me, with my gaze being taken higher and higher, at last I found what I was looking for, hovering directly above my head was a solitary skylark. It was in the summer of '76 that I first laid on my back in the middle of a field and watched in admiration as a skylark flew up from her nest beside me and slowly rose further and further above me up towards the heavens, all the while giving itself away with its distinctive song. The unfortunate thing is that it also brings back the other memories which surround this incident. As a hay fever sufferer, it wasn't my smartest move to spend the afternoon in the middle of a hay field in July. What also makes it worse is that I should've been in Mrs. Consadines history class at the time, but as I hadn't done my homework, I decided that pulling a sickie, was my most appropriate course of action. I can still remember my Granma's words as I walked through the back door at 3:00 o'clock, with my eyes streaming. "You're home early, you haven't been playing hooky have you?" What, me? Never!

After wading through the piles of necessary paperwork and red tape included in our planning application, and patiently coping with the months of waiting around for decisions to be made, so we could progress to the next stage, at last we received the green light from Planning, for our farm Teashop. In the short term, whilst we sourced the right builder for the job, we took the chance to progress things in a number of other areas. One such area involved Wendy talking to the local East Riding Council to seek permission to serve cream teas outside, in a tea garden, as and when the weather was fine, which she did for around ten weeks. We feel really lucky to be able to live out here in the country and are keen to have others enjoy that same peace and tranquility that we live amongst, and at times share the beautiful surroundings we have around us. I happened to have a rather fortuitous meeting at the local waste disposal centre, whilst I was in the process of clearing out some rubbish from the barn. I stumbled across a chap who noticed our Ginger Cow logo on the Landrover and started up a conversation with me, asking what the Ginger Cow was all about. Cutting a long story short, after being introduced to his wife, who runs the local food network, we were invited to a very productive networking event at Bishop Burton College. This enabled us to make some really worthwhile contacts to source local products and services, for the Farm teashop, but also to gain information to help us moving forward. It's amazing what you can end up with whilst clearing out your rubbish. It was about this time that Wendy really started to get hold of things in a business sense. She was able to make real progress in highlighting products, suppliers and services which she could tap into, to start to build the business that she had dreamed of for so long.

Alongside all that Wendy was up to with her Teashop plans, I thought that I would seize the opportunity to hold our very own photography exhibition on the forthcoming May Day Bank Holiday, entitled 'The world around me'. I decided that I would run the exhibition from the Monday, through until the following Saturday and hopefully the weather would be kind to us, and we could have Wendy serving cream teas and suchlike outside in the garden. In pulling it all together I never realised that I had quite so many photographs to wade through, but then again I have been taking thousands of them over the last decade or so, and deciding on which to exhibit was always going to be a challenge to say the least. I had this vision in my head that I could stack bales of hay, around the barn to create a gallery wall, up to around head height and this would then work perfectly as a back drop for my photos to be mounted. I worked out how many bales I would need to get my proposed wall built, checked how many I already had and then spoke nicely to Gordon Layton, my friendly local hay supplier, who was able to provide the remaining number I required. Before we could even think of setting things up I had a rather large job on my hands, I needed to tidy the barn and needed a fine day in order to tackle the task.

When the very next fine day came along, I set to work emptying what I could out of the barn and clearing out any rubbish which may have accumulated over the recent weeks. Most of that rubbish went up to the top of the Green Mile via the quad trailer, for my next bonfire. Once the place was cleared out, I then needed to sweep it out, wall to wall. Now that's not too tough an ask at all, you might think, but for this hayfever sufferer, who I may say is definitely allergic to dust, it may pose more of a problem than I would want really. What the heck I thought, and just cracked on anyway. I wasn't long into the mammoth sweep when amidst the ever billowing clouds of dust, my mind transported me back once again to being a kid, I was probably around 8 or 9 years old. At the time we lived in prison officers' quarters, in a home which, with others, backed onto Kirkham Open Prison. Now because it was an open prison, we would often see inmates around the small estate, doing gardening or maintenance work to keep the place looking good. One such inmate I remember was Jack. Jack would spend his time outside the prison gate, picking up litter and sweeping the kerb edges. It was back then, when watching Jack use his sweeping brush, that I cottoned on to the fact that every couple of pushes of his brush, he would tap the brush head on the road, without even breaking his flow, in order to free up any debris and dust from the brushes bristles, which then ensured it didn't clog up and meant that he didn't need to go over and sweep the same spot twice. I immediately changed the way I was using my sweeping brush and as the clouds of dust slowly started to settle down I could see that this was a far more efficient way to get the job done.

After much deliberation I settled on a number of photo prints which in my mind represented the beauty of the world around us, through my eyes, including landscapes, wildlife and seascapes. Images would be represented from both town and country, from as far afield as Australia and America, to those closer to home in Scotland, The Lakes, The Dales and good old Yorkshire too! After siting posters around the place and taking advantage of the wonders of social media, we opened our doors for business on the Monday morning. Business started briskly, which surprised both Wendy and I and that positive start continued on all the way through the week, until the close of play on the Saturday, when the gallery doors were shut. Although the exhibition was closed after a week, the 'Tea Garden' continued for a further nine weeks and was a roaring success, which gave us a great deal to think about. We learned such a lot during that busy period, but primarily we learned from our experiences that the Farm Teashop could, if we were smart about things, become the success that Wendy had dreamt for so long that it could be.

Since this adventure began and we changed our way of life, we have only managed to be away from the farm overnight just once, and other than that we have only been out for a full day on a few occasions. Our 31st wedding anniversary was fast approaching and so I was keen to make it special, but as usual, that's easier said than done. It wasn't like in the past when we could head to the Dales or the Lakes for a few days to celebrate, so what could I do that was a little different. I racked my brain trying to think of a way to celebrate those 31 fantastic years with Mrs. McKenna. It took a while but eventually I came up with the perfect way to commemorate our day and give her a right good treat too! I'll take her away. Our anniversary was on the Tuesday and things didn't go ever so well as I had been out in search of a 'Timepiece'. Well, that's what you're supposed to buy on your 31st anniversary, well according to the internet, that's what it told me. Well, to say the clock I bought didn't go down well, is a bit of an understatement, but hey there was time yet, I'm sure I could turn things around. Because we had a really busy few weeks on the farm, I'd decided that I would plan the big surprise for the weekend, especially if I was taking her away.

Thankfully, I got lucky and managed to book a table for the Friday night at 'The Pipe and Glass', in South Dalton, but of course I didn't let on to Wendy that this was happening, after all it would spoil the surprise. The Friday evening came and although she was suspicious, she went along with my plans. She later told me that she thought we were getting all 'dolled up' to go for fish and chips, as we often do and then she thought we'd go and sit in the car in our usual spot, up on the Wolds to eat it. Well, that wasn't the end of my plans, no, not by a long shot. After a fantastic dinner we set off for the second part of my plan to unfold. In preparing our night away there was a lot to consider, who would feed the animals and collect the eggs, who would bake the fresh scones and set the tables for the next morning? In short, we weren't able to go too far from home, and the result was that I took a slight detour as we drove into the farmyard on our return and immediately continued through another gate and up the green mile, through the paddocks to where I had pitched a very small two man tent. We had reached our destination, and this is where I had planned for us to spend the night! It wasn't a lavish hotel with everything laid on for her and it wasn't in some distant foreign clime, with a sun-drenched beach outside the window, but Wendy has said for months that she wanted to camp out either in a tent or under the stars and so it's just as well that I was on hand to ensure that her dreams would come true.

The air bed was in place, the new sleeping bags were unrolled and our daughters had followed my meticulous instructions and kindly made Wendy's favourite cheesecake dessert, which was sitting waiting for us, alongside the chilled drinks, outside the front of the tent. Even though it was a warm evening, there were concerns about 'catching our death', but no fear, because we were sweating cobs all night! The reason was, in my haste, I had bought an inflatable air bed which was just a fraction too big for the tent, but fear not, I squished it in, until it fitted. The unfortunate thing was that once it was inside the tent and the door was zipped up, it reduced the space considerably and we ended up almost a foot off the ground, which is quite high in a two man tent. Bearing in mind that Wendy hasn't been camping in any one of our 31 years of married life, I think I did alright pulling off this 'night away'. It was just beautiful to wake up to the sun streaming into the tent, the rustling of woodland creatures awakening from their slumbers and the dawn chorus outside the tent, in all its glory, I didn't care at all that due to being hunched up all night, I couldn't walk upright until several hours later. Later that day, just because I was now on a roll and wanted to be even more spontaneous, whilst celebrating our special week, we managed to get a very short one day holiday squeezed in too, well, a day out to Filey. I always said I could show her a good time!

For most of the weekdays and many of the weekends too over the last 30 odd years, before moving into Long Meadow Farm I had dressed smartly and worn a suit and tie to work. Since our big leap to the country that has drastically changed. One evening as I finished putting the cows through yet another enduring end-of-day catch up with me, I was walking back towards the house when the security light flashed on. Just at that moment I looked to my right and caught a glimpse of myself in Wendy's car window. Now I appreciate that doing what I do, means that I have nobody to impress, not even the animals, because they couldn't give a hang what I look like. I had indeed slowly but surely turned into the tramp my family had been saying that I was. For some months the women folk I live with said that I was going downhill, and I received many comments from them about my deteriorating appearance, and most of those comments were not very complimentary at all, but I just put that down to them being just a little jealous of my sense of fashion. After glimpsing my reflection the other evening, it appears though, that I may have somewhat misjudged them and I have in fact let myself go! In my defence, there is a very valid excuse, well I think so anyway.

From being young I never really found it a problem staying up late and over much of the last 20 years I have been getting up around 5:30 or 6:00am. It has never caused me an issue, but of course that was when work meant I was sitting in a car, at a desk or talking to people for much of my working day. So, since taking that leap in February 2014, my body has been given the shock of its life. Let me explain.

Although I don't think I have ever been lazy, I can never recollect consciously volunteering for any hard graft, ever. Prior to our adventure beginning, we considered many pros and cons relating to the move, the change of lifestyle, the sacrifices we would be making and of course the hard physical work we would need to undertake. Well, I can honestly say I underestimated that last point. I never appreciated just how much work it takes to keep a smallholding running, as well as setting up a business at the same time. The thing is though I am just so dog tired, all the time! I have considered curling up on the haystack or in the stable for a sly 40 winks, but haven't resorted to that yet. For years I used to get up early and run and thrive on being out there, but since our move, for me the running has stopped, due to a complete lack of energy. What makes it worse is, that I used to get it in the neck from Wendy for allowing running to take up so much of my time and now after years of chasing her to come with me, she runs every day, alone! One of her favourite places to run is up the 'Green Mile', which is the stretch of grass which runs between the paddocks behind us. The down side to her running there is that she is wearing out a line in the grass and as much as I ask her to run in a different line each day, my suggestion unsurprisingly always falls on deaf ears.

As I've mentioned previously, from the day 'Pip' our first unexpected lamb was rejected in spring last year, her mother was referred to as 'Useless Mother'. That was until 2:00pm on 29th April 2015, when she became the star performer from our little flock. Not only had she given birth to our third set of twins, but they were both female. As a result of this event we organised a competition to name the 2 lambs and their mother, as 'Useless Mother' really wasn't a very fitting name any more. After a fantastic response from far and wide, we came up with a winner and with the result being that the family are now known as, Delilah (the ewe) and Daffodil and Daisy, her twins (Daffodil having the darker markings on her face). They were the cutest pair of twin lambs you could ever imagine and although they were only very small at birth, they grew up fast, in fact too fast!

They were undoubtedly the most mischievous lambs we had that year, and because there are 2 of them, it just makes it double trouble. They are the ones who led the other lambs into trouble and got away with far too much around the place. Whilst the lambs are only small, they could squeeze under or through the post and rail fencing and as a result were constantly organising expeditions out of their field into neighbouring fields, including visiting 'Dad' in his nearby home. When they took the gang to visit Dad, Daffodil and Daisy were the only ones he allowed to clamber all over him and they regularly did, without him even moving a muscle. Time and again I had to go in search of these renegade lambs and then set about trying to get them back home to their mothers.

After, one of my many eventful evenings, chasing them across fields, I was considering that there must be a better way, without quite so much running around. That's when I started to try different ways of rounding them all back up. I did lots of shouting, I tried various hand waving and clapping techniques, but as much as each would catch the lambs' attention, they would just ignore my rantings and none of these ways would bring them back to where I wanted them to be. It was then that I witnessed a miracle, my prayers were answered and it all happened before my very eyes. I had been tracking down a gang of 7 lambs, including Daffodil and Daisy, when I spotted them, in the cattle field. In a moment of sheer desperation, I raised my fingers to my mouth, and I just whistled. I hoped that maybe it would do a better job of getting their attention, but what happened next was just like magic. As the sound of my whistle suddenly hit their ears, they all, in unison stopped dead and then they all turned and without any delay ran full tilt across the 2 fields. The ground between themselves and their mothers was soon covered and as they squeezed back through and under the fences they didn't hesitate once until they were once again reunited with their mothers. Well, that's a bit lucky I thought, but no it wasn't luck, because it worked every time, from then on in. All the same, I was looking forward to the day when they couldn't squeeze their chubby little bodies through the fences any more.

The births that year on the farm hadn't finished yet and as we were coming towards the end of June, we still had Stacey, our pregnant Pygmy goat yet to give birth. I recall just popping in for a routine check, whilst passing the stables, and lo and behold, what I found was that this little lady was already pushing. I immediately abandoned my proposed cattle grooming session, which the ladies weren't too enamoured about, and then Wendy and I went to see if we could help our little goat give birth. We had been told many times that goat births are very similar to sheep and react in a very similar way to labour. After only a few minutes and after not much pushing at all, the highlight of our week happened in front of our eyes, when 'Bambi' was born. From the very beginning Stacey was, and still is, a very good mother to her little girl, very attentive and protective and would always try and join in with Bambi, when she was having one of her mad half hours.

After putting off the cows' grooming session to oversee Bambi's birth, I rescheduled this long awaited event. You see, when it gets to early summer, the cattle are well on the way to losing their winter coats, and as this happens their coats end up with lots of knots. Now as the father of four daughters, I'm very well versed in dealing with knots when those bath and hair-washing nights come around. Many a time have I had to comb and brush through little girls' long hair to make sure it has no tangles in it, but I must say that's the full extent of my hair duties. Sorting out a pony tail or a plait never ended up the way that they should, if I was left in charge.

So it was then back to pampering the cattle. When grooming them, I can stand in the field and take care of Monica and Morag, without any trouble at all, but the other two are a little timid and tend to walk away whilst I'm trying to give them a comb. Monica and Morag will stand there all day getting groomed if you let them. Monica will lift up her chin and turn around so you can get at her other side and if you happen to walk away before she's finished with you, she'll just follow you, so you do have to be a bit sharpish, because if she gets near to you before you get out the gate, you may well get her horn stuck right up your whatchamacallit, for your trouble. Anyway after sorting Monica and Morag out I put Lyndsey and Flora firstly into the field pen and then they would be going through the race, so that they're in a controlled environment, enough to groom them properly and get rid of their knots. Lyndsey went first and all went well and she came out the other end looking good and so finally I just had Flora to take care of. Flora, it seemed hadn't read the script and felt that being so cute shouldn't stop her being a moody cow, literally, deciding that she wasn't following the others into the race. After several minutes trying to shift her, she was having none of it, and with one quick flick of her back leg, kicked out and just caught my shin. Well, I certainly felt it, but thankfully there wasn't too much damage and I decided to give her a few minutes to calm down. Before long we were all sorted and they were all looking beautiful as I moved them through into the long grass in our top field. That kick I got from Flora has, so far, touch wood, been the only slight injury I've had from any of the cattle, from either hoof or horn, so I'm doing alright I think, so far.

Now just going back to pony tails for a minute. Over the past few years we have been pestered by our daughters that we should get a pony. It has never been something that came into our thinking, as we didn't have the time, the space or the money to take a ride down that little road, but lately of course, things have changed, because we now have the space. We also decided recently that we would do some homework on Shetland Ponies and, once we had all the facts we would then consider if it was time to add to our growing family of animals. We nearly found what we were looking for, about 6 weeks ago and thought we were onto a winner, but it wasn't to be and afterwards were a little disheartened that things didn't work out as we intended. Well, it's been said to me many times, "as one door closes, another one opens" and sure enough, a little patience was all that was required.

It was on a beautiful sunny afternoon whilst Wendy was serving cream teas in the garden and we were just winding down from a busy day, when a lovely couple noticed us as they were passing in their car. They decided they would pop in for a look and see what this home-made ice cream was all about. I was pottering away round the back in the farm yard when the chap wandered around, with his ice cream and was looking at our animals. We soon got chatting about all sorts of things and what our plans were and what we were getting up to, when out of the blue he asked if we had any horses. I said no, but we had recently been considering and tentatively looking to bring on board a miniature shetland pony, but hadn't been successful so far. "Well", he said, "Would you like two of them?" At that, I was a little taken aback. He went on to explain his story. For the last decade or so his health had been deteriorating badly and although he had been breeding mini shetland ponies for almost thirty years, the concerns with his health meant it was time to find a new home for his 'little girls'. I later found out that for more than two years he had been seeking the right home for them and when he arrived at our place and he spoke with us, he said that he felt like his prayers had been answered. After Wendy and I spoke, we made arrangements to go and meet the two ponies and as you would expect they were beautiful. That was it, our decision was made, they were joining the McKenna family.

As I'm sure you can imagine we were doing a lot of reading up ahead of their arrival, and on the Friday evening our daughter Evie and I took the Landy and trailer and headed over to pick them up. After negotiating the narrow drive and squeezing the trailer through the garden gate, I was able to turn it around, load the little ladies up and then we promptly set off once again to bring Maisie and Lucy home. Maisie at the time was fourteen and her daughter Lucy was nine and we could see that it was quite a struggle for the couple to part with their precious ponies, but we assured them that we would take great care of them and from that day to this they have been pampered regularly, but not with too many treats, of course! Quite often Shetland ponies can be a bit snappy, but in all the time we have had them we haven't had any of that at all, they are little angels.

As the growing season continues through the summer months each year, it often turns out that we need to move the animals from pasture to pasture to make use of the new grass, and it helps to give each of the fields a rest for a time. After moving the cattle to the top field, we shifted the ewes and recent lambs into the field alongside the oak trees, as the grass needed bringing down. We moved them across on the Saturday and by Sunday afternoon we had already experienced a mishap in the new field. The accident involved one of the lambs, the one we called 'Flash' because he was dark in colouring, but had a white zig zag flashed along his side, much like Flash Gordon had on his vest, all those years ago. What had happened was that he had knocked off one of his horns, leaving the softer tissue exposed and bleeding profusely. He had either caught it in the stock netting fence or had been a little over boisterous with one of his brothers or sisters, when butting heads. I called and had a brief discussion with our vets, after which I set off to track him down and administer the necessary first aid. If only I had seen into the future and left the sheep in the field where they were, you know, the one with the field pen in the corner, but no, I had to move them all into the largest of our fields. This field had lots of nice long grass, but was somewhat overgrown and had lots of nettles and a bucket load of thistles too, almost as tall as me, thrown in for good measure. I had been trying to catch the lamb, using all sorts of methods for literally hours, on and off, and I was to say the least, jiggered. As he was just a young lamb, he hadn't quite cottoned on to following the feed bucket like the older ones do, but I wished that he had that day. After several hours I threw in the towel and waited for willing reinforcements, some with younger legs I hoped. Our daughter Evie had been out somewhere but when she got back got in, I gave her one of my best 'I need your help' speeches and surprisingly, it worked. She quickly got changed, we made a plan of action and that plan involved my lasso. I hoped that all those cowboy films I watched when I was growing up, would help me to catch this runaway lamb. Well, after only 20 minutes we had 'Flash' in our grasp. We calmed him down, stopped the bleeding, sprayed the magic spray onto the affected area and bandaged up his head and before we knew it, the little wounded soldier was soon off on his way again.

As you can imagine, we have learned so much over the last few years about so many things, but what never ceases to amaze me is just how smart farm animals can be. One evening, as I was walking past the pig pen, I was alerted by some commotion across the field. I stopped to take a closer look and couldn't believe what I was seeing. The three chestnut trees which are either inside or overhang the pen were now in full bloom, and the young chestnuts were growing larger by the week. Under one of the chestnut trees, there were our four pigs, not your ordinary every day pigs, but clearly very smart porkers. They had worked out that on their own they couldn't manage to reach the tasty treats, which were just beyond their grasp, but if they helped each other and jumped up onto the shoulders of their sister, they may just be able to get to where they needed to be. They soon worked out that even on the shoulders of others, they were still slightly short of the target. So after working out that it wasn't quite enough, they encouraged the pig underneath to jump up, with her sister on her back and only then did it enable the pig, on the shoulders to reach the supper which dangled above them. The amazing thing was, that not only did they do this the once, but all 4 pigs took a turn to have some of this late evening supper and funnily enough, all of our pigs since then have taken the same route to reach this forbidden fruit too.

One of my favourite things about living where we do, is the chance we get daily, to see the wildlife which is all around us. I have so many favourites I know, but what is really special is to witness the swallows bringing up their families. A few months ago they arrived back on the farm and very quickly they got down to rebuilding their nests and laying their eggs. At the time we had 4 swallow families who lived on the farm. One family in the pig house, one family in the front field shelter and one in each of the stables. After some weeks of waiting the eggs hatched and the hard work began, as the parents shuttled back and forth, in and out of the nests, bringing the grub for their little ones. After a further period of patient waiting, the parents managed to coax their bairns out of the nest, in order that they could take that first leap of faith and fly, but this was all a surprise to me. Just going about my chores in the early morning sunshine, I walked blindly into one of the stables and yet another special experience unfolded before my eyes. I looked up initially as I did each time I entered the stables and the normal scene which greeted me, with the five open mouths chirping for food, had changed and all five of them were perched on the edge of the nest, with their big eyes looking down with trepidation. It looked like they were awaiting their next instruction from Mum or Dad, who were sitting on the beams above my head and the young 'uns weren't budging until they got the word. Well, it seems that word came pretty quickly after, as almost immediately the five fledgling swallows leapt from their perch and commenced flying in circles around and around my head. I just stood and watched them as they periodically stopped flying and clung to the walls momentarily before they once again leapt off the wall and continued flying in circles. After a few minutes they must've got bored of the view below and followed their parents over the stable door and out into the farmyard.

From April through until September time we have the pleasure of their company out here on the farm, and my goodness it is a pleasure. Each day during the time they're with us, you can see the swallows flying up and down the paddocks and skimming across the tops of the spring barley, or the wheat in the neighbouring fields. Absolutely beautiful! With all the broods combined, the largest number of swallows I've been able to count together in one spot, was on one Saturday evening in September, when there was 77 of them all lined up along one of our cattle field fences. The very next morning they had vanished on their travels back to South Africa, which amazes me each time I think about how far they travel, and they're so small too. Boo, one of our Border Terriers regularly tries to chase and catch the swallows, as they clip the tops of the blades of grass on the green mile. As quick as she is and she does catch many things that move around here with her speed, she 'aint got a prayer, with that little challenge!

8 WHAT'S THAT SQUEAK?

I could see across the field that Wispa, our Southdown x Jacobs, just wasn't herself. I had watched her for a couple of hours as she was spending too much time on the deck, and when she was up, she was having one long itch along the fencing. Immediately alarm bells rang in my head…we have a problem. I hurried over to her and began to check her out and it didn't take more than a few seconds for me to confirm what I had already suspected. As the weather starts to get warmer, green bottle flies hatch and go in search of damp wool or dirty bottoms on sheep and other animals, as these are perfect places to lay their eggs. Once the eggs hatch, which is soon after they're laid, the maggots then eat their way into the animals flesh and at the same time release dangerous toxins. This condition is called 'Flystrike' and if they are not caught up with very quickly the animal can soon die. I treat all our sheep with a spray, in order that we don't have any problems when the weather starts to warm up. We quickly treated Wispa with injections and as horrible as it is, we had to first cut away the wool around the affected area and then remove every last maggot that we could find. This could only be done by systematically squeezing each and every one of them out of the poor sheep's flesh. We struggled over the next 24 hours to keep her alive, but early on the Sunday morning we lost Wispa.

It was a nightmare we never expected, and at that moment, I made a promise that I would never find my animals succumbing to this dreadful condition again. I wrapped her up and made the necessary call for her to be picked up as soon as possible, which was arranged for the very next day. Now, just for a moment I want you to picture the scene. It was a lovely sunny day, and Wendy's Tea Garden was full to bustin' with customers sitting enjoying the food and the surroundings. I had been busy up the field cleaning out the hen house, when unbeknown to me the truck arrived to pick up Wispa. The driver, who unfortunately had a close resemblance to Quasimodo, had opened the gate and backed up onto our drive, without any of us noticing him at all. By the time he was noticed, it was too late and he had wandered around the side of the barn and announced to all our customers, "I've come f'ot sheep!" As I was busying away up with the hens, I noticed him appear in the Tea Garden and ran as fast as I could back down the green mile and through the gate to where he was. I got 'the look' from Wendy and immediately escorted him around the back of the barn and we took the other route through the barn and picked up Wispa on the way. Not a nice experience at all, and one which I aim not to be repeating ever. Luckily, it didn't appear to put anyone off their Cream Teas, but you never know.

With the improving weather, and it being the right time of year again, late one afternoon our Wendy and I set off, armed with all the necessary tools required to gather as much elderflower as we could carry, in as many baskets and buckets as we could lay our hands on. Thankfully, we don't need to walk too far to stumble across vast amounts of the stuff. So, after getting all my instructions, "only the large heads in full bloom and not those past their best", (whatever that means) we cracked on and soon had every basket and bucket filled to bustin'. The most amazing thing was, that neither of us got stung by the abundant amounts of nettles in the same hedgerows. Wendy was soon getting on with making her Elderflower Cordial, which I must say, is delicious, and that's probably why she sells truckloads of the stuff. You see, that's something else that she'd never even thought about doing until we planned to move into the country.

The time had soon come around when Monica and Lyndsey, two of our 'Highlands' were off on their travels, but they were only leaving for a couple of months, as they were off to have a party with Mr. Bull, down beside Sheffield. We were once again full of hope after Monica had failed to get in calf the previous year, but this time things were going to be different. We only send the highland heifers to the bull after three years of age and so Flora and Morag were left behind on this occasion. It also gave us the opportunity to wean Morag off her mother, whilst Monica was away. We now just had to sit back and await their return in ten weeks.

Whilst the two cows were away, I took the opportunity to spend more time with Flora and Morag, the two younger cows, as they were often the ones who were pushed out of the way by the older ones, when I went to see the cows each day. On one of these days whilst talking to them, the sun was beaming down as I sat on the fence in the corner of the field, and I was admiring these lovely yellow flowers we are blessed with in abundance around the farm, but I was oblivious to what evil lurked behind their oh, so innocent appearance. How was I to know what damage they could do? This townie was just learning the ropes. In fact this was no ordinary plant, it was ragwort and I had no idea that ragwort poisoning could have a disastrous effect on horses, cattle and other animals. Well, the very next day after being given this wake up call, I got Sam, who luckily was over helping out, to walk the length and breadth of our eight acres and dig up every last root of the plant and build a bonfire with it. Let me tell you, it took him a while, but we had a mighty fine bonfire to torch at the end of the day.

On some days, as we all do, I try and pinch a few extra minutes in bed, ahead of heading out to get my chores underway. On the day in question, I wasn't even properly awake that morning, as I staggered out the door, excited for the day ahead. Without even thinking about it I stood on the front step and automatically popped my right foot into my boot and this was quickly followed by me sliding my left foot into my other boot. Squelch! went my foot as my toes reached the end of the boot and immediately I pulled out my foot. I picked the boot up and before I even tipped it upside down, I instinctively knew what was hiding in the darkness below. Mr. Toad, in his search for a cosy bed for the night had snuggled down in there, not thinking for a moment that he was going to be rudely awakened by my size six and a half foot, descending upon his head early the next morning. Luckily, he was still in one piece and as I said goodbye and let him loose in the flower bed, he hopped away merrily, with an obvious lesson being learned that morning, for me and him.

One of the benefits of having our little farm has been the fact that we can organise to do family things together. Since moving to the farm we have been able to have bonfires, picnics, Easter egg hunts, Halloween events and we've been able to organise sporting events too, like playing football or rounders. As we get more and more organised, we will hopefully be able to arrange even more fun activities too. So, the time was fast approaching when we were to start building Wendy's teashop. We hunted for some time to get the right builder in to do the work and in the end settled on a company which had been recommended to us by friends. Even before their work could commence we needed to undertake a lot of preparatory work. Due to planning guidelines we needed to build the teashop within an existing structure, our barn, and as a result, we needed to clear a whole host of trees and shrubs, which were firmly rooted in place outside where the new front door was to be located. It's a shame that we had to lose so many in the process, including a beautiful mature magnolia, which we had hoped we could keep, but even cutting it back, it would've blocked much of the light which we hoped would come streaming through all the glass at the front of the new building. It was great at long last to see things starting to move and watching the professionals at work doing their jobs was quite exciting really after so much talk, we were now seeing some action. All it took was a digger, a chainsaw and a box of matches, with some graft thrown in for good measure of course and in a matter of hours the trees and shrubs which had been in our way, were out, cut up and torched on the spot. And to think that normally, I would have got in a couple of large skips to get rid of the bulk of the tree waste and then with the help of my trusty quad and trailer, I would have burned the rest up at the top of the green mile. This time though, not on your nelly! In a matter of hours, the place was bare and all that was left was level, bare soil. Easy I thought, why didn't I think of that!

The other work which I needed to get done ahead of the building commencing, was to get the new entrance cut through the field hedge, the new road put down and the two entrances kerbed and tarmacked. Whilst having the professionals on-site, I spoke to them nicely and arranged to have a rather large obstacle, my enormous compost heap, shifted, which would have taken me literally weeks to move, posts included. Within an hour it had disappeared, leaving no trace of where it had once stood, much to the disgust of the rat family who had suddenly lost their home and were now scurrying about frantically seeking an alternative, deep dark hole to disappear down. Sorry, rats, you'll get no welcome around here! Before long we had the block work up, stud walls going in and ceiling beams in place, the teashop was taking shape. I must be a right pain in the neck and I know that, because whenever work is being done on site by contractors, I'm there, right at the core, in their faces, asking questions and checking things are being done as I would have them done, and I'm a right fussy devil too!

With so much now going on, it had reminded me what it's like to work under pressure. Back in the spring we decided that we would, as part of our planning application, go ahead with having self-catering accommodation on site for people to rent and stay on the farm. We toyed with caravans and camping pods and other such ideas, but in the end plumped for a Shepherd's Hut. Which in a nut shell is a self-contained shed, on wheels. Again we trawled the internet and did lots of homework until we found who we were looking for, 'The Yorkshire Hut Company', who were quite local and had a great reputation for their work. We sat down with Pennie and Kevin from the hut company several times and discussed all the options available to us, before agreeing just what would go into our hut and exactly how it would look. In the end we plumped for one hut with a double bed and a three quarter bunk above, and a log burner to keep it cosy on those long winter nights. We agreed on a fully plumbed-in shower and toilet, electric lights and sockets, a fridge, a sink and for good measure Pennie, being the artist that she is, even etched and painted our 'Ginger Cow' logo onto the cupboard doors. Now, Ahead of our shepherd's hut being delivered in the spring we needed to get one of our fields landscaped in readiness for its arrival. In preparation for that happening, I had arranged for the field to be rotovated, ploughed and levelled, and then I could get it seeded to grass. That's where the pressure starts to come into effect, as I needed to get a couple of jobs taken care of before the tractor work could even begin.

Surrounding the field in question there is almost 300 metres of fencing. Now, this wasn't ever going to be just an easy-to-shift fence, well for me anyway, as the 5x3 posts have been buried a couple of feet into the ground, topped with a rail and over the years have had several layers of stock netting and chicken wire attached to the posts, to keep livestock secure. So that the best job can be made of the ploughing, I have been removing all of the old fencing and my goodness has it been hard work, especially when you know you have a deadline looming. Thankfully, parts of the job were made a whole lot easier by utilising my land rover and the quad to the full. I would tie my length of rope around some fencing, with the other end onto the back of the quad and then hit the throttle. It's quite a satisfying sound, listening to the engine growl and the stock netting snap away from the fence posts and snake behind you like a leaping cobra. Then, after starting to shift 200+ fence posts by hand, I thought to myself, there must be a better way, and indeed there was! I ran down to the house, grabbed my Landrover keys, jumped into my wagon and took her up the field to work. So as the sun was beaming down on that late October day, Landy and I removed all of the fence posts. 'How did you do that Shaun?' I hear you cry. If I'm really honest, it wasn't the most difficult job in the world, as I just slowly drove my jalopy at each post in turn, giving them a whack with the bumper. Most just became loose and I could jump out and remove each post as I went along, but some posts decided to become a little awkward and so they just snapped where they stood and I later covered up any remains and left that part undergound to rot over time. It was quite fortuitous as it happens, as we were hosting a large bonfire at our place only a few days later, so the majority of the old posts helped to build the mother of all bonfires in the top field.

Another of my deadline jobs, was to cut back many of the overhanging oak trees, in order that a tractor could reach into the field edges and corners and take care of the rotovating and power harrowing, which needed to be done ahead of me seeding it. I had visions of me standing on top of my rickety old step ladders, trying to make the most of every single inch of my 5' 6" (and a half) frame, whilst trying to control the chainsaw in the process. Never a good idea! Thankfully, I was offered the use of a more suitable tool to get the job done, rather than risk losing a limb in the process. In the end, the job which I feared would never get completed satisfactorily, was again done and dusted in a couple of hours and I once again learned that with the right tools, tasks can be made so much easier.

I couldn't believe it, but the time had come around again, and they just seem to come along so fast, it's another of those big days. It was once again time for Piggy McDoodle and friends, to leave the farm and take that trip to their final destination. Unlike last years' experience which took many frustrating hours to get the pigs into the trailer, this time around it took no more than 20 seconds to have the cargo on board and the doors secured.

Undoubtedly, I had learned a great deal from the last years challenge. With a sense of pride and a bit of a smile on my face, I stood there in the pouring rain, thinking to myself how much of an anti-climax I had just witnessed. So much meticulous planning had been put in place with the many potential calamities and obstacles having been considered, and after just 20 seconds, we were done dusted and ready to go! Now, that's progress for you! All that was left to do was to go and pick our pork up later in the week. This time around we wanted to get some of the pork cured for ham and bacon and so as usual, we did lots of asking around and a number of people suggested the same place. So, on the Thursday afternoon, Wendy and I picked up the pork and then travelled over to Sutton-on-Forest, to visit Val, who was going to take care of that little job for us. Eventually, curing our own meat will be another experience Wendy would like to go through herself, but this time around, we'll see how Val gets on. After picking up our porkers from our local abattoir and butchers, and after dropping some of the meat off to be cured, we headed through the busy teatime traffic for home. What greeted us at home wasn't at all what we were expecting. Although our daughter and my parents were supposed to be at home, the place was in complete darkness. I walked in and immediately flicked the switch to turn the light on, but alas, nothing! "Oh, flamin' Noras, there's a power cut!" I shouted. I did all the normal checks that you do in these situations and then called an electrician we've used before, for some over-the-phone assistance, but still no joy. What confused me though, was that although the house was in total darkness the power was on in the barn, with the lights, freezers etc. all working fine. I called our neighbour who explained that there had been a very short power cut in the afternoon, but had only lasted minutes. By this time our 2 older girls had arrived home from work and soon decided to head out to McDonalds for their tea, and it also meant that Naomi could get her homework done, with the aid of their Wi-Fi. I then arranged for an engineer to come out from the power supply company to see if they could help to track down the problem.

Luckily the engineer soon arrived, but as I was too busy explaining the problem, I forgot to mention that in our kitchen, Wendy, myself, and my Ma n' Pa, were in the middle of bagging up several pigs worth of pork with only candle light for assistance. I'm not sure exactly what he thought was going on in our kitchen, but the look on his face told a story. He immediately scanned the length of our long wooden table, which was piled high with a couple of freezers worth of pork, including chops, sausages, pork joints, belly pork and mince. Before he had the chance to say anything though, I swiftly whisked him out of there to check the fuse box in the barn, at which point he found out what the problem was. The mains switch which turns on the power into the house had been switched off, how I don't know, but that's all it was. All he did to sort out the issue was to flick a switch and boy oh boy, did I look a muppet! He did go off with a pound of sausages and a lovely rib joint for his trouble, so he was a happy bunny. After the girls called us, to get a power update, they soon arrived home with news of their visit. It seems the Manager heard them talking about their power cut dilemma, whilst they were ordering and took pity on them. In fact he gave them free meals, which was a very nice thing for him to do.

I'm not sure why it happens, but more often than not, when we have an animal related mishap, it very quickly turns from one issue into more. It's like the animals see me running around like a lunatic and think, hey, he's getting in a flap, let's have a bit of fun. Here are a couple of incidents which reflect what I'm talking about. I know that I won't be thanked for mentioning one of these and I will get more earache as a result, but I firstly have to mention something which happened whilst we were tagging the year's lambs. We started with the ewe lambs, firstly penning them up with their mothers and whilst Wendy grabbed the first lamb, 'Badger's bairn', I loaded up the tagging tool. As I turned my back to pick up the tags, I heard an almighty shriek and quickly turned around, just in time to witness a handful and a half of Wendy's hair disappearing into the side of the lamb's mouth. The lamb just looked like she was just sitting chewing the cud and chillin' out. Let me tell you now, Wendy was not a happy soul, to say the least. The lamb had a growing mouthful of hair and with the lamb between her knees, Wendy had one hand hanging onto it and the other hand was frantically trying to pull her hair out of the young 'uns mouth, whilst at the same time, checking for bald patches. All the while the lamb just stared up at her and munched away contently, without a care in the world. I'm afraid, as you can imagine, I didn't help the situation at all. Well you have to laugh don't you!

I have no idea why at all, but I have been told on a number of occasions over the years that bad luck follows me around. I should have realised at the time that I hadn't been involved in any dramas for at least a day or two, so I should have expected that something was about to happen, and indeed it did. The day had started, as it does, like any other, nothing unusual, up at around 6 and quickly out to take care of the animals. Each day I work through my routine, which used to start with the pigs, but now the ponies are let out and looked after first, and then I work my way through all the residents until I finally get to the cows, last but not least. Everything was moving along nicely and I was well down the menagerie list, and with the sun now rapidly on the rise, it was turning into a cracking day, or so I thought! After dealing with the sheep, I glanced over to the cattle, who were next on my list, but something appeared out of place. Without fail, each morning, I am met with a welcoming party at the field gate, with Monica, Lyndsey, Flora and Morag all lined up and ready to greet their breakfast. Well, for some reason, today was different, there were only 3 of them at the gate and Flora was missing. Where was she? I quickly cast my eyes across the field, scanning all four corners...

one, two, three, and before I got to the fourth corner I spotted her. She was loitering beside the crush gate, which the cattle often use to take care of those hard to reach itches, but the confusing thing was, the cows were all in the top field and so couldn't reach the gate itself, as there's a fence in between. Besides, Flora is so keen on her grub and is normally first over to meet me, so this was unusual, especially for this lady, and so I was really confused.

I dropped what I was doing and ran across the field to get a closer look, but before I had got half way over, my running slowed to a walk and in fact, my concern turned into laughter as I could see exactly what Flora's problem was. To explain a little, the part of the fence which runs alongside the front of the race has a half rail removed, to allow the crush gate to open and close easily. Well, with this half rail missing it has created a gap. Not any ordinary gap, but a gap just big enough for a two year old highland cow to somehow squeeze her head through to almost reach the grass in the neighbouring field. The problem was, once through, it wasn't nearly as easy for her to get her head back through that same hole, as I was about to find out. Have you ever tried or even thought about trying to push a Highland cow back through a hole that wasn't quite big enough to get their horns through. Take it from me, it 'aint easy! As I pushed one way, she pushed the other, as I turned her horns vertically, she wanted them horizontal and she's not a little lass isn't our Flora, she's got some beef behind her, I'll tell you. For some reason, it just took me back to my primary school days once again and made me think about when my teacher, Mrs. J had tried to retrieve that little ball of plasticine from up my nose, with me doing anything but cooperating with her. Anyway, eventually, I just had to turn to brute force to sort the situation out, and show her who was boss. I'm sure she'll thank me for it one day.

I suppose it's not really something that you think about until you are in a position to need it, and that time soon arrived. After seeking recommendations, we were able to make the arrangements to get our Highland cattle a bit of a pedicure, and although Wendy is up for most jobs on the farm, this was a little beyond her extensive capabilities. We therefore called in the cavalry in the form of the Yorkshire Foot Trimmers. Although I had researched online and seen pictures of how they would take care of our cows' feet, I was excited to be able to see Mandy and her team in action. The cows were penned in and ready when the trimmers arrived, and after backing their trailer up to the gate, they set to and within an hour, they were all done and dusted. In short, they just walked each of the cattle from the pen and race into a crush, which sat alongside their trailer. They then strapped the cow's legs in, making each cow comfortable, then they pressed a button which lifted and rolled the cow onto its side, on the back of the trailer. The cows were content and stress-free and it enabled the trimmers to work safely on their hooves, without fear of a kick in the shins, or even worse, anything up to 1800lbs parking itself on their toes. The cows appeared to enjoy the experience and it was great to see them skipping around the field afterwards, all that pampering had clearly sent them a bit giddy.

Talking of feet, both Wendy and I could do with getting our feet checked out and sorted, as we have both been suffering from foot ailments since moving onto the farm, but just haven't had the time to sort the problems out. We believe that the cause of these tiresome ailments is far too much welly wearing. We have changed wellies several times, but still the pain continues. Wendy is suffering from really sore callouses on the ball of each of her feet and I have been having to deal with extremely painful heels. As you can imagine, it has often somewhat hampered our activity around the farm, but we soldier on regardless. Well you can't be going through life continually moaning about things, can you? We have just had to improvise and change our walking technique in order to walk pain free. Wendy walks primarily on her heals, to take weight off the painful callouses on the front of her feet and I'm just the opposite, walking more on my toes than on my heels, because walking on my heels just hurts too much. I suppose we now just see all the pain we go through as part and parcel of our new life, but we do get a few funny looks when we are walking in pain.

Autumn was now upon us and after much discussion I decided that this year we would enlist the help of a Charollais tup to father our lambs. My thinking was, that we would get larger, more commercial lambs, which would've been so much better for the freezer, but that was before I thought about the women I live with, who apparently can't eat lamb anymore! So, I set off bright and early on the Thursday morning, to pick up the charollais tup who was coming to stay with us for a couple of months. Well only a few hours later, I was on my way back up the motorway, in the old Landy, with not one, but two tups, who were laid down in the back keeping me company. I was offered the loan of two of them and thought that with a little healthy competition between them, it may ensure that one way or another we'd have some nice lambs come April. When we got back to the farm I had to quickly mix up some 'Raddle' which I had been given and then I needed to smear it onto the tup's chest. I was given some to try, as an alternative to using a harness and a block of chalk, which I'd used previously. By using the 'Raddle' or chalk, it enables us to see more easily which of our ewes have been getting romanced by the tups. It didn't take very long at all for the Ewes to get noticed, so I soon disappeared and left them to make their introductions and become better acquainted.

Eventually, all the preliminary work had been completed on our proposed Shepherd's hut field and it was time to get it seeded, if we were going to get any grass on it by spring, as it was now December. I spoke to a number of people locally who strongly recommended that December wasn't a good time at all to be grass seeding a field, but of course I knew better, or did I? I discussed my plight with the local seed merchant in Cranswick, who told me that he thought he had just the seed for the job. This was seed from New Zealand and would grow in temperatures down to minus 3 degrees. "That'll do for me" I said and arranged for three bags to get delivered ASAP. I was later talking to a farming neighbour and mentioned that I was hoping to get a field reseeded with grass soon, but I had no clue as to how I was going to accomplish this with any sort of proficiency. He went on to tell me about a handy contraption called the 'Seed Fiddle' which they used to use back in the old days. In fact, I've since found out that the gadget was first introduced around the 1850s, but thought nothing more about it. Anyway, I was talking to one of my friendly farmers, Gordon, who was going to rotovate and harrow my field for me, when he again asked how I was going to seed the field. "By hand" I replied. "I've got something which may help you out", he said, "come around and you can borrow it". I got myself around there sharpish and after getting his grandson to climb up into the heavens, inside one of his sheds, he fished out what he was talking about. Well, blow me down, there it was in front of me, a real-life 'seed fiddle'. What were the chances of that happening? I couldn't contain my excitement and soon after getting the field power harrowed, I was out there, with the seed fiddle under my arm, excitedly marching up and down that field. Initially I walked up and down in lines from top to bottom and then I did the same, but from side-to-side, across the field's width. I tried to make sure that each row overlapped as best I could, so that everywhere got an even spread of seed. All that was left to do then, was just wait and see what the results were in the spring.

At the time I can remember thinking that maybe it's a look that'll catch on. Maybe people will grow to love the curly eyebrow look! But really and more importantly, I should've been much more concerned about how soon my eyebrows would grow back! I had once again been involved in one of my favourite pastimes, burning things. People often say it must be a 'man' thing and that may be true, but for me there is definitely a fascination with flames. I've had it since I was a very young boy, probably around nine or ten, I suppose. I can recall sitting, on a summer day, high up near the top of an old oak tree, with some friends, doing not a lot, but messing about with matches, which we'd bought from the local garage. More often than not I have a bonfire on the build and it's usually made up of garden waste and tree branches, but on this occasion I had been burning piles of plain old rubbish! This time though, it wasn't just the rubbish which got caught by the flames. Unfortunately, because I'm really stupid, on one of my many, getting-too-close-for-comfort visits to the fire, I got knocked back several feet, by the heat, but this time the flames had caught my fringe, eyebrows and eyelashes. I immediately ran my hands across my face and head, as the strong smell of burning ginger hair wafted past me. One day I'll learn!

If I had a pound for every time I've said that, I'd be a wealthy man. There are so many lessons to be learned and it appears that I only catch on after the event. I really should think more before I jump in with both feet. Another example of this was the night when I nipped across into the barn to pick up some logs for the fire. Well, as it was pouring down I couldn't be bothered with putting my boots on and messing about with all that lacing up, for just a few minutes. My wellies were nowhere in sight, so, I grabbed Wendy's wellies and squeezed into them, well I was in a hurry and wasn't really bothered what I looked like, it was dark and it wasn't a fashion show, was it? As I rushed into the barn I didn't turn any of the lights on, as I was only hanging around for a moment and so thought I would just use my phone torch to get what I wanted, then get out. Things so often never go to plan, when I'm involved, just why is that? I had only been in the barn for a moment, when I heard the squeak of a mouse, well I say a mouse, but it may have even been a rat. I ignored it, I didn't have time to be checking out what animal it was, but the thing was, whatever animal it may have been, it was doing all in its power to make sure it got noticed. It was following me as I made my way around the barn in the dark. Every corner I turned it seemed to be there and I was just intrigued to find out just what animal it actually was. As so often happens in these situations, each time I stopped, it stopped and just kept still and then each time I continued to walk on, it seemed to move once more. The creature was playing a game with me and I wasn't in the mood for any game. Eventually, after almost twenty minutes of hunting, I tracked down the culprit. Much to my disgust or maybe just relief, I found that it wasn't any kind of reject from 'Tales of the Riverbank' which had been following me around the barn, but was in fact Wendy's squeaky welly, that I'd nicked! Well, it just goes to show, that's what I get for snaffling her wellies.

Christmas time was here once more and Wendy and I were all excited for a particular weekend in December to arrive. You see, the thing was, we were taking our 7 grandchildren (at the time), onto the Santa Express steam train, which runs from Pickering Station, and we couldn't wait. Over the years we have spoken about doing it so many times, but have never got around to sorting it out, and now that we had 7 grandchildren, we've got things organised. The funny thing is, if Christmas had been a few months further away, we would be taking 8 grandchildren with us, as we have another one on the way in the New Year. We rarely go out very far, as I've said before and so wanted the day to go well. We arranged with all our kids and their families to meet at a certain time in the station carpark and surprisingly enough, it all worked to plan. Before long the fifteen of us boarded the train and we were soon off to visit Santa. After a little while it was our turn for each of our grandkids to take the long walk through the train, all eagerly heading off to meet Santa Claus in person. The kids were so excited, but then again so were Nanna and Grandpa and do you know, he really did look like the main man too! Looking back to that weekend trip and as Christmas was fast approaching, it got me thinking about how Christmas has changed for us over the years, and particularly since leaving our old world behind. It has definitely become far more simple and the cost of Christmas has reduced drastically. I know that we never went mad at all at Christmas, because things can get out of hand very easily, if you don't watch your spending. If I'm honest, I have often been referred to as a bit of a tightwad, so expensive gifts were never really where it was at with me. More recently we have tried to consider the cost more and think about the individuals we are giving gifts to, instead of just buying for buying sake.

Last year was our first Christmas on the farm and Wendy's gifts were being thought about for weeks ahead of the big day. "Oh, I don't need anything" she'd say, but I knew that come Christmas morning if there wasn't something special for Mrs.M, I'd be for the high jump! She rarely wore jewellery, she had all the perfume she needed, with clothes I'd make the wrong choices anyway, so don't bother trying, and so this year I thought about smaller things, but things that were really quite special. I won't go into all the details other than to say, that things went down very well, surprisingly, as it appears that she did have a favourite gift in mind and the item she liked most cost barely a few pounds. "What was it"? I hear you cry. It was a plain old hand whisk, for all the baking she does. The funny thing is that she's never used it for baking, not even once and that's because she's found a far more useful way to utilise it, let me explain. One evening, there I was standing at the kitchen sink, again, just minding my own business, when I heard a strange gurgling sound coming from upstairs. Our bathroom is directly above the kitchen and so unfortunately you hear all that goes on above you, in stereo sound, including this gurgling noise. Now Wendy likes a lot of bubbles when she has a bath and so what was she doing to cause that gurgling sound I was hearing? Well, I ran up the stairs, only to be greeted by a view I didn't expect. Wendy, was leaning over the bath and was utilising my much considered Christmas gift, the hand whisk, like a mad woman, to agitate the bathwater and bubble bath sufficiently to create lots of foam for her to have a nice deep, bubble filled bath. Whoever would have thought that you could have so much fun with a whisk? So, when Christmas next comes around in your house, remember, it's not the cost of a gift that counts, but it's the joy it gives, and of course its usefulness that counts!

For me, I knew what I was hoping to get from Santa, that Christmas. Whilst out checking the animals one evening, I had accidentally dropped my torch into the ditch, rendering it useless. At the time I never realised how dropping it would come back to haunt me, but that's exactly what it did. For months we had been losing our Muscovy ducks, as many had disappeared without trace. Although we had a range of suitable homes available for them, they had always preferred to roost outdoors, as I've said before, in the trees, on the stable roof, wherever they fancied really. We have suspected for some time that they have been taken by a fox, but also considered that other predators could also have taken them or they have all just flown away, to live their life elsewhere in pastures new. Up to this point, as much as we have searched high and low, we have never found any evidence or had any proof either way, but that all changed just days ahead of Christmas. As I start my rounds each morning in the dark, Tuesday was much the same as any other day. After dealing with all the farm animals, I made my way back to the house to pick up the 3 dogs, to take them out for a run. As the sun had by this time risen, I was able to see in full technicolor what was greeting me on the lawn beside the house. The sight that welcomed me left me in no doubt that Mr. Fox had in fact come calling and had caught our ducks off guard. The remains of one of our remaining 3 ducks was strewn across the lawn and our second male was missing and was never seen again, leaving only our little female to tell the tale of the night before. Following the traumatic goings on of that night, we have, as a matter of course been coaxing our remaining duck into the barn for safe shelter, each evening. That in the main hadn't been too arduous a task, until the night that it absolutely poured down. Darkness had fallen, the rest of the animals were locked up for the night, which left only our solitary duck with her head under her wing, standing on one leg, roosting on the fence between the sheep fields. I crept towards her, to try to take her off the fence, but unfortunately, on this night Miss Duck was in no mood to be taken quietly, which was never going to be a good thing on a very wet, very dark night, without a torch! She then spent the next 30 minutes giving me the run around. All I could see was a faint white blur, as she was flying from fence to fence, across the fields, each time deciding to shift herself, only when I got close enough to maybe grab hold of her. It was like she was determined to visit as many of our neighbours as she could, whilst making things as difficult as possible, for me. Eventually I got her to fly back into the farmyard, where I could calmly and without any sudden movements, slowly walk her back into the barn for the night. Guess what I purchased later that very same, eventful evening?

We were still preparing for Christmas and so I was once again got dragged out shopping, which I know isn't a regular thing around here, thank goodness, but all the same it's not my favourite pastime. On our list of people to buy for were Maisie and Lucy, the Shetland Ponies. Now I know they are a hardy breed and have an extremely thick coat, but I was talked into getting them each a coat for the winter, just in case the temperatures really plummeted. I was quite surprised that they weren't too expensive and we were able to get them both a coat to match, so they would look very swish! After rushing to get the rest of our shopping, we excitedly hurried home, gave them both a good groom and decided to let Lucy try her coat on first. You see she hates anyone going near her back end and so it was going to be quite a challenge to get her new coat fastened on, or so we thought! In fact it went like a dream, without any hiccups at all. It fitted really well and she looked a right bobby dazzler too, but that's when things got all interesting. Although we thought Lucy looked great, her mother, Maisie, clearly didn't like Lucy's new look at all and so began running round and around the enclosure, trying to get away from Lucy, who was now intent on chasing her mother, whom she thought was running away from her. Each time Lucy went near her, she would just gallop away, without hesitation. It was as though Maisie didn't recognise her little girl, at all. This continued all afternoon, but as dusk fell, it was time for them to go into their stable, and somehow I had to get them both into the same stable, but without Maisie having a right old strop! Even though there were a few moans and a fair bit of chasing too, I managed to get them both in for the night. I stood outside for a few minutes, just listening, hoping that there wasn't going to be any kicking off as I walked away but things just settled down and luckily by the morning, they were back to being the best of friends again.

9 REINFORCEMENTS TO THE RESCUE

One of the most rewarding things about living our dream has been the opportunity which we have been afforded, to meet people. In so many instances these, often chance meetings, have proved to be such a blessing to us. Life has introduced to us to so many characters, wonderful people who are just going about their daily lives, unaware that they are an inspiration to many they come into contact with, and are touching the lives of those around them.

I would like to tell you about one such inspiration who we met in the summer of 2014. We first came into contact with Margaret Whittaker, who at the time had purchased some of our eggs from Wendy's cart outside the gate. At that time we didn't meet her face-to-face, but were amused by the note she had left inside our egg money jar. The note was an I.O.U which was telling us that she owed us around 76p and would return at a later date to clear her debt. The note had been written on the back of a reminder card. Now this wasn't any ordinary reminder card, it was in fact a reminder for her exercise class. There's nothing surprising about that you might think, but you see the thing is, at that time we were unaware that Margaret was actually in her 86th year… and she went to exercise classes! A few weeks later, true to her word she rolled up at our door with the outstanding coppers in hand and if truth be told, she was brought back by her daughter and son, who wanted to see what this Ginger Cow was about, that their mother was blathering on about.

Margaret has become a regular at The Ginger Cow Company ever since, but is now more of a friend than a customer, calling by regularly and each time she visits she unknowingly brightens up our day. How she has packed so much into her life, I don't know. On many an occasion we have taken her by the arm and walked around the farm as she has recounted tales from her early years in Merseyside, told us of her links to 'Auld Reekie' and countless experiences whilst working in the mental health arena. On a regular basis Margaret has entertained us with anecdotes from her time singing for the BBC in her youth, and her adventures as she has travelled across the globe. We have been given gardening advice and tips, had fresh cuttings from her garden and gifts hand-delivered to our postbox, many times. Wendy regularly receives letters from Margaret, each one brightening up her day and these are typed up on an old type writer, which I'm sure would have many a tale to tell if it could speak!

Like so many of our lovely customers in the summer months, she has brought family and friends for a visit. More often than not though, you could observe that solitary figure perched on a bench, under a parasol, tackling yet another of those crosswords, which never appeared to put up much of a fight at all, and all the while she was drinking in the peace and tranquility around her. For someone who could on the face of it, appear to be rather fragile and frail, she does in fact have an enthusiasm and vigour for life which is a credit to a lady of such mature years. Maybe the secret to her vim and vigour lies in what she has told us she gets up to in the early hours of the morning, in her beautiful secluded garden, when she rolls in the early morning dew, in her birthday suit. I've often considered, when the weather is warm that I might just give it a go myself, because if it works for Margaret, then it may just work for me!

Christmas Day arrived at Long Meadow Farm once more, and Wendy thought it would be a great idea to christen the new tea shop, which was almost at completion stage, with only the snagging list to go through. We decided that we could line all the new tables up along the middle and all 20 of us we were having for dinner could comfortably fit around it. It was a really lovely day and everyone enjoyed themselves, especially all the grandchildren. After the very busy Christmas Day which we had, I left my chores a little later than usual the next morning and waited until it was just starting to become light. It had been raining for most of Christmas Day and the rain was still falling the next morning and I could clearly see the amount of water which had fallen, was now standing in the fields. I walked around the outside of the barn and teashop and even there we had standing water and as it was still pouring, I decided it would be wise to speak to one of the friendly farmers I know, to see if I could borrow a pump from him, as I thought if the rain continued, the pump would help to keep the levels down.

As I drove back through the gate, I couldn't believe what I was seeing. In the short time I had been away collecting the pump, the water level had risen by six to eight inches and was now filling up inside our new teashop. I ran through the torrent which was now raging around the barn end and across the bridge towards the house. Thankfully, it was being diverted off the bridge and into the beck, so wasn't at that stage heading for the house. I just opened the front door and shouted "The water is in the shop, the water is in the shop, get towels NOW" I then waded back over the bridge to get the pump set up and working. Within minutes, I turned to see Wendy, Olivia, Evie and Naomi, all in their PJ's, wading through the water-filled barn, with piles of towels under each arm to try and stem the tide, which by this time was running through the new kitchen and into the toilets too. I called our Jake, who lived 10 minutes away, in Sutton-on-Derwent and he came over to help, but our Sam, who had twice tried to come over, had to turn back to Brandsby, due to flooding. I called our neighbours across the road, Matthew and Sarah, and got them out of bed to come and muck in and we posted an urgent plea on our 'Ginger Cow' Facebook page and on the local Pocklington Facebook page to try and muster up additional manpower.

With Wendy now in tears, and the water levels still rising as it rapidly flowed downhill, off the fields, I did think we were fighting a losing battle. O, ye of little faith! Isn't it so often the case, that when you think all is lost, you need to keep fighting because things can be turned around, just when you don't expect it? Wendy was in the kitchen with Sarah and the girls and said that she was going to say a prayer to ask for more help, because boy oh, boy we needed it. Within minutes it was like the world and their brother arrived at 'The Ginger Cow'. We had cars stopping and people jumping out and asking what they could do to help. We had Steven and Emma, who were other neighbours of ours, who we had never even spoken to, turned up with their two boys, a digger and another large water pump and before we knew it, we had 3 pumps on the go and literally dozens of people, with more arriving all the time. Many of these people we wouldn't know them if we fell over them, but they were now all at our place, over 80 of them in total throughout the day, working hard to stem the rising tide and bring the water levels down. I just don't know where they were all coming from. Before long, with shovels, and with the digger, two trenches had been dug which then allowed the water to disperse from the garden into the main ditches, along the road side and could then flow away as it normally does, downstream. The tide had turned, yet still more people were arriving, from Holme on Spalding Moor, Everingham, Bielby, Pocklington, Barnby Moor, Market Weighton, Sutton on Derwent, Driffield and Hull. People were travelling miles to help. As some left, further waves and waves of help just kept appearing. Those who were turning up, were arriving with sacks, bin bags, shovels, towels and food as well, to be honest, I don't think I've ever seen so many Christmas biscuits in one place, ever.

So many angels tuned up on that Boxing day, some staying all day, changing their plans in the process to help others in need. Family meals were delayed, playing with a new Lego set was put off until later, planned rounds of golf were cancelled and the bargains hoped for during the scheduled retail therapy were no doubt missed out on, and one man even chose to stay rather than spend extra quality time with his mother-in-law. Now that is going the extra mile. It's extremely humbling to see what was set aside to help us in or hour of need and we will be forever grateful for that. For some weeks after we were trying to get things dried out and at the same time were working hard to ensure it didn't happen again. Initially I went to speak to our neighbour Steven, down the lane, the one who had brought a digger in on the day of the flood, to enquire about using the digger skills of one of their sons, James, who was keen to help out. We then arranged for James to come over with the digger in tow, to create a rather large barrier between the fields and our place. After taking advice we then put a long term plan in place for the future, so the problem didn't arise again. 10 tons of planings were added to the end of the car parking area and French drains were sited from the fields into our new ditch, which ran under the car park. The ground level was raised over a foot around the Teashop with drains and gulleys also being put in place to aid the removal of any surface water. Additionally and most importantly we put a new ditch along our furthest perimeter fence line, to capture any surface water which would have ordinarily made its way across the fields towards our property, but not anymore. We have had no more water trouble since and any surface water disappears very quickly through the sandy well drained soil that we have around here.

Well it may have been a new year, but the dramas kept coming thick and fast as we moved into 2016. It was early one morning, as these things often are, (why is that?) whilst out sorting the animals and getting organised for the day ahead, when I noticed that 'Badger', one of our Shetland sheep, had become a little standoffish and believe me with her appetite, this was not like her at all. After a little bit of running around, well far too much really, I managed to take a look at her and could see that her left eye was infected. I've learned over the last couple of years to take care of many issues myself with the animals, but this was something that needed to be dealt with by the professionals. I called our local vet and Angus soon arrived and very quickly established that she had in fact cut the eyeball itself and as a result would need to be operated on, and undoubtedly she would be losing her eye in the process. The only way we can think that she damaged the eye, was whilst feeding. The sheep all put their heads through the sides of the hay feeder and with Badger being just a little greedier than many, she shoves her head right deep into the middle of the hay and somehow it looks as though a piece of hay has gone straight into her eye, piercing the eyeball in the process.

All the plans were made ahead of her being operated on and after keeping her indoors for a couple of days and off food and water for a time, it was time to take her for the operation. As Wendy was keen to ensure that 'Badger' didn't do a runner, around Market Weighton, both she and my Dad came along, to ensure that all went to plan. Wendy sat in the back of the Landy with Badger, to continue her nursing duties whilst we travelled and to take hold of her as we reached our destination, so she couldn't engineer an escape attempt and for whatever reason, make a bid for freedom. In my view though, that was never going to happen, as she has far too cushy a life at our place and gets the best of the best, all year round. We drove around the area for twenty minutes and everything went according to plan. She was back in a field in little over an hour and was quickly on the mend. After a few days on her own, she then returned to the flock and her stitches were taken out a fortnight later. There have been no long term issues with her, following the accident and operation and she copes extremely well with just the one eye, which is a credit to her.

It felt like we were working our way through the busiest few months I can remember. Alongside the building work and the recent puddle trouble we had our 7th and 8th grandchildren being born, Lily Mavis and Tabitha Hope. We had one of our sons Jake and his family moving house and all the decorating and babysitting duties that goes with that territory. So, with all that going on, we had to do a little bit of jiggery pokery around the place with jobs. I had my days planned out each week, with school pick-ups and painting, tip runs and bedtime stories, all thrown into the mix, but I had a plan and was confident that everything would get sorted. Dusk was falling and the light was almost gone after another long day, I found myself daydreaming as I was travelling back through the fog and drizzle, over the Wolds from our son's new family home in Fridaythorpe, keen to get home and sort my animals out for the night. As I came down the home side of the hill, I managed to pick up a phone signal so I could call home to check how things were. Wendy answered the phone, but before I had even got half a dozen words out of my mouth I was cut off, which I must say, isn't unusual at all. "You have nothing to do when you get in, it's all done!" I was hearing the words, but it just wasn't registering in my head. How could this be? The womenfolk don't shift animals, they don't take trailer loads of hay out to the cows, what was she talking about? I hurried on through what was now darkness, keen to get home and understand what had happened in order that all my jobs were sorted and the residents of 'Long Meadow Farm' who had a bed, were in fact, all tucked up and cosy, bedded down for the night.

Well, the answer to my question came very quickly after arriving home, never underestimate the fairer sex. Would I ever? All that needed to be accomplished had in fact been taken care of by Wendy and two of our daughters. Not only had the laying hens, ponies, duck, goats and pet hens all been put to bed, but before the goats and Ponies had been tucked up for the night, their stables had also been cleaned out, as this too was my Saturday job. They had also taken bales of hay and feed out to the three groups of sheep, but they had also taken it upon themselves to reintroduce 'Badger', our now one eyed sheep, back into the flock, with the other ewes. Finally, considering the fact that Wendy was terrified of the cattle not that long ago, something to do with the size of them and the big pointy things on their heads, they had also filled the trailer with bales of hay and with Olivia taking charge of the quad and the other two on rounding up and gate duties, they were able, between them to fill the ring feeder with a fresh supply of hay. I was honestly lost for words and very grateful, but very proud of them too! I also believe that what went on during the previous 24 hours had been a massive turning point around our place. Firstly, I knew that if I keeled over tomorrow, I now know that my family would be able to cope in my absence and also, if they'd done it once, there ain't no excuse next time I need their help, is there?

I get the chance to think a lot, whilst doing what I'm doing around the farm. Often I don't have people to talk to or to distract me, which is nice, and also important when I'm concentrating and thinking about important matters in my life. I remember considering one such important matter as I was working in the vegetable patch one afternoon. I was looking back on how my day-to-day look has changed since leaving our old life in suburbia behind. It soon led me to working out that I had worn a business suit, a nicely starched and pressed white shirt and a tie regularly, at least 5 if not 6 days a week, for almost 32 years. Back then I didn't really give it a second thought, as it became second nature, you know, it's what was expected of me, working out in the corporate world. Oh, how things have changed. From those days when I was so keen on a nice sharp crease down my trouser legs, hated tramlines and was always turned out with a whiskerless chin, to be blunt, I had turned into a right dosser. I seem to have gone from smelling of your average, mid-range aftershaves, to smelling of any number of farmyard fragrances. Although my look probably did change very quickly, I really didn't appreciate just how far downhill it had actually gone. That was until the day I had to pop into our local supermarket in Pocklington, for some bits n' bobs, for Wendy.

So, get your imagination head on and picture the scene, I was standing in the middle of the cereal aisle, but without causing a blockage or inhibiting the flow of trolley-pushing happy shoppers, when not one, but two shoppers happened to physically slow down and glance me up and down. At that moment I did consider whether I should ask the obvious question as to their sudden interest in my attire and being the redhead that I am, it did take a fair amount of self-control to not make some sarcastic, wholly inappropriate remark, but I'm pleased to say, I resisted the urge. I was a little narked though as it had really put me off deciding which cereal to choose and I'm always rubbish at choosing at the best of times. I eventually made my choice, no surprise, cornflakes again, and then hurriedly got myself through the self-service checkout. It was only then, as I walked out of the store that I got my latest wake up call. This was the second time of course, the last time it happened, when it was the reflection in Wendy's car window that startled me, but this time it was as I walked past all the full size, nicely polished, plate glass windows, that I could see for myself what a complete tramp that I had turned into. My black woolly hat, neatly adorned with pieces of hay, pulled down over my eyebrows, my smelly coat with more holes than coat, my burgundy jeans slouching much too far down my rear, and wellies which could have done with a good clean several months ago. I did feel comfy though and I'm not doing anyone any harm really, am I? I know it gets right on the girls' wick at home, particularly the hat situation, but the thing is, I can scrub up well if I really need to, I'm happy and besides, I can call it my just a bit more than a midlife crisis, can't I!

Just for a moment I want to go back and talk about wellies. Wendy and I have had an ongoing battle about wellies, ever since we moved into Long Meadow Farm. From Wendy's point of view they shouldn't be entering our house kitchen at all, but for me we live on a farm and to mess about taking them off and then putting them back on only moments later, after popping into the house for something is ridiculous. There was a time when I seemed to be always getting a thick ear, for messing up her kitchen floor, but those days are over, because I have learned to clean up after myself. If I leave no trace of my misdemeanour, then I am able to dodge any potential ear-bashing which could've been coming my way and life is once again sweet.

As part of our ongoing groundworks ahead of opening the teashop, we needed to arrange for a large tree to be taken down by a couple of professional 'Tree fellas', who clearly knew what they were doing. Afterwards I was left with a nice pile of wood and had planned to quickly make my way to the nearest axe retailer, to buy a whopper of an axe. My plan was then to turn the pile of wood into stove sized logs for burning. Well, as I often would, when I had professionals around doing jobs, I took the opportunity to get some tips for future reference. Very quickly, after talking to Sam the 'Tree Fella', I knew what kind of axe to buy, which was very different from the one I would have bought and after a demonstration I also knew how to efficiently cut through large rings of tree trunk too. I was shown how if you get your axe stuck in a piece of wood, I should not do as I normally would and hit it harder and harder until its completely stuck fast, but instead, flip the log over onto it's back, whilst still stuck to the axe and then hit the back of the axe against the chopping base. By doing this, the weight of the log assists you in splitting it into two, just like magic. As you can guess I was kept busy chopping wood for some time after. In fact, if I'm honest, I had quite a number of unsuspecting visitors, including our sons, my daughter's fiancé and my brother-in-law too, chopping wood as a result, marvelous! If I had a spare half hour or more I would grab my splitter axe and chop a few logs and I find it's a very satisfying and rather therapeutic too.

As you would expect, I've been learning new stuff every day since we moved out here, and for whatever reason some things just stick in your mind, even if you're not using the information regularly. One such thing was when

I was told by a farmer friend, that farmers should always carry in their pocket, 'a knife, a piece of string and a shilling'. Well that got me thinking about what rubbish I keep in my pockets. I decided to go through the pockets of my overalls, my work jacket and my jeans, just to see what hidden gems I might find. The first thing I found, in abundance, in several pockets was copious amounts of baling string. You see, it's not that long ago when I wouldn't have appreciated that string, because I didn't even know what baling string was, let alone how useful it is. But now there's not many days go by in which I don't use some of that very useful string. Some of its uses have included securing temporary fencing, fixing gaps in stock netting, tying back shrubs and bundling logs and branches, for more easily transporting them. My most supportive use for baling string has been when I have used it to keep my trousers up, on a couple of occasions, when I have misplaced my belts and it has worked a treat!

I then pulled out my trusty knife, which I purchased back in October 2013 in Keswick, when we'd last had the chance to go away. At the time I was thinking ahead and thought I was bound to need a good knife on the farm, and indeed I do. I use it very regularly, especially at feeding time, for cutting the strings around the bales of hay. I moved onto another pocket and found some cash, not a lot and no shillings I'm afraid, but then again they wouldn't be overly useful in buying anything nowadays. It is funny, but when I do have any cash, which isn't very often, I don't keep that cash in the same pocket as my knife. Why, you may well ask yourself. It's very like me, but it's so the coins don't scratch my knife, I'm funny like that. So, my pocket raiding continued with half a pocket of rifle pellets, a range of different sized screws, nails, nuts, bolts and miscellaneous fixings, which I think are always good to have on hand. One top pocket was just full of old receipts and a felt tip pen. In another I found a number of dog poo bags, unused thankfully, although there has been the odd occasion when a used parcel has been forgotten about for a day or two. I went on to find a couple of pieces of broken pottery in one pocket and an old button, all which I will have picked up whilst visiting the hens, oh and my hanky, which has probably been in my pocket since that great hayfever-suffering-summer of 1976. It was no wonder I'd been walking like the hunchback of Notre Dame with that little lot weighing me down, it was definitely time for a clear out!

Through our local vets, we often get invited to attend evening meetings, when an external speaker comes in and talks about a particular subject which they believe farmers and smallholders may find useful. On one such occasion, I was able to attend an evening laid on at the local rugby club. The aim of the evening was to remind cattle owners of ways to deal with various conditions caused by stress, and a drug company had been invited to come and talk about these things. Well, I don't mind saying, by the end of the evening it was me who was stressed, never mind the cattle, anyway I'll come onto that.

I arrived in good time, for a change and walked into a busy room and was promptly handed a raffle ticket, which enabled me to get a free drink to start the evening, now that was a welcome bonus I never expected for a start. I quickly scanned around the room to see if I knew anyone. I recognised a number of people, and of course the vets themselves, but caught the eye of a gentleman sitting towards the back, who looked like he knew what he was doing when it came to cattle, and so I thought that's where I would park myself for the evening. The gentleman's name was John and he had been farming since he was 15 although he was now over 70. With all those years of experience I couldn't let this opportunity pass me by to tap into all that knowledge whilst we were waiting for the talk to begin, so that's just what I did.

It wasn't long before the room was full and it was time for things to commence. As I sat there my eyes scanned around the room, as I was thinking to myself how much I looked and felt like a fish out of water. In the corporate world I had been involved in many a large meeting and countless conference sessions, so the group size wasn't an issue at all, but on this occasion, I didn't know squat at all about the subject of the evening. In reality, I probably didn't look out of place, but I just thought I looked that way, compared to a room full of seasoned dairy and beef cattle farmers. I'm sure that most of them will have been doing the job since they were young and it was definitely one of the occasions when I wished that somehow I'd got into this farming lark, way before I did. Before I knew it, the talk was coming to an end and we were able to chat some more. By this time I had been introduced to Terry, who was sitting on my left. So, picture the scene, there I was sitting between Terry and John, with my head turning first to the left and then to the right, listening to these two proper farmers, talking about their cattle. Just to observe the passion they had for their animals was a real joy. After a little while we were told that the food would shortly be getting served. FOOD! What d'ya mean Food! Nobody told me about food. I had already had my tea and besides I had chores to run and I had to get to the supermarket before it shut, what a nightmare! I then made a big mistake and I looked over to where they were laying the food out and my goodness, that glance was a glance too far, and definitely a bad idea. There was pie and mash and peas and gravy and there was this soft lad having to rush off to get to the shop before it shut, it's no wonder I was stressed leaving all that good grub behind!

We were just coming out of the tail end of winter now, and I was longing for a bit of sun to brighten things up around the farm, and to give the grass a nudge too of course. I check the weather via my phone far too many times in a day, but when those smiley yellow suns appeared on my phone screen I was overjoyed, in fact I couldn't contain my excitement. So many outdoor jobs which had been stacking up for far too long, can at last be tackled, (does that sound convincing?) From first thing one morning, because the weather was nicer, I was able to keep the doors open and I had been hard at it, painting these doors, including the entrance to our new toilets for the teashop. I don't know about you, but when I am intensely focusing on a job and concentrating hard, for some reason I always stick out my tongue, heaven knows why. Anyway, I was knelt down, painting the bottom edge of a door, listening to some tunes on the music player thingy, when I seriously got the fright of my life. Out of the blue I was startled by an extremely loud, totally unexpected, ear piercing squawk. Unbeknown to me, Phin', one of our resident pheasants had crept round the outside of the barn, unaware that I was only a couple of feet away from him and, after filling his lungs and puffing out his chest he let out that almighty squawk at the top of his voice, to let all the other local boys know that this was indeed his patch. Unfortunately for me, by doing that, he had inadvertently scared me witless, in the process and I'll tell you what, I needed a lie down afterwards too!

Well after a pig-free six months, the time had come for our latest porkers to arrive. Initially, we had two pigs delivered, with a further three or four arriving around late April time. We could have taken more in together, but one thing we have learned over the months is to stagger the time when they are ready for the freezer. To add to the mix, we needed to make sure that we had a nice big porker ready for action at the end of June. That's because Evie, one of our daughters and her husband to be, Joe, came to me earlier in the spring and asked "Dad, can we have a hog roast at the wedding?" and my response was, as you'd expect "Of course you can my dear", well with me being the ever-so-obliging Father, I had to say yes, didn't I? So, in late June when they get married we'll have a hog roast on the big day, but we just didn't tell the pig! As it happened, very soon after the two pigs arrived, we stumbled over a bit of a problem. These pigs were unlike any others we had experienced in our short time rearing pigs, they were tame! So that posed us a bit of a problem. I am definitely a bit of a softie, probably too soft in fact, but the decision was taken to hang onto these two pigs and arrange for an alternative pig for the big day, a pig which we wouldn't see until it looked tasty. As the two were staying, we named them both. The pig which was previously known as the bridal pig, was named 'Precious' and her sidekick was from then onwards, called 'Petal'.

As the weather now seemed to be turning for the better and after a run of a few dry days, I was able to get down to business. As it was that time of year again, I had been talking once again about clearing the ditch through our farmyard for far too long, so it was time to get on and get it sorted. I had arranged for a friendly neighbour with a digger to come and do the job, but as part of the deal I needed the silt and leaves which would come out of the ditch to be moved elsewhere on the farm. Well, that's when things got exciting, as, for the first time ever, I got the chance to drive a dumper truck.

Bearing in mind that I spent many, many hours playing on building sites as a kid, obviously, when I shouldn't have been anywhere near them, (Don't tell me mother!) I had sat on countless dumpers, but to drive one, well that was something else. It was great fun, but ended far too soon. Only 30 dumper loads later and we were done. The ditch was cleared, the water flowing beautifully and the ducks had broad grins in their faces at the prospect of all this free running water to play in and the bonus was that nobody got sprayed with mud on this occasion either. If I'm honest, I've been looking for other excuses ever since to hire a dumper truck, but without any good enough reason as yet.

Ever since I was a little boy, probably about 7 or 8 years old, I have loved finding things out in the fields whilst out playing with friends. Clay pipes, pieces of pottery, old bullet cartridges, all of which I would normally tuck away in the back of one of my drawers, until my mother had a clear-out. Well, similar experiences have happened to me since moving onto the farm.

Firstly, I was introduced to the word 'Shoddy'! I had often heard the word throughout my life and understood that it meant that something was of poor quality or was referring to bad workmanship. But where did the word come from? Soon after we moved out here, I started to regularly find buttons in the soil. When fencing was being put in, when I was digging the veg patch, whilst clearing mole hills, even just walking through to the hen house, they just kept surfacing in the soil. They were so easily noticeable as they were round, flat and stood out on the top of the earth. These buttons were often the same size and were often from the same manufacturer, 'Archibald and Co. London', who from a bit of research appeared to be a manufacturer of army or forces uniform buttons. I wondered, was there a button factory in our location at some point in time? I didn't do a great deal about it, but some weeks later, more buttons appeared in our new paddock, as I was checking how the new grass was coming along. This time it was a different kind of button, as it looked like a uniform dress button. So I undertook some further investigation and once again and spoke to the Layton family, particularly Angela, whose family have farmed this area, including, many years ago, the land which we now live on, to see if I could find out more about these buttons.

'Shoddy', appears to originate in the Batley area of West Yorkshire and as far back as the 1800's and is the name given to scraps of inferior woolen yarn which was mixed with new wool to produce cheap cloth. Anyway, any parts of the rags or cloth that was not suitable to use would be left to rot and then sold on to farmers as 'Shoddy', to fertilise their crops. Angela, was telling me that after the war she remembers truckloads of 'Shoddy' being delivered from West Yorkshire and it would be ploughed into the fields to support the growth of crops, and in their case it was sugar beet. Very often, old forces uniforms were used as part of this process, as there was an abundance of them at that time. That's surely why in fact I have kept finding all these uniform buttons. Buttons aren't the only thing that I've come across out here though.

After recently getting the ditch through the garden cleared out, I was walking through the yard early one morning and as the reflection on the water cleared, I spotted something in the now deeper, clearer ditch. It appeared to be a bottle and after jumping in and fishing it out, I could see for myself that it was in fact no ordinary cast away coke bottle or alike, it was an old glass bottle. I gave it a gentle wash in the outside sink, to see if I could get a clearer view of what it actually was. The neck of the bottle had been pinched together during the manufacturing process and rattling about in the neck was a glass marble. Well, to say the least, this little fella was excited, just like all those years ago as an 8 year old, finding his first clay pipe. So, after a little homework on the internet and talking to Gordon Layton once again, it was established that this was an old lemonade bottle from a factory in York and was maybe up to 80 years old. At the time I can remember picturing in my mind, some young farm worker, rattling along on his horse drawn trailer, kicking up clouds of dust, with the hot sun beaming down, finishing his lunch and tossing the bottle aside, as he returned his trailer of newly baled hay down the lane past our farm house to their barn! I do love finding treasures like that and I keep them all safe, stashed away in some drawer or on a shelf. Heaven knows why, because they are just dust collectors really, but each item has a history and a story behind it, even if it's just a story that's in my head. I suppose that's why I hang on to so much rubbish!

One of my favourite things, is to spend time with the livestock when all the hustle and bustle of the day has subsided and it's all peaceful and quiet. On one such lovely night with a crisp clear sky overhead and an almost-full moon shining brightly, as it wasn't cold, I thought I would visit our pregnant ewes and just sit and watch them for a while. I climbed over the fence, nobody even moved a muscle, so I just sat down amongst them and crossed my legs. It immediately transported me back to around 1969 when I was doing much the same thing, just without the field full of sheep, back in Mrs. Jenkins primary school class. Back then we would all sit on the floor with our little black plimsolls on and our legs crossed, all keenly watching that old TV on a stand. More often than not we would be watching programs about history or geography, but I used to love the old black and white footage about farming even back then, and I'm sure that a lot of the time I will have been daydreaming anyway. So, back to the sheep. Whilst sitting amongst them I was highly amused by both the sight and sound of them all chewing the cud in unison. It was so relaxing just watching their jaws going ten to the dozen, all in time with each other. Before I knew it over an hour had passed, and it was way past my bedtime. The funny thing is that, as always happens, when I got back into the house, nobody had missed me, in fact nobody had even noticed that I had disappeared for all that time.

Time was pressing on and the grass on my new field was growing great guns. For weeks I had been chasing around trying to locate someone who could roll my recently seeded grass field, in preparation for our shepherd's hut arriving. In the end I thought, sack it, I'll just do it myself, so I went and hired a ride-on roller and cracked on with the job. If I am honest, this was what I had been trying to avoid, once again I was shying away from another new experience for me, driving this big ride-on roller. I had been awaiting a dry spell, well even a few days without rain would have been a bonus around here. The roller was delivered, but I held back my excitement until lunchtime, waiting until every last drop of the dew had disappeared from the ground. I started her up and drove the roller down to the field and initially I sat for 10 minutes planning my work route, well I wouldn't want to get caught up in any of the dozens of overhanging trees which surround the field, would I. I placed my headphones on my head, so as usual I could listen to my tunes, I straightened my sunglasses, turned my music up and off I went. Well as is so often the case, it wasn't very long until things went pear shaped and my plans went swiftly downhill. How on earth was I to know that the turning circle was the size of a football field. What happened was that when I had trundled across the field for the first time, I left it just a little too late to start to turn the vehicle and as I hadn't realised that you can't make sharp turns on this monster, I promptly ploughed through the undergrowth on the opposite side of the field and crashed through the overhanging trees. There was a number of almighty cracks, my headphones flew one way, the sunglasses launched themselves into the nettles and just for a moment, I maybe, sort of, lost control. I looked around to see if anyone had witnessed this carnage and thankfully no observers were present, phew! Luckily, there were no further mishaps that day and my field looked lovely and surprisingly was really, quite flat.

10 JEREMY'S JUMPER

It might seem a bit of a nonsense with Wendy planning to soon open up a teashop, but baking was never one of those things that I associated with her in our previous life. It would come about from time-to-time and although she was a very good baker, I never got to sample her delights with any regularity. I'm sure that with 6 kids it was often more convenient to just buy what we needed from the supermarket. Thankfully, that has all changed and everyone in the house agrees that her new-found love for baking is a very welcome addition around here. I'm a lucky man to be able to walk into the house around 8am after sorting the animals out, to be greeted with the almost heavenly smell of freshly baked hot cross buns, banana bread and a Victoria sponge too, well you can't go wrong with that can you? Well that's unless I was thinking about my waistline and the fact that at the time, I had less than 100 days to get it into some sort of shape for Evie and Joe's wedding. I didn't want to end up being the fat lad on the big day, did I?

It was soon time for our shepherds hut to arrive on the farm. It was like a military operation getting the hut off the trailer onto its axles and wheels and into position, but Kevin clearly knew what he was doing and had probably been through the process, dozens of times. It was exciting to see the finished structure in place, after so much discussion and we had definitely made the right choices, across the board. It was then my job to get it plumbed in, the electric connected up and some additional landscaping sorted out around the outside. Then it was to be Wendy's job to sort the soft furnishings and finishing touches, to get it ready for all those lucky people to come and visit us down on the farm, in the months to come. Hospitality is yet another world we haven't ventured into previously, as neither of us have worked in that field at all, but if nothing else, we did know what good customer service was and we were determined to always endeavour to be delivering quality, at all costs.

Around that same time, our shepherd hut wasn't the only new arrival on the farm. Mabel came to stay too! I was out working, planting fruit trees at the time, when a car pulled in through the front gate and a lady got out and walked purposefully down the field towards Wendy, who was helping me out. You could see that this lady was on a mission, and after a little while I wandered over, as my nosiness had got the better of me. So, the story went that this lady, who had visited our place a few times during the previous summer, regularly helped out a small sheep farmer who was in the process of switching his sheep breeds, from Rylands to Texels. As part of this process, the remaining flock were going off to market or for meat, but he was keen to find a forever home for Mabel, who was fully grown, but was only the size of a young lamb. If we didn't taken her on, she would've run out of reprieves and would have been sent with the others to the abattoir. After discussing things with her friends they decided that they should speak to us and maybe we would be able to let her have her new forever home, right here at our place. Well, on the Saturday, I went to have a look at her and then thought for all of about 5 seconds after which I promptly picked up the woolly ball of fluff, popped her into the back of the Landrover and brought her back to the farm. We quickly gave her all her injections, checked her over, gave her feet a trim and before we knew it, she had settled in with the other sheep really well and has been thriving ever since.

It was soon time to take care of the next stage of my grass-growing activities and this week it was time to encourage it all to grow. Spring had definitely arrived, but the grass needed plenty of TLC to get it moving, after the bleak winter months. I roped Wendy into dragging the chain harrow around the fields behind the quad, to liven things up and then it was time to get some much needed tillage onto it all to encourage that growth I needed. You see that was something else, I didn't know, what tillage was. I now know it's fertiliser and I had taken advice, and what I needed was a fertiliser mix called 20.10.10. which offers Nitrogen, Potash and Potassium to get things moving. Things didn't start ever so well as I had ordered a 600kg bag of the stuff which duly arrived for delivery, but the problem was that I thought they would have the means to lift the very large and very heavy sack off the back of the wagon, but they didn't. It took brute force once again to get it shifted, all 600kgs of it. With the welcome assistance of the driver, he and I just shoved the sack off the side of the truck onto the new carpark and thankfully the sack never split, but I was then on the clock to get all 600kgs shifted and onto the fields as soon as possible. Within days the fields were growing nicely and turning a much brighter shade of green, so it appeared to be a job well done.

With the grass taking its time growing up to this point, we had been relying on using our new hay feeder to keep the sheep satisfied until it did start to get a shift on. Last year I purchased a different hay feeder for the sheep, which was really too big for them, but I thought it would save me filling it up as often. In actual fact it was for the larger round bales and I have no means of lifting these larger bales into that feeder, so in the short term I just used the smaller bales to fill it up. It kept the sheep well fed throughout the winter, but it also ensured that on a daily basis, lots of hay was wasted. The sheep stick their heads inside it, pulling out hay all the while and in some cases they have been clambering inside, which all adds up to lots of hay finding its way onto the floor, which is then trampled on and the sheep cover it in unmentionables. The end result has been, that over winter the wasted hay has built up in layers and each of these layers has just covered the earlier layer which had been previously messed on by the sheep.

As you can only imagine, after clearing the top layer, the smell was horrendous, indeed it was a treat for the olfactory senses, but you soon became numb to the whiff! We utilised an array of hand tools to get the job sorted and many times thought about getting a digger in to assist things along, but the sense of achievement we got from completing the job far outweighed any aches and pains gained in the process. Well, that's what I kept saying to myself! Each day, whilst undertaking this little chore, our merry band of volunteers whom I had dragged in to assist in this work, were banned from going anywhere near the house. Food was brought out to us, but we had been instructed to stand an agreed safe distance away, until they had left the area. At the end of each day, before being allowed into the house, those who were staying had to strip off at the door and make a dash, up the stairs to the bathroom for a nice long hot shower, before we could mix with any of the other residents in the farmhouse. I did draw the line at being hosed outside first though, which had been encouraged a number of times. Really, this was quite a bonus for me, well, with a house full of women I'm invariably down the priority order for use of the bathroom and so to be in there before any of them was quite a thrill I can tell you. I'm now even considering seeking out smelly jobs on a regular basis, in order that I can balance out the bathroom rota a little more in my favour. To really put the lid on a completely nasty week, if shifting all that muck wasn't bad enough, an additional spanner was thrown into the mix to wind things up even further. I was only eating a lettuce leaf from the salad we were having for tea, when I lost one of my crowns. I was never going to go half measures on this at all and as it turned out it was one of my front teeth. As I couldn't continue looking like 'Nosferatu' or a reject from the 'Hammer House of Horrors', I immediately got myself to the dentist to get it sorted out and thankfully, sort it they did. Such a sight would not have been good for business at all.

The alarm sounded, reminding us to once again get up and check on the pregnant ewes. It was lambing time once more and as I walked across the fields I could see that things had moved on and a further 2 lambs had literally just been born. I was a little confused though, not difficult I know, but Badger was cleaning up both of the newborn lambs, but Coco was cleaning up one of the lambs also. It was a bit of a conundrum and I just had to work out who belonged to who. After a few minutes moving them all into the lambing pens and observing things, I eventually got to the bottom of it. The twin girls were in fact both Badgers bairns, but Coco was well into labour herself and apparently she had just wanted to assist her friend in the cleanup operation of her lambs. Without much of a break, and with strong winds and rain now upon us, Coco then gave birth to another girl herself, a beautiful grey and white patched ewe lamb, very cute!

It was now stretching into late afternoon, the delivery ward was empty and then Baa Baa's labour began. After a couple of hours she was still struggling on and although her lamb's nose and toes were on show, they were going nowhere fast and had hardly moved at all for some time. It was time for me to intervene at this point and each time she had a contraction and started pushing I would take hold of the lamb's legs and pull, all the time being aware that I didn't want to dislocate anything in the process or cause her damage, by my actions. Ultimately, brute force was what did the trick and the lamb's legs which had somehow been trapped against the back of the pelvis, were pulled free, and out he slipped like an ice pop on a summer's day and what a whopper he was too! I was extremely relieved when I could see that both mother and lamb were all well and then left them to bond for a little while, before I moved them into the next pen. I gave Wendy a call and she took the tea off the stove and hurriedly came out to see the latest newborn. As she walked past the shelter in the next door field, she noticed that one of Delilah's twins looked lethargic and listless. She picked her up and she was cold, it was clear that for whatever reason, she hadn't been feeding and her temperature had dropped rapidly. I wrapped the little one in my jacket whilst Wendy ran back to the house to make up a bottle and to get blankets to wrap her up. I called Andrew, from our local vets practice and minutes later he was out in the field establishing that Mum had in fact got mastitis, and the lambs had hypothermia.

Both of the lambs were soon wrapped up by the stove in our kitchen and things looked like they were turning a corner, with both of the poorly lambs now feeding from a bottle. Our vet loaned us a heat lamp and a pen made from straw bales was built inside our barn for Delilah and her twins, where the heat lamp could be sited and they could all be kept together in the warm. Our only other challenge was then getting Delilah out of the field into the barn, while all the time she was frantically chasing around the field looking for her babies. After only an hour and a half, I had her cornered, in the shelter. I was completely jiggered but knew that I had this chance to grab her and could reunite her with her lambs. All other sheep in the shelter made a hasty exit, except Delilah and me and one rugby tackle later I had her. I then tried to call home for assistance, but as only happens to me, my phone battery died…typical!

I pulled her out of the shelter, got off my knees and carried her into the barn. Very soon the family were reunited and we checked on them throughout the night, but early the next day the little ewe lamb sadly passed away. The remaining twin boy continued on the bottle being fed at regular intervals for over a week and things looked like they were on the up, but our most pressing concern was how we were going to get Jeremy, as we called him, back onto feeding from his mother. As a side note, he was named Jeremy, because Wendy thought that he looked like a rabbit and she thought that Jeremy was a good name for a rabbit. Who was I to argue, so it stuck!

So to look after Delilah too and treat her for the mastitis she was suffering with, it meant regularly injecting her with a course of antibiotics for her infected udder. Alongside those injections, I also got the job of emptying the same infected udder several times each day, to clear it out and to relieve the pressure on her too. I did get a few awkward looks from people who happened to call around whilst this little job was underway. Over a number of days, while we had Delilah on her backside, we took the opportunity to latch Jeremy onto her, hoping that this would enable him to keep some sort of bond with her until she could feed him properly herself. Well, the perseverance paid off and after almost 10 full days, I'm very pleased to report that the bottle feeding was stopped and Delilah was going it alone. So, with the weather warming up a little at the time, we decided that the best course of action was to move the pair back out into the pasture with the other ewes and lambs. Just to be on the safe side and to keep Jeremy warm outside, Wendy cut up a pair of wellie socks and made a rather fetching blue woolly jumper for our Jeremy. It definitely did the trick and both ewe and lamb started to thrive from that moment on.

Now, I understand that in the bird world, thrushes are in decline generally, but we have one who lives on the farm who is, to say the least, a persistent little lady, who is doing all she can to ensure that the species don't die out. The only problem is that she has taken it upon herself to build her nest on the top of the rear wheel of my Landrover. This has happened not once, not twice, but on four separate occasions. I physically removed the nest on three occasions before driving off the driveway and on the fourth occasion, the wind destroyed it. She has since attempted to build on two of our daughters car wheels also. It's such a shame, because she was making such a fantastic job of it too, but due to the mountain of rubbish I needed to take to the tip, I couldn't take Wendy's car to shift it all or wait any longer. She wasn't the only bird we had encounters with around that time as within a few weeks of each other, we had blue tits, house sparrows, wrens and pied wagtails, all moving into nests on the side of the house. That's quite a mix of families really. In addition to these nest builders, Wendy and I are always excited to have the swallows return from their winter break and one evening we were walking up what we call the green mile, between the paddocks, and literally out of nowhere, down they came, a pair of swallows tearing down the field towards us. They continued to swoop up and down, turning sharply, narrowly escaping a collision. This was our first sighting of the swallows back on the farm that year, what amazing stuff nature is!

It was just another one of those occasions when I walked away from being reprimanded, it was no doubt, once again for shirking my domestic responsibilities around the home, but as I walked down the staircase I heard a noise. It wasn't a noise we hear very often at all around here, but none the less I immediately recognised what it was, as the sound was coming from Wendy's incubator, in the downstairs hallway. Quickly, I jumped down the remaining stairs, knelt down and peered inside the top of the box. Without giving it a second thought, I opened my cake hole and bellowed…"Duckling!" Within seconds and just like magic, I had been surrounded by the women folk of the family, who immediately began to oooh and aaaah, all over this little bundle of yellow fluff as it staggered around the inside of the incubator. It also appeared that there were even more of them on their way to hatching too. Well, of course in all that excitement I had been conveniently relieved of my place in the doghouse, which was indeed a bonus! Ultimately, 5 ducklings were born over the following 24 hours, but unfortunately one of them died very soon after birth. The remaining ducklings thrived, growing fast and over the coming months were all rehomed!

It seems as though we see things come around in cycles on the farm and one of these cycles involves both life and death. With the ups and downs of lambing going on, unfortunately losing one lamb and then it was one of the ducklings who died, things were rounded off just the other day when I came across a dead tawny owl. Now this was something I certainly didn't expect. It was just laid under a tree, looking just like it was asleep, without a mark on it. It got me thinking as to why or how it had died. An hour or so later I was talking to our neighbour's who too had found a deceased tawny owl and again it had no visible signs of distress on it at all. Now that really got me thinking, could these owls, both found within 1000 meters of each other have died from the same cause? And if so, could they have in fact been poisoned? From around 8.45pm that night, as I was going about my work I was listening out intently for the sound of tawny owls calling. I wanted to make sure that our local tawny family hadn't, as yet been wiped out. It wasn't long at all until I could hear a male tawny calling and in fact he went on calling all night and if truth be known, it was the same every night for weeks, right outside our bedroom window! It certainly sounded like he was grieving for his mate who had sadly passed away.

Preparations were now all underway for the forthcoming opening of The Ginger Cow Teashop and over many weeks, Wendy and our daughter Evie had been very busy contacting local producers, in order that they could stock the Teashop shelves with lots of wonderful local goodies. As part of our planning guidance, we need to source local produce from the area. In doing all their homework, what surprised us most of all, was the wide, yet diverse range of fantastic local foods which are being found, almost right on our doorstep. Everything from cakes, to crisps, to chorizo, from biscuits, to bread, to beautiful fruit juice. Ice cream, chocolate, preserves, the list goes on. Many of these suppliers have kindly forwarded samples, which obviously I had to try, after which my only question was, "Why have we been eating so much mass produced fodder, with far too many food miles behind them, when there is so much quality, so close to home?" Yes, we maybe need to look a little harder, yes we may need to pay a few pence more, but my goodness you can certainly taste the difference! Having said that, after getting a chance to try some of those samples we received, I've had precious little chance to get near the results coming out of the Teashop kitchen ever since, barely even a sniff!

Looking back, at the time I thought it was such a great idea, to be able to seed my grass field so late in the year, December in fact, and still have it grow through the winter. That was great news at the beginning, when I was really keen for it to start growing and in fact it was growing really well, but things have progressed. I soon found myself in a position where the grass was doing just a little too well! I was regularly finding that I would jump on the ride-on mower to start cutting this new lawn, but after cutting a strip from one end of the field to the other, I would turn back around and the grass which had just been cut appeared to already be growing and reaching for the skies once more. It amazed me, I could almost stand and watch it grow, it was growing so rapidly. Luckily we were fencing off one end of the field as a paddock for livestock, so they will get a right good feed out of there, but at the other end where our shepherd's hut is sited, it needs cutting every few days, oh what a joy! The positives that came out of it are, that it's taught me that I do need to think much more carefully about the longer term with some of my decision making, Oh and we have a lovely lush pasture too.

A few months back in early spring, I purchased a few tons of fodder beet from a neighbour. Both the sheep and cattle love it, but last week the Highlands took things to a whole new level. On a daily basis, I would throw a few beets down the field for them, but as they clearly enjoyed it so much I decided, in my wisdom, that on this one day, I would throw them a few extras. Great idea, they'll love them! And indeed they did love them, but oh dear! Shaun's messed up again. Well, not me exactly, but it was more the cattle that were messed up. That was the day that I found out that even a little too much fodder beet can have a massive detrimental impact on their delicate bellies, and when their bellies are upset, I certainly know about it. It wasn't all of them, it was in the main, only Monica and Lyndsey. I was quite concerned about the two of them as they did more laying down than ever before, but with an upset stomach, I suppose I would too. Initially I wasn't sure what the problem was, but took advice, took any remains of fodder out of the field and over the coming days, things settled down and thankfully they firmed up too, thank goodness! You can be sure that I won't be repeating that little treat any time soon.

As I've said before, these mishaps rarely happen in the singular and so when one occurs, we generally just sit back and await the others following, in whatever form they may take. The wait wasn't long at all on this occasion as it happens and only days after 'fodderfest', we had something else to deal with. It was pouring down with rain, which didn't help things at all, but I was fine and dry as I was just coming to the end of cleaning out the stables. As I was about to close the stable door and walk away, I glanced across towards the house and saw Wendy jumping up and down, waving her arms and shouting. Now, because I had my old tunes turned up far too loud (one of the benefits of having distant neighbours) I didn't have a clue what she was saying, but almost immediately I saw what the problem was for myself. Firstly I saw 'Boo', one of our dogs disappear out of sight and then I witnessed a rather larger creature with big black spots go lumbering around past the trampoline in hot pursuit. It immediately became so much clearer, as I could see for myself that the three dogs were having a whale of a time with the 3 pigs who had taken it upon themselves to escape from their normal playground into our garden. This was the first time that we found that the pigs somehow knew when I was recharging the battery for the electric fence, and took full advantage of the situation, by digging their way out to freedom. Only moments later, I had grabbed their feed bucket whilst Wendy ran over the bridge to shut the front gate, or who knows what mayhem they may have caused if they had got out onto the open road. With a bucket of food in hand, the temptation for them was far too great, and they were soon back home. In the end all I was left with was unsightly patches on our lawn, where three little piggy snouts had been digging with all their might, and three disappointed border terriers, who were keen to play some more had to go and seek out entertainment elsewhere. I soon established where they had escaped from and fixed the fencing and returned the newly charged battery to its rightful position, outside their front gate. This fiasco wasn't going to happen again in a hurry, or was it?

With all this unforeseen activity going on, it was just a distraction that we really could've done without, as we were trying to progress things towards our projected opening date of July 4th for the Teashop, Shepherds Hut accommodation and Farm Tours to be up and running. Just this week, we have had the groundworks getting underway with water, waste and electric being installed in a variety of places, additional fencing and gates going in, electricians in the teashop finishing off, a decorator brightening up the outside of the barn and after five months of waiting, our additional electric supply has been connected up and completed. One thing that really amazed me in all the work which needed to be done ahead of opening is just how important it is to have all parties communicating with each other. The area that slowed us down most of all, as well as costing us an arm and a leg was the electric board, or whatever fancy name they have now. I never realised that such a large organisation could be so disjointed, by having so many different departments involved in one relatively small job. We had a team arrive and check out the job, another team arrived to double check measurements etc., another team put signs up and safety barriers, another team came to dig the trench, (well the trench which was outside the garden anyway, as I had to get the trench dug that's on my property) then one team came to lay the cables, another to come and joint the cable, another team to connect one end up, another gang to connect our end up, another team to fill the external trench, another lot to come and move the barriers and then finally after far too many phone calls harassing them, another team arrived with topsoil and grass seed, to restore our lawn outside the gate to its former glory. Phew! I'm glad we don't have that to deal with very often.

Ahead of time, I never really thought what we would do with all the soil that came out of the holes, but when the time came I had to come up with a plan. We had three waste tanks put in on the farm, with one to look after the house, replacing an ancient septic tank, one for the new shepherd's hut and a whopper for the teashop kitchen and toilets. Each tank required a hole to be excavated which went down almost 3 metres and various pipes and electric cables laid to ensure all worked correctly. I am so glad we brought in the professionals for such a job, because I've since heard so many horror stories where things have gone badly wrong. We had waited well into May before these tanks were installed, as the water table had been so high over the winter and so in digging these large holes we were still coming across water at just short of a meter in depth. The professionals we used shored up the sides of each hole in turn with steel and once the tanks, which had been filled with water to weigh them down, had been dropped into the empty hole, freshly mixed concrete was then poured into the holes to secure them, ahead of quickly whipping out the steel plates before they were cemented in place for the eternities. Before long we were finding that we were running out of the big jobs which needed doing, and to say that it was a good feeling is an understatement.

But just when you think that things are starting to settle down around the farm, something comes along to remind me, that I need always to be prepared for the unknown and to expect the unexpected. The normal, everyday activities are always there to take up your time and where animals are concerned, there's always a job to do. On this occasion it was the lambs who decided that this was their week to start giving me the runaround. Last week it was the wandering pigs, but with the lambs they are a completely different kettle of fish. There are more of them, for a start, they aren't controlled by food quite as much, they are quicker and lambs definitely have mischief as their middle name. The thing I would never have expected to happen, is what happened on Friday. That was when I first noticed that the lambs had executed their escape plan to a 'T' and they had taken themselves en masse to visit the Highlands up in the top field. Now, you may recall that around this same time last year, I had experienced a similar nightmare trying to gather the lambs back in, shouting, clapping and far too much running around, but this year I decided that I would try out last year's winning technique from the beginning. As I walked through the trees I clocked them across the field nibbling away on the grass and I just stood unnoticed and watched them for a few moments. I lifted my fingers up slowly to my mouth, licked my lips and whistled! It worked like magic, in unison each of the lambs ears pricked up and after a very brief pause, every one of them galloped back across the two fields along their escape route and under the field gates in between, back to their mothers. It worked like an absolute dream and thankfully this method has worked well almost every time since.

When it gets to around the middle of the year we need to make a few decisions regarding our livestock numbers on the farm. We are only very small and only have so much land to do all that we want to do and as a result only so much grass is grown, so it's important that we don't overstock ourselves, exhaust the pasture we have and go on to create problems for ourselves. As a result we need to whittle down our sheep numbers and bid farewell to a number of them. We have generally found that it's mostly the young, year old males and the odd female who we sell on to other farms. I would definitely get some of these meaty lambs into our freezer, as I know they've had a good life and are very well fed and cared for, but as I live with a house full of women, who apparently don't eat lamb, I don't get a say in the matter, for now, but we'll see what the future has in store, won't we?

Another reason we cut down our stock numbers is to accommodate a few new residents at Long Meadow Farm. It was time for us to take a drive up to Sutton-under-Whitestone, to visit a gentleman who breeds a vast array of wild and wonderful creatures. He showed us around his place and around every corner there were so many beautiful animals. It would have been so tempting to consider many of the animals he had, but in the end, we just want to best utilise the space and surroundings we have, in a way which isn't putting too much additional pressure on ourselves, our workload or the surroundings and resources were have on the farm. After a great deal of discussion, we bought a couple of young llamas, who we arranged to be delivered a couple of weeks after our visit. The weather was unseasonably good to us for a change and the beautiful weather had been around for almost a full week when things all changed for the worst, I didn't expect the rain to come back like this, but it did. The timing wasn't good at all, as I had jobs stacking up and it undoubtedly hampers things, a lot, especially when you are on the clock, preparing for your daughter's wedding and the forthcoming opening of Wendy's Teashop. There is always a positive in these things though and this occasion was to be no different.

When the rain began to fall, Monica and the other Highland cows' mood suddenly improved miraculously, which was long overdue too. As much as they are outdoors all year and have no problems at all with snow, rain, ice, wind, hail or fog, they just don't get on with the warm weather. With their thick coats on, it just drains them and they really can't be bothered to do anything as a result, so they lounge around in the shade until the sun goes down. If you think about it, I suppose it could be likened to my brothers and myself, wearing our snorkel parkas, with the hoods zipped up, every day, throughout that wonderful summer of '76. Not a nice thought at all. Like always though, we just work around the weather out there, because it comes with the territory and we're living our dream and having heaps of fun in the process.

With the rain and the sunshine taking turns around here, the whole place was really greening up, the flowers were out in full bloom and the farm was a picture. I recall, standing back on the top of the hill by our front hedge and admiring the place, whilst at the same time I was checking that my newly planted fruit trees, which had just gone in were all straight and spaced evenly up the car park, that's OCD for you. The very next morning whilst out on my rounds, I noticed that some of the lambs had taken it upon themselves to venture out of the front field towards the road, rather than heading up to visit the cows which was their normal route. I didn't foresee too much of a problem with that, I whistled and they returned as normal, they couldn't get into much bother out there on the car park, could they? Very quickly I saw for myself that in fact these marauding munchers could not only get into bother, but they already had done by taking a liking to the lovely, cherry, apple, plum and pear trees which I had planted, only the day before! The problem was that the ground is uneven in many places and the lambs will continually find the bigger gaps to squeeze their chubby little bodies through, to go and explore other parts of the farm. It was a continual chore, each day having to block up yet another gap under the bottom rail, so as to nip their break outs in the bud. As each year comes along it always gets to that stage that I long for those woolly wanderers to be just that bit too big to fit through any gaps at all! As a result of their exploits, I have realised the best way to deal with the problem is to just crack on and fatten them up as soon as I can and so they were put on extra rations from the very next day, just to help things along a little of course.

The Thursday evening arrived and I got a call to say that our Llamas were only minutes away. I soon guided the truck, up the green mile to their new home. I had been running around all day, trying to get their new shelter completed. I had done my homework and I wanted to be able to move it around their paddock if required and thankfully, I had completed my task around 5.00pm. They arrived just after 6pm, but before letting the Llamas loose in their paddock, I felt it wise to get a head collar on both of them, so I could start to halter train them from day one. I do want them trained up and handled regularly. So, the head collar went on the first one easily, that was the male, and then it came to the second and that seemed to go well too, which scared me a little, as things were unusually going surprisingly well. With the help of the breeder, I then took the first one through the gate into their new paddock, while he brought the second one in from the truck. Now, it's funny, but Wendy had mentioned any number of times over the days leading up to their arrival, that she couldn't wait to see these llamas chasing me around the field. Well, unfortunately for Wendy, that didn't happen quite as she'd hoped, but what did happen was enough to give her a chuckle anyway. As I walked my llama further into the field, for some reason she got spooked by something, (that's the llama, not Wendy) and as she was a little jumpy she leapt several times, heading through the undergrowth, with little old me hanging onto her head collar for dear life, which subsequently came off in my hand. Now, in hindsight, I could have or should have let go, but I didn't and as I got up off the ground to dust myself off, I looked across to see Wendy in stitches, doubled up with laughter. I'm glad that she had found it amusing, but I am equally pleased that she didn't have her phone with her to video the experience!

Well you'd think that was the end of an eventful day, but unfortunately it wasn't. That evening, just as it was getting dark, as I was walking back through the yard, I saw out of the corner of my eye, something running across the new flagstones, outside the teashop. I ran over and watched in horror as a mole headed down a hole and under the new patio. Not on your flamin' nelly, I thought. Uncharacteristically I did some quick thinking and quickly flipped over the new corner slab and just as he dug down with all his might, I was able to catch the furry little devil by his tail, before he got away. If he and his family had got settled under there and under my newly laid turf, I daren't think what damage they could have caused, it would have been a nightmare!

In preparation for opening our doors to the public, we had to ensure that all was in place to keep everyone safe and happy. As part of all the checks we needed to undertake, we were required to prepare a risk assessment of our site. Following this assessment, we then needed to place signage around the farm to inform our visitors of any action they need to take and to highlight any warnings which we were required to bring to their attention. It's the world we live in, but in the end we placed signs for not feeding the animals;

where the animals are dangerous and to stand well back; to wash hands, in a particular manner; to be aware that the ground is uneven; that water was ahead, that no entry was authorized; to close gates after you; to walk over a disinfectant mat; that smoking was not allowed; that parents needed to take responsibility for their own children and the list goes on. We have always been keen to do things by the book and to ensure that what we do is all above board, but it was getting ridiculous. Our motto has always been to get it done right, the first time around!

As has been said before, it has long been a part of Wendy's dream to open a little tea shop and it's been great to take a step back and watch her stretch her wings to bring all her ideas to fruition in our little part of paradise, right here in the East Riding of Yorkshire. You see, after running a hairdressing salon from her late teens, then getting married at 20 she subsequently spent her time raising our 6 children for 30 odd years. During that time it's been me out in the world of work, whilst she has coped with far more nappies, teething troubles and school runs than most people and now I see it as her time to shine. It has been wonderful to watch her step up to challenges that inevitably have come up, and it has been hard at times to not interfere, but to let her discover for herself the way through an impasse which may have arisen. It has been difficult at times to get it into my head that it doesn't matter if I have been through many of the challenges before, it's more important to be there if needed, than take away these learning experiences she has been going through. Whether it has been fitting out the inside of the teashop, working with producers and suppliers, getting labels printed, sorting out payroll or recruiting staff, she has stepped up and taken the opportunity to grow through it all with both hands. After all, if we both came out the other end of this adventure, having squandered too many of the experiences, then I think we would have missed out on a great deal. This whole experience we are going through is strengthening both of us and we are both learning so much from the adventure.

Well, our Evie and Joe's big day soon arrived and the house was awash with laughter, fancy hair do's and frocks. All the preparation was done, the teepees were up, the hog roast was organised, the ice cream van was arranged and all we needed to worry about was the weather. After the service, which was held in Beverley, everyone made their way back to the farm, for the celebrations afterwards. The weather almost held out for us, and apart from a 10 minute downpour of rain, it made no difference to the day at all. I'd been given my orders, the night before the wedding, by Monica, one of our highlands, that she wanted to get involved with the festivities and needed to look her best, so she wanted a bit of a 'DO' for the wedding herself. So, up I was, even brighter and even earlier, in order to get her looking all beautiful and at her best, for the big day. As well as Monica, the bride was beautiful, the groom scrubbed up well too and once again, it was another proud moment in the life of this Dad!

I know I'm a bit of a moaner and have in the past found time to whinge about our friendly, neighbourhood bunnies, but soon after the wedding, things unfortunately were once again taken to a whole new level. I have tried for so long to be patient and tolerant and to embrace them sharing our little patch of heaven, but on this occasion, they crossed the line. There I was just tootling down the lane in Wendy's mini, singing away to Cilla's greatest hits, just loving life as you do, when a little orange light appeared on the dashboard in front of me. Oh no! What now. What on earth did it mean? All it said was 4x4! When I could, I stopped and called the garage for advice, who then explained that the car would need to go in to get checked out. It was all arranged and the next day, only a short while after dropping it off, I got a call and then soon after it was followed by a video (technology eh?) showing that apparently someone had cut a cable under the vehicle and they had apparently ruled out rodent damage. I immediately disagreed with them, in my head, as I instantly knew how this damage had occurred. You see we have a regular visitor, the same one who chooses to dig up my new turf in the garden. On many occasions, from our front window, we have seen Mr. Rabbit hop under Wendy's car, as you can see his silhouette as he stands on his back legs, having what we thought was just a nosey about. How wrong we were. What he had done is he had bitten clean through the cable and nibbled away on a couple of others too during his regular visits. The thing is though, that I'm now minus £150 and it's time for 'Roger' to move on! As it happens, nature has a way of catching up in these situations and I didn't have to do a lot of chasing to track the bunny down. Only a few weeks later I spotted him across the road from the farm and like a number of other rabbits I'd seen over recent weeks, he had been struck down with myxomatosis, which appears to once again be on the up. Following this discovery, the only action I therefore needed to take was to put him out of his misery and take care of his remains. Not a nice job at all, but unfortunately a necessary one all the same.

11 'HIGHLY COMMENDED'

After so many months, wading our way through planning, after constructing the building, decorating, shop fitting it out, filling it with stock and getting to grips with a new till system, 'The Ginger Cow Teashop' was, as Fireman Sam would say, 'ready for action!' We advertised the fact that we were opening up on July 4th 2016 and sure enough there was a queue of cars outside the gate, as I opened it up on the very first morning. With a great deal of trepidation, Mrs. McKenna started to set out her stall and welcome her new customers in to see for themselves what she was offering in her exciting new venture. Bearing in mind that Wendy had never even worked in a teashop or a cafe, this was much more of a mighty leap than a step into the unknown.

I've said it before and I'm sure that I'll say it again, but human nature is a wonderful thing. In the few days after opening the Teashop, we were at the receiving end of so many kind words, heartfelt cards and beautiful gifts from so many, who were wishing us well. It never ceases to amaze me the lengths people go to in order to pass on good wishes, to say thank you, or just to encourage you to keep going, when things are tough.

Can I tell you about just one of these acts of kindness we experienced, at the time? In our first summer on the farm, whilst Wendy had the opportunity to put a few tables out in the garden and serve cream teas and sandwiches, we had a really good response from people coming to sample her delights. Some people would come back again and some people would come back many times. One such lady, brought her daughters, on other occasions she brought her friends and on one occasion, she even brought her hubby! Well, on one of these occasions, whilst in conversation, the lady spoke to us about her hobby, which was needle felting and explained how some months before, she had been bitten by the bug. We even gave her a big bag of hair, it being the result of one of my coo grooming sessions, so she could use it in her work. Wendy subsequently bought some things from her, for our home, some felted cattle and pigs and do you know, they are so lifelike, just much smaller than the real thing. Anyway, after being opened up for only a few days, this lady, who we'll call Maxine, because that's her name, reappears once again with her family. You could see she was excited to be back and said that she had brought us a little something. A little something! She, no word of a lie must have spent weeks and months on this little something. What she brought us was a handmade replica of a Highland Cow, which she had made. We needed to find somewhere fitting for this beautiful gift and so it soon had pride of place on a prominent shelf at the back of the Teashop.

I really hadn't realised just how jealous some animals can get. Grooming time came quickly around again and I was hell bent on getting all of our highlands groomed and all the knots taken out of their coats. Now when I say knots, I mean knots! It's the remainder of their winter coat, which had been coming off for quite some weeks. We have 4 daughters and as a result I've experienced many a knot or a tangle on bath night when the girls were having their hair washed, but this is a whole different kettle of fish, let me tell you. So, there I was sorting out Morag's coat, minding my own business, when all I could hear was Maisie and Lucy, the ponies, in the next field moaning a bucket load. What on earth's up with them? I kept going, but they kept whinnying, I think that's a real word, but eventually, although I wasn't sure, I thought I had worked out what the problem was. I downed tools, walked through to the top field and promptly escorted the ponies down the green mile and back to the stable area. I then brought out the box holding all their grooming paraphernalia and only then did they finally shut up! I was correct in my thinking and all the time they had been moaning, they had just been jealous that it was the cows turn to be groomed and not theirs. Before long I was on my way back up the green mile with the ponies, to then continue with the job I had started some 90 minutes earlier, in the cow field.

Over many months we had slowly but surely lost all of our Muscovy ducks to Mr. Fox, but it was agreed that we really needed to have ducks on the farm, as we felt that ducks were an important part of the farm family. We once again did a little searching and eventually, after considering many types, we settled on Aylesbury ducks. We sourced a lovely looking pair over in South Yorkshire, so one Sunday afternoon, Wendy and I took a little drive over there to pick them up. Over the next few weeks, Frank and Betty settled in really well, they behaved themselves, which is unusual around here I know, but all the same they did. After a few weeks Betty thought that she had laid sufficient eggs to sit on, so that's exactly what she did and a month or so later, she proudly marched out of the duck house with 7 yellow bundles of fluff behind her. They were very quickly growing and so again we needed to decide on a plan. We couldn't keep all these ducklings, as they all grow up and then there'll be more babies and before we knew it there would be dozens of them around the place. The thing is, we only have so much space available and overcrowding can lead to many problems.

I can remember doing my rounds early on that sunny morning, when I thought, I've really done it this time, Betty hates me! That morning I went to let her, Frank and the ducklings out of their home and for the first time, her threats became a reality and she did bite me. It obviously didn't hurt and if I had been in her position I'd have probably attempted a far worse punishment. You see, the night before, three of her ducklings went to live with another family and as you can imagine, she wasn't ever so happy about it at all. We had been talking to some of our neighbors up the lane some weeks before, who were keen to have some ducklings for their children and they already had hens, so ducks would fit in really well down there, and besides they're a lovely family too, which always helps. As it happens, a couple of them then disappeared over the period of a week and we think that they had been taken by predators. We have stoats, weasels, buzzards, red kites and owls, as well as Mr. Fox too, so there's no shortage of potential culprits, I'm sure. For several days I just dodged Betty, whenever I could, just to let her calm down, which eventually she did, thank goodness.

For some reason I had drawn the short straw once again, and I had been left with Olivia's car, which needed 2 new tyres fitting. "I'll take Mums car to work today" she said, "Can you speak to the garage and see if they can sort it, today, thanks, bye" and off she went. Kids, who'd have 'em! Now that doesn't on the face of it sound a big ask, but as I had a busy day planned, it was due to be showers most of the day and there was a mile and a bit walk home after dropping it off and then back to pick it up later, it all added to the task. Well, as it happened, I didn't mind at all really and in fact it was as I strolled, reminiscing along the lane that I was reminded of things I had learned many years ago whilst walking down very similar lanes as a boy.

There were many really important, life changing skills and experiences which I can still remember almost 50 years on. Tell us, tell us, I hear you cry!

Well, have you ever given someone a Chinese haircut? Well that's what we called it. It's when you pull up a stalk of foxtail grass, strip the seeds off its head and then ever so gently thrust the remaining stalk into your brother's hair, or any other unsuspecting victim. You then slowly twist the stalk and then pull, Ouch! Your victim, is left with a sore head and minus a handful of hairs. It was also back then that I learned, and I don't know or understand why it was the case, but whenever we saw an ambulance go by, we had to find and touch something green. Also, I learned that if you pick a broad leaf blade of grass or a privet leaf, place it between the inside edges of your two thumbs and blow through it, you can whistle. Endless hours of fun can be had with a blade of grass, so if you haven't done it before, give it a try. I remember climbing trees for fresh, ripe damsons, plums and pears, there were plenty of apples too, but I was never a fan of apples. I never did find out whose fruit it was that we were pilfering and I'm certain that I'll have to answer for all these misdemeanours one day. Just walking down that lane made me think about just how lucky I was, to be able to spend so much time in the outdoors and down those, almost vehicle-free lanes back in the day, without the many concerns and worries that would be raised in today's health and safety conscious world. We used to love going out as kids with either one of our Granmas, who would walk our legs off all day for miles down these lanes, teaching us songs that I can still remember to this day, as we marched along.

Oh how time flies, our wedding anniversary had come round again, but unlike last year's stay in the two-man tent we decided to give our shepherd's hut a trial run before our paying guests started to arrive in the coming weeks. Thankfully we got an even better sleep than in the tent and it was all that we anticipated it would be and more, so we were sure our paying visitors were going to love it. I did wake up to an unexpected additional job, thanks to Gavin the goat. I knew that their stable door needed some attention and yes, I had been putting it off for some weeks, but Gavin's patience had obviously run out, but his method of bringing it to my attention was a little unorthodox, to say the least. He had for whatever reason, decided that the best course of action to highlight the situation was to just take a good run up and park his head through it at pace. He was unscathed, thanks goodness, but the door definitely needed some work doing to it, which I promptly attended to.

Summer arrived at last and with the beautiful weather, it brings a whole different set of obstacles to overcome. One of the challenges which we had to deal with involved Precious the pig. She's the pig that we bought for the hog roast at Evie and Joe's recent wedding, but luckily for her, she and Petal had got a reprieve. Well the thing is, that like all of the animals in the warmer weather, they would go through gallons of water each day, with it being so warm and that's where the problem begins. For some reason, Precious got it into her head that it was a bit of a game with the water trough. Whenever it got filled up, which is very regularly in the summer, she sticks her nose, which is the size of a shovel, underneath it and tips the whole thing over, leaving it empty and needing to be refilled. So here's my dilemma, how do I tell a 100 kilo pig, "please piggy, piggy, don't keep turning the trough over", because however hard I try, that 'aint ever going to work. I changed the position around the field, wedging it up against the fence, making it more difficult to tip up, but to no avail. I made sure she got to drink from it first, allowing her to get her fill and then chased her away so the others could get a drink in peace, but she just meandered straight back and flipped it over. I've tried weighing it down with blocks, to discourage her, but that hasn't worked either. Now I know that initially it may have been that she started to tip it up so that she could drench the area thus turning it into a mud bath for her to wallow in, out in the sun, but I think it's just become a bit of a habit now. My concern is, that I obviously didn't want her or our other pigs to become dehydrated as a result of her actions, so in my next Saturday column in the Yorkshire Post I asked for any suggestions readers may have to get around the problem would be very welcome. Sure enough I got the response I was after, and a few weeks later I went to collect some cast iron pig feeders to use in the pig pen and do you know, they've worked a treat ever since!

I came across something in the greenhouse this week which I hadn't seen for many a year, but once again it whisked me back to being a kid, cabbage white caterpillars. Isn't it funny what triggers memories? I'm not sure why at all, but there seemed to be a constant stream of two particular things which kept recurring around the farm, one was childhood memories and the other was just general drama. It wouldn't be the same if we didn't experience one on a regular basis and on this occasion it involved sheep, well one sheep in particular. I noticed Brock, one of Badger's young twins sitting alone in the sun, at the opposite side of the field to the rest of the sheep, who were all in the shade. I watched her each time I passed by and for whatever reason she always seemed to be on her own. I did think the worst, with the flies catching up with Wispa the previous year, so I penned the sheep up, so I could take a closer look at her. On one hand, what I found was a relief, but on the other it was a mess. Brock had somehow caught her horn on something, or she and her brother Stanley had been having a bit of a scrap. Her horn was hanging off and blood was pouring down her face. For most livestock-related problems around here, we just deal with it ourselves and so I set to work patching her up and in the end she could easily have been mistaken for Pirate Captain Jack Sparrow. Within twenty four hours she was doing very well once again, even without one horn. At the time, I wasn't sure if the stump that was left would continue to grow or not, but it did and although she's a bit lopsided as a result, she's still beautiful either way!

Ooh, we could hardly contain the excitement, we were having our first paying guests come and stay in our Shepherd Hut. We were really keen to make sure that all was perfect for them, even down to Wendy getting me to put the hot water bottles in their bed, around about 3.30pm, just ahead of their arrival and I know what you're thinking, "but it's the middle of summer!" Well apparently it was all part of the Ginger Cow service they would receive, whether it was summer or not. So, things had been going so well, right up until their very last night with us, that's when at 2am our new alarm which had been fitted in the Teashop started sounding. I flew out of bed and was over there in a flash. I had it turned off in seconds and checked that all was well, before going back to bed. It later transpired that there had been a brief power cut, which had in fact set the alarm off, so thankfully nobody was attempting to rob us blind. It was then on our mind for the rest of the night that the alarm had woken up our guests and disturbed their sleep. You can cope with owls-a-hooting, Cows-a-mooing and hens-a-clucking, out here in the sticks, but a racket like our burglar alarm would wake anyone from their slumbers. Well that's what we thought, but in fact we were wrong, they had a great night's kip and slept like logs all night, not hearing a thing. Wendy's only response to the news was, "I told you the aloe vera mattress was worth all that money".

Wendy and her new team of staff were now a few weeks into service in the Teashop, but already we had experienced a right 'to do' down on the farm. Wendy had it seemed picked up quite a nasty repetitive strain injury in her wrist. Unfortunately, I think it's going to take some time for it to really heal properly too, as there's a continuing need for her to be using that wrist going forward. Well, as always it appears that she likes to give everyone good value for money and with this in mind she likes to serve nice big 'doorstep' sandwiches in the teashop and on one particular day, she had seen a run of customers all wanting these very same doorsteps. This meant she was hard at it most of the day cutting dozens of slices of bread and in fact it has been much the same story for the previous 3 weeks. The result of all this doorstep activity meant that she had injured herself quite badly with all that effort. On the positive side though, the wrist did get better in time and the customers continued to love the sarnies!

Since moving out t'country, we have been blessed with so much, but one of my favourite blessings, sad as it may seem, was the chance to get a tan, well a 'Farmers Tan' to be exact. Being a 'Ginge' has always meant that I had to daub endless gallons of sunblock on and steer clear of the sun whenever possible. In reality though, I was always forgetting to put sunblock on and countless times I fried as a result. I can remember one of the worst occasions was when as a youth I took part in a sponsored walk from Hull to Hornsea along the 19 mile stretch of old railway line and with the sun on my back all the way, my back and the backs of my legs were crimson by the end of the day. I recall that we had a footy match that same evening and it hurt every time I bent my legs, but hey ho, that's what happens when you're young and stupid! Anyway, dodging the sun hasn't always been that practical these days, with so much to be done outside. I do continue to put suncream on, as I should, but I think that because I am outside most of the day every day, my skin has become more used to the sun. The result is that I now get a proper tan and thankfully I'm a much less pasty little redhead than I ever was before, which I think is a real bonus for me.

As it was now coming towards the end of the summer, it was that time of year again, the time of year when we need to start thinking ahead towards decisions that needed to be made over the coming months, before it got too late and we missed the boat on some things. For instance, when do I send some of my highlands off to visit the bull? and which coo's shall I send? What 'tup' shall we bring in to party with our ewes in November? When shall I take our next pigs off for slaughter? Do we bring in a billy goat for 'Stacy' and maybe 'Bambi' to have kids? All of these things need to be thought about ahead of time and with everything else that's going on, it's easy to forget and let things slip. As it happens we were ahead of the game on all these decisions and were well on with our preparations. When the time came, we decided that with regards to the Highlands, it was time for Monica to have a rest from calving, she's nineteen now and needed to be able to put her feet up. For the last two years we had attempted to get Monica in calf, but not been lucky on either occasion, so we arranged to have Lyndsey, who is five and Flora who is four to get picked up and go and spend ten weeks or so down in South Yorkshire with Pete Fletcher's new Highland Bull.

With regards to finding a tup for our ewes, I waited until the 'Rare breeds sale' was on in Murton and I took a trip over to see who and what was on offer. I walked up and down the rows of Tups, picking out the Shetlands and making a note as I went. I then went to have a good look at each of them in turn and gave each of them a bit of a test. Having had a little bit of experience up to this point, I wanted an animal who could do the job we wanted him to obviously, but also one who would behave himself and not wreck the place in the process. As I stood in front of each of the tup pens, I would reach out and touch the head of the sheep and gently push their head or stroke their forehead. If the Tup then pushed back or took a step back to give me a charge, then I just did a Dionne Warwick and walked on by. It may have been a ridiculous way to choose a sheep, but it worked for me. I walked out of the auction with a beautiful Shetland Tup, costing me 45 guineas, whom we call 'Mac', or 'Maximus' on a Sunday. He also happens to be the closest colour I could find on the day to ginger, which for me was the icing on the cake. With regards to the pigs taking a trip, we decided that we needed another freezer before the pigs could go, but soon enough I was on my travels, taking just two of them off on their journey. If you remember, two of them had been given a reprieve after the wedding hog roast and so certainly for now those two were staying put on the farm. We decided that with the goats we would leave bringing a 'billy' in until the beginning of the New Year, so that the goats could have their kids when the weather had hopefully warmed up a little.

A few years ago, we were asked by some friends in Cherry Burton, if we would have room for a little white bantam out at our place. The story was, that over some months the bantam had got really noisy and our friends were concerned that this noise was going to upset their neighbours, on their street. Of course we said yes and that it wouldn't be a problem and she came to live with our gang out here. From the moment Layla arrived we have had very little noise from her at all and the only noise we have got out of her is when she gets broody and decides to park herself on a nest full of eggs, for no good reason at all, as all of the eggs are in fact unfertilised and so will come to nothing anyway. She doesn't have too many chicken friends around the farmyard, for whatever reason and was spending most of her days with Frank and Betty the ducks, but she is a contented little soul. Anyway, out of the blue, we received another heart felt plea from our friend in Cherry Burton, who asked once again if we could accommodate another little white bantam and again it was for the same reason, she was just too noisy for the neighbourhood. As you'd expect, again said yes, but what was really interesting was that this new bantam Henrietta, was Layla's sister! Now bearing in mind, that they hadn't seen each other for two years, it was quite an emotional moment. When Henrietta arrived and their eyes met across the farmyard, it was like 'Long Lost Families', down at the 'Ginger Cow'. Well, I can report that they have been inseparable ever since and together they tootle around the farm in total silence, so I don't know where all that noise they were making went to....aren't animals funny!

Throughout that summer we experienced a very busy old time with the Teashop full to busting most days, both inside and out, Monday to Saturday and the car park rammed full, but luckily doing the job it was supposed to be doing. Social media was going bananas and from the countless reviews that we were receiving, customers were definitely going away happy and their expectations were being met, so all in all the hard work was paying off. In preparation for opening up the Teashop, Wendy had toiled over her menu, not being certain that what was on there was what the customers were after, but clearly the food was hitting the mark and, with the specials board also available, alongside the daily menu, things were doing extremely well. This was confirmed late that summer when the Teashop was nominated for a food award by the 'Beverley Food Festival' and the 'East Riding Local Food Network', in the category, 'Best Cafe/Teashop'. For weeks the Teashop staff were awaiting the arrival of the judges, who would be coming to sample the delights on offer and out of the blue, that day arrived. Inevitably, it was pouring with rain and the teashop was full. We had two sets of customers waiting for a table already and it hadn't even got to lunchtime yet. A further two ladies turned up, but were happy to wait for a table to become available. Soon enough, things progressed and Wendy was able to get everyone seated and served.

I can remember doing a bit of washing up for Wendy, when Olivia, our daughter who works with Wendy, burst through the kitchen door and blurted out, "The judges are in and they want to speak to the owner". Wendy immediately looked at me, but I looked her right in the eyes and said, "This is your day and your teashop, go and welcome them, answer any questions they may have and make it happen!" So, Wendy turned and immediately walked through that swinging kitchen door, whilst switching on her brightest smile and turning on her charm, in front of a packed teashop she did us all proud. Eventually, the judges left, after they had been talked to death, but whatever she had said had obviously done the trick, as a few weeks later

Wendy and her team, got their glad rags on and went for a night out at the awards ceremony at Tickton Grange, near Beverley. The teashop category was way down the list and so there was a long wait for them all. The moment finally arrived and in the end 'The Ginger Cow Teashop' had been pipped to the post by another teashop at South Cave, but an additional award was to be given for a teashop which was seen as 'Highly Commended' and guess who won that award? So, after only 6 weeks, 'The Ginger Cow' had been nominated and after only 10 weeks, they had been given this award, which isn't bad, considering that the winners were very well established and had been in business for a number of years.

Since opening the teashop, we have taken the opportunity to share what we have with others, which included the animals. We do this by taking visitors on a guided tour around the farm, introducing them to the animals, letting them feed some of them and telling them stories about the animals and our experiences with them. We would run the tours 3 times a day at 11am, 1pm and 3 pm, with average numbers of around ten visitors on each tour. We have had a real cross section of visitors keen to see the animals, from the youngest children in pushchairs all the way through to our many pensioner visitors, either as a group or with grand kids in tow. It's always funny, as I stand and go through the health and safety information before we start the tour, invariably we see at least one harassed mother or grandparent rushing down the car park dragging kids behind them cursing as they go and complaining about the traffic making them late. It never fails to make me chuckle. As the tours were going so well and we were being requested to run them for schools, we decided to start branching out and began setting up bespoke visits for these larger groups to come and take a tour. From then we had both schools and groups like 'Beavers' coming to see the animals. It never ceased to amaze me just how many people love the Highland Cows and how many people both young and old have never been so close to many of the animals we have on the farm. To see the reaction of many people when meeting the animals was rewarding in itself.

It was almost closing time in the teashop late one afternoon. I had pinched a few minutes to sit and park myself, after being busy with jobs all day, and with the sun on my back it felt good, just to catch my breath and chat to a friend I hadn't seen for some time. As we chatted, momentarily my attention was caught and my eyes for some reason were drawn up to the top of the barn. That's when things very quickly unfolded in front of me, but it all happened within a flash of a second. From my left I watched a sparrow hawk dart from out of view across the top of the barn and snatch one of our young swallows, who were taking a well-earned breather from their 'Dinner catching' tuition with mum and dad. I couldn't believe what I had seen, I'm sure I was sitting with my mouth wide open, not listening to a word my friend was saying. The hawk, swiftly flew up into one of our poplars, I'm sure just to secure his prey and quickly moved on through the trees. I explained what had just played out before my eyes, but he just kept on, talking! It was only after this had happened that I began thinking about not only this event which I'd witnessed, but many other instances when opposition has played a part in our life, since moving out here to the country.

I more than understand that there is opposition in all things, but I was considering how we have coped with things as we have encountered problems over the last couple of years. I'm sure, like most, we have become stronger as a result of many of the experiences that we have been through, and living with the elements will always play a big part in teaching me patience, as I learn to live with it rather than against it. Working with animals, with their own minds, has and will continue, I'm sure, to pose problems, but in many cases we have again learned to work with them rather than against them. Building trust, in my view has been key to making positive strides forward in working with livestock and that can often take some time, to achieve the desired results. We have unfortunately seen over the last 2 years all 15 of our Muscovy ducks fall to the local fox, and again we have learned from the situation, even if that lesson is, choose ducks who will live in a home rather than roosting on top of the barn or stables overnight. At this time of year we all have to put up with flies and wasps causing us issues and have taken steps to protect our livestock from the flies. By this time in the summer, we had so far removed four wasps' nests with a view of trying to protecting our visitors, but I understand that anywhere cream teas are, those wasps won't be too far away. Unfortunately, some pests are more difficult to deal with. That summer, alongside the teashop opening, we had once again opened our small 'Shop-in-a-shed', where we were selling gifts and crafts, many of which had been made by our daughters. Sadly, opposition had once again reared its head, as already we had seen shop items taken, whilst our backs had been turned and even some of the china sugar bowls which were sited on each table, had gone walkabout too. I just hoped that their need was much greater than ours.

Although it hadn't been long since they had arrived out here, the llamas, Marguerita (Marj) and Miguel appeared to be settling in quite well. It was only a couple of weeks ago that I was spending ages trying to encourage them across the field, in order that they would come and say hello to any visitors we had. Now, they can't help themselves. They are just so nosey, or inquisitive and although they are still not fans of being stroked, they do love to get up very close and personal. Now we were aware up front that Llamas spit, but thankfully, we have only witnessed Marj spitting and so far that spitting has only ever been reserved for Miguel, and that's because she's a greedy girl and wants to eat his grub as well as her own. We were unsure when we were going to get Miguel 'seen too' by the vet, but we may just have left things that bit too long, let me explain. I was showing a group of around

9 or 10 ladies, with their kids in pushchairs around the animal tour one sunny afternoon at the end of the summer, when I said as we left the pony field, "now let's go and see who's around this corner, shall we?" Then as we walked around the corner of the trees towards the Llama enclosure, I stopped dead in my tracks, as the Llamas appeared to be in no mood for either visitors or lunch, as they were engaged in other more strenuous activities, if you know what I mean. Some of the children were asking questions, the mothers were all just in hysterics and I was just standing red-faced, trying to explain that the Llamas weren't in any mood for lunch that day. Oh, the things I continue to put myself through. I'm sure that I've been irreversibly scarred with some of these sights that I've seen around here and the Llama episode was soon followed up by another experience which I'm sure will stay with me for a very long time.

Early one morning, just as I was finishing my jobs, I noticed that the pigs could do with their water topping up with fresh water, so I once again unwound the hosepipe and dragged it through the yard. I started topping up the trough when I could hear that clicking sound which I instantly recognised, it was the sound of something shorting out the electric fence around the pig enclosure. It normally occurs when the long grass around the perimeter strays that bit too close to the electric wire and causes the problem. I started to walk in the direction of the clicking and that's when I was caught by surprise by the sight that beheld me. My eyes had followed the wire along at almost ground level for some distance until I noticed an obstruction which was causing the problem. I continued to walk along the outside of the fence, so as to get a better view of the object. As I got closer, that's when I caught sight of the offending obstruction, a big fat toad. There he was, strewn across the electric fence, looking like 'Shughie McFee' in the 'Great Escape', (remember, when he made a last ditch attempt to try and get over the barbed wire perimeter fence?) I hate to see animals die unnecessarily, but to end his life this way was just so sad. I'm sure that, as well as having nightmares reliving the experience, almost certainly each time I come across a toad, I will once again be reminded of this life that was snuffed out, way before his time!

Out in the sticks and especially doing what we're doing, you can't help but take more notice of the seasons and the length of days and daylight. I couldn't believe how quickly the days were becoming shorter at the end of our second summer. It was already beginning to get dark and it was well before nine o'clock. Alongside the day's shortening, another sign that autumn is well on its way was the abundance of conkers on our chestnut trees. Before I knew it, I couldn't stop myself from picking up a nice stick or two to bring down those prize winning conkers, ahead of any strong winds spoiling my fun and doing it for me. With 8 grandchildren, that's a lot of conkers I needed to collect, so I thought it best that I started sooner rather than later!

It was now evening time and I'd left the ponies out as long as I could, before bringing them in because sometimes they had a habit of moaning a bucket load if I brought them in too early. And even though they'd had extra time out in the field, for some reason Maisie and Lucy, were not in any mood to be coming easily, and clearly wanted to stay out longer. I could see that this was the case, as they were just plainly ignoring me. That's when after trying all my normal methods of rounding them up, I had a thought. I don't know where it came from, but all the same I thought I'd give it a go. Maybe, if I changed my accent and called them in their native tongue, it might help. So, that's just what I did and instead of calling them with my normal, bit of allsorts accent, I put a heavy Scottish accent on, with them being Shetland ponies of course and do you know, without even a thought, they trotted over immediately. I wondered, would this work elsewhere around the farm, so as I marched the ponies back to the stables, I gave it a try, firstly with the Highland Cattle and the Shetland sheep and do you know, it definitely had very positive results in both cases. Obviously, I had to undertake more robust research to test my thinking out a little more, but it was looking very promising so far.

It was late in the day, when I wandered down the car park to lock up and move our sign from outside the gate, but that was when I noticed that something was missing. To be truthful and it's sad to say, but I was surprised that they had both lasted all summer and as long as they did. Well, ask yourself, why would anyone in their right mind choose to steal one of our signs from outside the entrance gate? For a laugh? Nobody would get much for its scrap metal value and would be no use to them unless they had a business called 'The Ginger Cow' and required visitors to take the next right turn. If I had stood and thought about it long enough, I would have got seriously wound up, so I made the conscious decision to not think about it, and just moved on with my life, just without my sign!

It was just one of those days, I had so much to get done and really not enough hours to catch up with everything. Firstly, I needed to nip out to the local farm supplies shop. I'll take Wendy's car, I thought, it's a little Mini and it was just easier than taking my Landrover, and besides, I parked the Landrover in the main carpark, to show customers which way we wanted them to park their cars, so if I move it, then we were bound to get cars parked in all sorts of wild and wonderful places. Anyway, taking Wendy's Mini was a big mistake! After using her car, which really isn't a problem at all, I happened to misplace her car keys, which as you can imagine, certainly is a problem. Now although we have 2 sets of keys, they do cost such a lot to replace, so of course I searched everywhere. I even resorted to having a rummage through all of our wheelie bins, just in case. I could track their whereabouts up until lunchtime, but that's when it all went hazy and eventually I gave up. Rolling forward four weeks, still the keys hadn't turned up and there I was walking the dogs one morning, through the wooded area behind the house, which just so happened to also be the home to my hammock. As I passed the hammock I walked over to see what debris had fallen into it from the trees above during the windy spell we'd just experienced over the previous week. In fact there was no debris in it at all, only a set of car keys, in a puddle of water. A wave of relief came over me, yet there was grief too, as they were sitting in this puddle of water! I immediately ran around the outside of the house, through the garden, past the trampoline, dodging the clothes hanging on the washing line, just to get close enough to the Mini to press the 'unlock' button and test if it was still working. Hurray! It was, soggy or not. That's when my memory came flooding back. A few weeks earlier, probably around four weeks or so, there was one day, after working extra hard, I thought I deserved a treat and I had slipped away early one afternoon for a sly forty winks in the hammock. That must have been when the keys dropped out of my pocket and I was none the wiser.

Funnily enough though, I wasn't the only one to be in the dog house that week because Scout, one of our border terriers, got into bother that week too. I'm not sure if many people know but Scout has won a coveted award, one he is extremely proud of. A couple of years ago, we presented him with the award for being 'The laziest bone-idle hound on the planet'. He was presented with this title as he chooses to not walk more than half a dozen metres away from our front door, when he wants to go for a wee. Unfortunately, Simon our friendly neighbourhood gardener chose to park his strimming helmet, right in the middle of Scouts favourite weeing spot and of course, strimming helmet or not, that was never going to deter our Scout, when he needed to go, he'd go! So Scout decided in his wisdom that it would be a good idea for him to cock his leg up Simon's very favourite helmet. Luckily, Simon did see the funny side, but as you'd expect, Scout was suitably reprimanded for this outrageous behaviour.

12 MY HAMMOCK HAVEN

As you will have no doubt noticed, we are very accustomed to animals behaving badly from time to time on the farm, but I also think that on some occasions, these animals can sense fear in others and use that to wind things up. For example, there was an incident which occurred whilst taking visitors to see our animals at the end of last summer with a friend of mine who had brought his family to see the farm, and as it turned out, he was the only victim involved on the day. I won't mention his name for fear of embarrassment and the countless years of endless ribbing he would undoubtedly receive from his family and work colleagues as a result of such humiliation. Picture the scene once more.

The sun was still high in the sky, it was a beautiful day and we were coming towards the end of our farm tour. As we reached the conclusion of the tour, I mentioned, as I do that we needed to walk through the gate into our farm yard where we would see the ducks, goats and pigs, oh and of course that's where our pet hens live! Hens! The look of fear swept across his face as the colour immediately drained away. "It'll be fine", I said as I encouraged him through the gates, "they're too busy with dust baths to be bothered with you". I carried on to tell everyone about our goats, who were next up on the tour, "Come closer" I encouraged, but to no avail, he just responded with "I'll just stand over here, I'm fine". He couldn't have stood any further away from the hens if he'd tried. As I chatted on to the visitors, now explaining about our visiting swallows, I saw movement out the corner of my right eye, the hens were on the move, bath time was over. Before I knew it, things were quickly turning pear shaped, with 'Rita' our most inquisitive and at the time, evil grey hen leading the charge as three of our hens galloped across the yard towards our group of visitors. The visitors, both adults and children all began to ooh and aah at the hens, who were very cute, well I say all, when in fact, it was all of the visitors except one.

That one visitor appeared to be running for his life through the yard with Rita in hot pursuit. She was only being nosey and wouldn't have gone anywhere close to him really. At the time, because she was a morky little devil, rarely had anyone got close enough to her to even give her a stroke, but as he tried to escape her advances, all he was doing was panicking her even more. It was quite a sight and one I never expected to see, with this 40 something friend of mine running for fear of his life, round and round in circles, until he eventually got close enough to the gates to escape to safety. Following all that drama, no amount of encouragement was going to have an effect on him at all. "I'll just watch from here" was his continual response, as he stood leaning on the gates, from the safety of the other side. Those apparently vicious feathered creatures, who would have to wait for another day to get up close and personal with that pale faced 40 something.

Things were continuing to be very busy around the farm and there were only rare moments when I could relax and take in the sights and sounds of the wonderful nature around us. The weather was threatening to turn warmer and being the big Jessie that I am I had been waiting for an evening that was quite warm to spend a night in my much anticipated hammock. Around 9.00pm I said an early goodnight to the gang and ventured out, making my way through the trees at the back of our house to where I was to spend the night. I must at this point mention that there were a number of doubters around this neck of the woods. Those who believed that Dad was never going to spend a whole night outside, under the stars. I've done it many times before, when I was younger, I told them, in all manner of structures, several dens, a bivouac or two, straight under the stars and even in an igloo that me and our Chris built, but still their disbelief and doubting continued. Not at all being put off by these doubting Thomas' I soon got comfortable as the darkness started to fall. I watched the rooks coming in to roost and several 'Woodies' and I also noticed that 'Phin' the pheasant had returned to his favourite spot in the pine trees, after disappearing for some weeks. As the sun set and the light slowly vanished over the horizon I lay there and followed the tree trunks around me with my eyes, as they stretched upwards until they disappeared into the rapidly darkening heavens above me. Soon enough, I was in total darkness and the peace was blissful. I could hear the nocturnal residents of the wood going about their nighttime activities, these including rabbits, of course, hedgehogs, I'm sure and of course the Tawny family, who were talking to each other through the trees. After almost an hour in my little haven, my peace was suddenly shattered and that was when things took a rather unexpected turn for the worst.

Off in the distance it began. Beep, beep, beep, beep! I immediately recognised what the sound was. Beep, beep, beep, beep! It continued. Over the years, I had been stuck in numerous sets of roadworks, enough times to recognise what I was hearing. I thought, it's fine, it'll settle down, but no it continued, on and on and on it went. The nearest main road to us, which is around 1 mile away, across the fields was being resurfaced and the racket I could hear was the sound of the trucks reversing and moving about in the distance and this was I'm sure going to continue throughout the night, fantastic!

Well, being the ever-so-patient man I'm not, that was it. I tutted and sighed a few times, packed up my bits and then quietly made my way back home. As you can imagine, I was making every effort I could to not bump into any of my doubters, as I crept through the house and up the stairs. Thankfully I successfully dodged them, at least for that evening, but I'll tell you what, they let me know exactly what they thought the very next day!

It's not like I don't have enough to keep me occupied around here, but just as the days seemed to be getting shorter, for several nights I had the opportunity to play a new game. I suppose we could call it 'Hunt the Bantam' or two as it turned out. It had appeared to me that Layla and Henrietta had been getting on so well, since being reunited some weeks ago, but for some reason, things had all of a sudden seemed to fall apart. There was no more snuggling down together each evening in their cosy little home, not at all. I wasn't sure if they'd had a row, or whether they just needed their own space for a while, but whatever the reason, I wish they'd just sort themselves out. Each evening I had to set out, armed with my trusty torch, to track the pair of them down. I hunted far and wide around the farmyard, in all the usual places, and eventually I would track them down. Layla's favourite spot, was choosing to roost on the edge of one of our large potted hostas behind a large conifer and Henrietta more often than not chose to perch herself in the branches of a large magnolia tree. Each evening I would have to physically move them by hand and return them both to their home, for safety more than anything, as there's always a chance that Mr. Fox would come calling. Thankfully they sorted out their differences in the end and it's just as well, because it was becoming a real bind doing that every night, that's for sure!

I know that I've harped on about the swallows a number of times, but before we knew it, the time had come for them to be leaving us once again for South Africa. On the Saturday morning, even though it did take a while, I managed to count 77 of them, all comfortably perching along the fence line in the cow field. I'm glad that I did though, because the very next morning, every single one of them had left and not one of them had said "bye"!

In July the previous year, we thought it would be a good idea to purchase a caravan to do up. It wasn't the fanciest or most sturdy caravan I've ever seen, but the plan wasn't that we would set out on adventurous caravanning holidays across the nation, but that we would utilise the caravan around the farm. When we first brought it home the interior of the caravan was transformed to look beautiful, after lots of hard work on many parts, it looked wonderful and was awash with bunting and all sorts of little finishing touches.

Now all we needed to do was give the exterior a lick of paint and buy a few replacement bits and pieces and before we knew it, the job was sorted. Wendy, then had one of her brain waves and I must say, this was one of her better suggestions. With the Teashop now being very busy, and as we came into autumn, the weather wasn't so good and so we had moved the outdoor seating. Customers were therefore turning up and as there were no tables free inside the teashop they would just hang about outside or get a brew and sit in their car, until a table became available. Wendy's latest suggestion was to have the caravan brought down into the tea garden and then any customers who wanted to wait, could to do so inside the caravan, rather than in the rain, great idea!

With all this jiggery pokery going on with the caravan, it whisked me all the way back to the summer of 1978. You see, from 11 years old I had grown up in Hull, the centre of the universe when it came to caravan building and for a number of years we lived on Sutton Park, with major manufacturers on our doorstep. What I clearly remember more than anything was seeing fields and fields covered in caravans, all neatly lined up together, with barely any space between them. Well, there was a little space, in fact just enough space for young teenage boys to squeeze down the alleys between the caravans and then after choosing a caravan, we could then step inside and make ourselves comfortable to play cards. How did you get into the locked vans, I hear you ask. Well, we soon worked out that each door key was taped under each door step, but that may have been insider information we had acquired through someone's family member working for the company, but it's all a bit hazy. We used to have great fun back then spending time in our van whilst en route to our rope swing which was on the bank of the River Hull, at the back of Sutton Fields Industrial Estate, as it is today. Isn't it amazing how often very small things can whisk you away to times gone by and remind you of experiences from so many years before, or is it just me that likes to reminisce?

After being away for around 9 weeks, it was time for Lyndsey and Flora, two of our highland cattle to come home, after being away partying with the bull. I was in the barn, busying away with some jobs, on the day they returned. Off in the distance I heard that familiar squeak once more and immediately recognised it as Pete's trailer, on its way down the lane. I went to greet them as they pulled in through the gate and as I turned to walk down the field alongside them I looked up to the top field where I could see our other cows, Monica and Morag who were both trotting across the field to the fence, to welcome these new arrivals home. Now, I couldn't believe what I was witnessing here, firstly, how did they know what was going on and so quickly? The returning cattle were inside a trailer. Secondly, I don't think I have ever witnessed Monica move so fast in the two years since she had first arrived. All I can say is that whatever they thought about their two friends returning to the farm, it was definitely a big deal! Now all we can do is hope that all went well and their time away was productive, hopefully leading to them both having calves in the late summer next year, fingers crossed! Now I just have to resist the temptation of standing in the field staring at them both, convincing myself that they were putting weight on, let's just wait and see what happens shall we? It's really hard not to as this is the third time we have tried for calves and that would be three times without any success if things didn't work out this time too. To make things even worse, I've had one name chosen for many years, so here's hoping.

With the weather still being somewhat kind to us and the grass still growing, we decided to stop cutting 'the green mile' enabling it to get a bit of length on it. I then put up a post and rail fence around the small ditch, for safety sake and then sited a temporary fence half way down the mile, to secure the area. We then gated up the front of both the compost heap and also the log store, so that no over inquisitive sheep would come to any harm as a result of their adventuring and we were then able to turn the sheep out onto it, so they could literally have a field day. They spent the first 20 minutes just exploring, and disregarded the fact that there was all this lovely fresh grass for them, but then they well and truly settled into this new pasture. By shifting the sheep, we will be able to give the three fields they normally rotate around, a good rest and it may even get a little bit of fresh growing done itself, if the temperatures don't drop too much over the coming weeks.

Recently we came across a startling revelation. My parents have been heavily involved in doing family history and tracing our family tree for many years. As a result I was aware that we had a history, way back, in the fishing industry. That was interesting to me, but I never really thought much further than that. Well, on top of that fact, what has more recently come to light is, that our own very small leap into farming wasn't in fact the first venture into that world in the family. It turns out that my Great Grandfather, on my mother's side, Thomas Christie had a small farm in Echt, Aberdeenshire. Thomas was one of 12 bairns and in fact had 12 bairns himself too. He was born in 1844 and died in the early 1920's. I need to bear that in mind when I think things are getting tough around here, because, I'm sure that however hard it may feel for me, at times, it will, I'm sure have been a whole lot tougher back in his day, without the resources and technology we have at our disposal today. Plus, the fact that he was farming up in the North East of Scotland, which isn't very well known for having mild winters at all. Wendy also reminded me that in fact she had some farming in her family too, with her Grandfather being a farm manager for many years on farms in both Sancton and Kelfield amongst other places.

I'm not even sure whose idea it was to be honest and I don't ever remember signing up for this when we moved out here. What I had thought was a bit of a throwaway comment from somebody, very soon snowballed into what was soon to be known as our 'Halloween Spooktacular'. All of the half term week in October involved us running a fun event where kids could take part in various activities with hotdogs and refreshments thrown in. The place was awash with spider cookies, pumpkin treats, toffee apples and ghostly cupcakes. On top of all that, visitors had the chance to go on the farm trail with Sheriff Shaun. I swear, the things I've been roped into over the months. I wouldn't have minded, but I didn't even have my own sheriff badge, I had to borrow one from one of my grandsons, Noah.

Let me explain how it went. Just imagine that you are under 12 and you are assisting the sheriff of the county in apprehending the big bad guy, 'Rustlin Rodriguez', who, it so happens had been stealing our sheep. All the way around the farm we enlisted the help of all the animals and our resident witch who lives in the wood and Sarah the hairy legged spider also joined in to help us to catch the bandit. While the kids were eagerly searching for the bad guy, we had some unsuspecting somebody, who we had roped in to help and play the part of the rustler, who kept popping out from behind trees and then quickly disappearing again, all very pantomime like. It went down really well with the kids though, even if I did have to dress like a complete lunatic!

It was around this time that I was reminded of some unusual behaviour from our sheep. I don't think it's a characteristic which is seen only in Shetland sheep, but I'd be interested to find out. Although it doesn't happen with the whole flock, it does happen with several of them and we have seen it many times before, but I noticed it this week with our new tup 'Mac'. Let me tell you about what goes on. When you go and visit 'Mac' in his field, he trots up to you, we would then give him a rub on his head or squat down, give his forehead and cheeks a stroke, then give his neck a massage. It's then, when you start talking to him, that this behaviour reveals itself. That's when he begins to wag his tail, furiously. It's not just a one-off thing, as he keeps wagging it whilst you are talking to him. It's as though he does it when he is acknowledged by me and it's just like watching one of the dogs. You never know, in time, we may be able to get him to fetch a ball too!

As we have been trying to build a business to sustain us, out here in the country, we have sought to market ourselves in all sorts of ways, to get 'The Ginger Cow' name out to a wider audience. We have chosen not to go down the route of siting major signage on the closest main road and this was a conscious decision. On so many days we wouldn't be able to cope with any sort of increased numbers through the teashop doors and the more pressure there is on the Teashop staff as a result of more customers, the more pressure there would have been on my ears, so that ain't ever gonna happen if I can help it. We mainly focused on lots of social media to highlight what we did, and of course my column in the 'Yorkshire Post' has undoubtedly helped things along. Out of the blue one day, we had a bit of a surprise when we had a call from one of our local radio stations, Beverley FM, who wanted to come and interview Wendy about her Teashop, its rise in popularity and her recent success in the Beverley Food Festival and East Riding Local Food Network awards. It's been great to stand back and watch this lady bloom in a world which even six months before was so alien to her, I'm so very proud of what she has achieved!

With a great deal of anticipation the time had once again come around for tupping, when our new boy in town would be put in with the ewes. Our new tup, 'Mac' had been marching up and down that fence for a few weeks, ever since his arrival, with an array of ewes taking turns to flutter their eyelashes at him through the fence. So, after mixing the raddle up in an old beans can, Mac was suitably daubed and ready for action. I enlisted Wendy's help, for the next job and whilst we had all the sheep together we had timed it right so we could worm them all ahead of their spending time with Mac.

Now not all of the sheep were going in with Mac this year, as we had some of the recent lambs, who were too young and also 3 males too, so we needed to sort them out as well during this worming process. Anyway, we cracked on with the job, getting all of the sheep into the pen. That was easy, and then in small groups we would send them down the race until it was almost full, after which we would shut the gate behind them. Then from back to front we worked our way through the sheep, administering the dose of medicine into the mouths of the sheep, using the drench gun. We've done it many times, so the sheep know what's coming and Mrs. McKenna and I have things pretty well organised, or so I thought. There we were, down to the last batch of sheep and with only a few left to take care of, I was bent almost double, straddling Delilah's back, with her head in my hand, the drench gun nozzle was in her mouth and I was ready to dispense the medication. Unfortunately for me, when I squeezed the trigger on the drench gun the liquid decided not to behave itself at all and must have hit the back of her throat and shot back out of her mouth and as was my luck, it went straight into my left eye. As you can imagine it wasn't a good place to be with one eye shut, my face dripping with medicine and a ewe wedged between my knees, but it appeared that Mrs. McKenna for some reason happened to see the funny side of things, even if I didn't. It was one of those times you just got on with the job, so I wiped my eye with my shirt sleeve and cracked on until the job was finished.

Throughout the worming process we had been trying to sort the sheep into 2 groups, the 'Party' team and the 'Not-old-enough-to-party' team. The only problem was that some of the smaller sheep were still able to squeeze under the race fence and so had joined the party team in the field, which thankfully wasn't the field with the tup. I then stood at the gate into Mac's field and with Wendy sorting the sheep out as they came past her, I then allowed only the party flock through to see Mac and after only a few minutes, Wendy had them all sorted. That's when at last I was able to go and wash out my eye and hope to goodness that Mac was up to the job!

For many years, since being very young, when it's come to breakfast cereal options, I have to say I have been a cornflakes man. I have in the past, on and off dabbled with Weetabix, but over recent years I have been banned from going near those golden bricks of breakfast, for various reasons, none of which I will go into. I have to say though that over recent years there has been a significant change around here in my morning munching regime. After 53 years of running scared, I have eventually come to see the light and been truly converted to the delights of what I have previously referred to as gruel. It is of course the humble bowl of PORRIDGE! In the past, I could never understand why Goldilocks would go near the stuff, but somehow in recent times, I have become hooked in a big way to that bowl of oaty gorgeousness. What is really hard to take in all of this is the fact that for years growing up, I would do anything to steer clear of the stuff and would on many occasions come home from a long hard day, after toiling away in the school classroom, to find the porridge I hadn't eaten at breakfast time, staring up at me once again from the table, once again awaiting my return at tea time. Oh, how my Mother would torture us with that porridge, but now as my life has been transformed I've experienced a completely amazing turn around.

Once I get all my animal feeding and chores out of the way, I get myself back into the house for my breakfast ritual and generally this is how it goes. I get my special measuring mug out, which is an old enamel mug, the sort you use when you go camping and put one mug full of oats into a pan, add two mugs of water, and a dash of salt, but never, ever should sugar, treacle, jam or other such sweet additions ever be entertained. Slowly and ever so carefully I bring it to the boil and once those bubbles of air are struggling to force their way through the porridge it's time to put it into a bowl. This is where it starts getting technical, as it has to be a stone cold, china bowl and will be left to cool down. I have found that the time it takes for me to relight our old bosky coal burner is a sufficient amount of time for it to get to the right temperature for me. On a side note, when I was growing up, I could never really understand why the 3 bears would go out and leave their porridge to cool down, allowing Goldilocks to come and get tucked into it. It's funny because I understand it now. Once my porridge has cooled to the correct temperature, that's when I slowly pour, very cold, straight-from-the-fridge milk, around the edge of the bowl, then pause for just a moment before carefully giving the bowl a little twist and shake. If all has gone to plan, the milk has sneaked down the sides and underneath the porridge and my breakfast is now floating merrily and looking as appetising as any bowl of porridge ever could! De....licious!

I suppose I'm not really surprised, but it seems that all those rigorous checks I undertook to establish that we were buying a lovely placid Tup, back at October's Rare Breed Sale, may not have been as thorough as they should have been. It was once again feeding time on the farm and I had trekked up to the top field with some food for Mac and his ladies. I walked through the gate and gave a few of the sheep a cuddle, as I do, when they came running over and then continued to fill the feeder with their food. That's when out of nowhere, when my back was turned and I was looking the other way, I felt a thud into the side of my right thigh, as though I had been hit by a runaway Austin Allegro. The force of the impact sent me flying sideways, but luckily I had a row of sheep tight up against me which ensured I didn't go headlong into the dirt. I immediately turned in the direction of this impact, instinctively knowing even before looking that I had just experienced my first whack from Mac! He looked up at me with innocence in his eyes, like some kind of fluffy brown angel as though to say "What, me!", but I knew the truth. You can be sure I haven't let him get a run up at me since that day and to be honest he has behaved impeccably since that day, so I can't really complain can I?

I was sitting on the corner of the fence, up in the top field, just having some thinking time to myself. 2016 had been quite a year for the McKenna family and it seemed to have flown by. One way or another we had crammed so much into it and thankfully had achieved such a lot, as we had continued to build our life in the country. The year seemed to be flying even before it had begun, with us getting flooded out on the previous Boxing Day and thinking back, I still can't believe that we had so many good Samaritans turned up, out of the blue to help us out, in our hour of need. It wasn't long into the year when we were once again experiencing the highs and lows of lambing for the second time and this year unfortunately there was the low. Hypothermia and lambs isn't a good mix at all and since losing Jeremy's twin sister to the cold, we have been through it a hundred times in our heads, how could we have changed things or what could we have done differently, so as to not lose her. We can only learn from these many experiences and endeavour to make sure we are better prepared for the next time it may come around.

As spring was unfolding in 2016, we were furiously trying to get our vegetable patch up to last year's standard and at the same time get everything completed ahead of the Teashop opening. Seeding, fencing, paving, plumbing, turfing, painting, ditch digging, pruning, muck clearing, marketing, planting, bramble clearing, nettle spraying, shepherd's hut siting, gravel levelling, drain laying, tree felling, log chopping and hedge trimming, grass cutting have been a few of the tasks we have been working through, alongside our day-to-day jobs and not to mention getting a wedding arranged in between all of that!

So, this year we leapt into teashop world and it could so easily have been a struggle, with the severe lack of experience on our part, but as usual, our Wend' has pulled it out of the bag and she's won an award for her team's efforts too. The signs were good, with us being contacted almost every day in the weeks leading up to opening, with people requesting an opening date and on day one we had cars queueing up outside the gate. Once again, the support we have seen from people, from all over Yorkshire has been wonderful. We do see ourselves as being extremely blessed, living where we live and so it has always been in our thinking to share this adventure with others, which is why we opened up to the public and had our beautiful shepherd's hut built for people to stay. We took long enough just deciding on the right place to site our hut, in order that visitors could get the best views from their window, and have the most memorable experience from their stay on the farm. As we rolled into a new year, putting the past year's struggles behind us, we were excited at what's in store for us this coming year. We were looking forward to lots of youngsters being born on the farm in 2017. We could have a Highland calf or two, the same ones we have looked forward to for the past couple of years, but had no luck so far. We hoped for lots of lambs, a couple of pygmy goat kids, some ducklings and maybe even a baby Llama, you never know. Either way we were going to have a busy time, but we were excited for the new challenges ahead.

I had been hoping for better to be honest, but my New Year didn't get off to a great start at all. It was the very early hours of new year's day when it happened, and it has caused me a great deal of pain and discomfort ever since. I had been in such a great mood, after a quiet new year's eve, just chilling, with Wendy and the girls, we had played a daft game, had a laugh and performed the obligatory 'Old man's eye' as it's known as by our kids, or 'Auld Lang Syne', to the rest of the world and I decided in my wisdom to pop downstairs for a drink. Now before you go jumping to conclusions, it wasn't a drop of the strong stuff, because I never go near it, it's more likely to have been a Diet Coke. Well, I opened the kitchen door and as the lights were off and the switch is across the other side of the room, I paused for a moment to check that the 3 dogs were all tucked up in their bed and they were. I wouldn't want to be tripping up over any of them and doing them and more importantly me, any injury, but thankfully they were all snoozing soundly. I closed the door behind me and strode confidently into the darkness without another thought. I hadn't taken more than 4 steps when my bare left foot stepped on a foreign object on the floor. I had no warning at all and as I leapt into the air, yelling uncontrollably, ultimately collapsing heavily like the proverbial sack of spuds, I immediately knew what it was that I'd stepped on. You see, Wendy had spent hours pre-Christmas, searching for just the right gifts for all of the family, including Scout, Elsa and Boo, the dogs. Well, one of these gifts, was a meat-scented pork chop toy, which by the time New Year came along, it had received several hours of chew time and so was somewhat misshapen, with lots of sharp edges protruding from it, several of which were now impaled into my foot. As you can imagine, I wasn't best pleased at all and you will not be surprised to note that not one member of my family came to my aid, or even attended the scene of the accident, to seek after my welfare, but I have a long memory and so I do hope they bear that in mind!

During Christmas week, after a great deal of encouragement from the ewes, we decided that it was high time that we moved 'Mac' out of the front field where he had been spending the last couple of months with the ladies and shift him on to pastures new. So, one chilly morning, Wendy and I cracked on and got him moved. He was clearly excited to get in there and discover what was in store in his new pasture, that was until his new house mates came to see what all the fuss was about. Marguerita and Miguel the Llamas came lolloping across the paddock towards him. This was karma coming back to bite him in the behind, after relentlessly harassing the ewes for weeks, and of course I couldn't forget him giving me a whack as well. It was a joy to see him running for his life, round and around the field, with his tail between his legs, and all they wanted to do was to say 'Hello'. Over the following few days, things soon settled down, the bottom sniffing had ceased and they all appeared to be getting on fine.

The weather had been a bit manky for a few days with drizzle and dampness in abundance, and it so happened that I'd gone out to mend one of the rails in the front cow field. Whilst I was in with the Highlands, I noticed that the 3 younger cows had wet back ends, basically from the top of their backs, all the way back to their tails were soggy. Now, I knew that this wasn't from them cleaning themselves up, as they wouldn't have been able to reach that far with their tongue, so it flummoxed me a little and more importantly, if I'm honest I was concerned about it too. You see, I have seen this wet back end before and it's not a good sign. What happens is that if any of the cows are in season, then the other cows would be attempting to jump up on their backs and mount them. As a result this gives them a wet back, from their mucky hooves. If this was happening, then I could take it as read that any of them, who were getting jumped on and were in season, wouldn't in fact be pregnant and expecting a calf in the summer. So, I did panic just a little in my head, when I caught sight of their backs, and as I walked over for a closer look, I must say, I was cursing under my breath.

It was Lyndsey and Flora, who I was concerned about, as they were the ones who I had hoped were in calf, as they had been off getting romanced by the bull the previous summer. As I got nearer, I carefully looked them up and down, but I couldn't see anything which could tell me anything I didn't already know, so still no answers. Then, as I was stroking Morag, it hit me like the proverbial bolt out of the blue. Well actually it was her tail that hit me and it was 'smack', right across the kisser too! That's when the penny dropped and the answer hit me right in the face, literally. There I was, standing in the cow field with this muddy stripe right across my face, which I must say did stink too and that's when it dawned on me. By this time in the year, each of the cows are now eating hay from a feeder ring, which throughout the winter gets very muddy around it, with the mud and all their own mess too, it gets to be quite a quagmire really. As a result of this, their tail ends would then drag in the mess and throughout the day as they swish their tails around their sides and up onto their backs, they inevitably get soggy backs as a result…got it! What a relief that was, so I could continue dreaming that we would get these so longed for young 'uns in the summer after all, so my fingers were still firmly crossed!

Things are so often not what they at first seem to be around here. One Sunday evening I decided, whilst out with the dogs, to take them around our top field for a change, and whilst doing so I noticed something I hadn't seen before. I thought that there wasn't much around the place that I missed, but this was certainly something that I had. As I walked around the field perimeter I was looking to see how the grass was faring, to establish what attention it would need in the coming weeks to fertilise it, or certainly to liven it up. It was only then that I saw just how poor the grass in fact was. As fields go it has always produced good grass for the cattle and from a distance the field has continued to be green and so to me it had appeared fine, but as I say, things weren't as they seemed. On closer inspection I saw that a large percentage of the field was in fact moss, large patches of nasty, useless to my cows, moss. Upon stumbling on this news, I once again spoke to Gordon Layton, who has several decades more experience than I ever had in these matters and so arranged to get the whole field ploughed and subsequently power harrowed. Once it was completed, it looked great and before long it was all prepared and ready to be seeded, which was once again going to be sorted by hand with me and a little old fiddle. One way or another I needed some good grass on there for my cows by late spring, or latest by early summer, but I needed to bide my time and wait for the right time to get the grass into the ground, so I decided to wait for the right conditions to get the seed in place.

We seemed to be going from one bit of exciting news to another around here, and once again out of the blue we got a call from BBC Radio Leeds, asking if they could interview us live on air. On their mid-morning programme, they had been running a feature over the previous few weeks titled, 'New Year, New You', in which they had spoken about people's new year resolutions involving their health, exercise, new job, etc. and other life changes, which they may have made at the start of a new year. So, off we set to Leeds, bright and early on that Monday morning and as the traffic was good to us, before I knew it, we were there. After they sat us down and settled us in they checked some information about us and then we were straight into it, telling the story of our life-changing decision, live on air to their listeners. Hopefully we didn't come across as sounding too much like blithering idiots, and you know how so often you dislike the sound of your own voice, when you hear it back, well whatever the case we were told by many who heard us from the listener side of the radio, that we came across just fine. It was on the way home that day, that Wendy and I were discussing what had gone on and just how much we had actually accomplished over the previous two years and sometimes, because you are so close to it all, you can fail to see just how far you have traveled or appreciate all that has been achieved.

I was up extra early on that Monday morning, as there was lots to get done before I could go and pick up our special visitor. I had been discussing things for some weeks with Pete Fletcher, to establish just when our new short term resident was going to be available and that day had arrived. It didn't help at all that the temperature had once again dropped, my taps were frozen solid, the hosepipes lay like uncooked pieces of spaghetti and to cap it all, it was like walking through pea soup in the dense fog! After making sure all of our inmates were fed, watered and happy, the dogs had been walked and the stove in our kitchen was lit and all fired up, I was all set to leave. I grabbed what I needed, but as I made my way to the Landrover to head out I noticed that I'd missed something. All of the footpaths were very icy and so I started the Landy engine, to warm her up and whilst it was getting all cosy for me, I set about gritting all the areas, which were remotely slippy. Before long I was on my way, but soon realised that due to the fog, it was going to take a wee while longer than I had anticipated, to get safely to my destination, just south of Sheffield. There were a number of accidents which had held me up en route, but eventually arrived at Pete's place. Pete was the owner of my cattle, before me, but on this occasion it wasn't a cow I was coming for. The time had come for me to pick up 'Max'. After a chat we walked around to a pen inside his barn and although there were a few animals in there, my eyes immediately caught sight of the main man as he ran up to the side of the pen to greet us.

The gate was opened and Pete leaned over and picked up the cutest little Pygmy Billy Goat, you could ever imagine. You could just tell he was excited to come and spend time with Stacey and Bambi, our two pygmy goats. Straight away I thought, the women folk are going to be cooing over this one and guess what, that's exactly what happened. As soon as I got back to the farm and was walking him around to his holiday home, they were out of the Teashop before you could blink, fussing over him. Our two goats just watched from afar, in fact Stacey ran up their steps to get an even better view. Initially they looked confused and a little surprised as they watched me walk ever closer to their pen. Who was this mysterious, ever so short, dark and handsome stranger who was coming their way? Why was farmer Shaun bringing him here? We hoped that the answers to those questions would be answered very quickly in the coming days. I soon left them to become acquainted and went off to get on with my chores. Over the next few days Max settled down really well and both Stacey and Bambi, appeared to take to him, without much fuss. A few weeks later, it looked like things were changing in the goat pen and tempers were becoming a little frayed. Max started to become a little too boisterous with the ladies and particularly after teatime when they would have to endure his mad half hour when he would gallop around the pen, up and down the steps, over the tractor tyre and would frequently bounce off the walls, the stable doors and the fence, for no apparent reason. In the end it was time for him to leave, but by that time Stacey and Bambi were already growing sideways by the week and so it appeared that he had successfully completed his work. As cute as he was, the two other goats said that he had outstayed his welcome and they'd be glad of the peace and quiet afterwards.

One of the routine jobs I do each morning, whilst feeding the animals, is to check that nobody is unwell, that they are all in good nick and that all of them are generally behaving themselves, although that rarely happens. As we worked through springtime, I started to experience many more of our sheep having problems with their feet. Every couple of days I would come across another limper, who needed some attention. I would have to grab my box of tricks and deal with it, which normally only takes a few minutes, but the sheep and I could both do without the problem. I've been told many times by people in the know that it's because we are on sandy soil out here, on the edge of the Wolds and I can't do a great deal about that. How I would deal with the issue is, I would firstly round all of the sheep up and put them into the pen. I then grab the patient and turn him or her onto her backside, turning their head to the side, behind my leg, which helps them to stop wriggling and then I get on with the job. Ordinarily, when I see one of the sheep limping I make a mental note as to which foot I thought was causing the problem, and then check that foot first. Once I've assessed the damage, I aim to sort it! I would clean their feet up, particularly between their toes and then with my shears I trim any broken nail or excess which has grown over the underside of their foot. Once I have repeated these checks with all of their feet, I would then use my magic blue spray (or Alamycin to give it its correct name) on the affected areas of any sore feet and the job was done. I would then let them stand a little while, so that the spray dries properly and then they're back into the field, hopping and a-frolicking with their friends.

After biding my time over the last few weeks, I set out at the weekend, armed with my sacks of grass seed and the seed fiddle I had borrowed from Gordon Layton, with the aim of getting our top field seeded by hand. Once again, using the right tools made light work of the job, but I'll tell you what, I was ready for a sit-down at the end of it. With our soil being so sandy, you're forever sinking in it as you're traipsing up and down the field. It's like walking for ruddy miles along the beach at Fraisthorpe, but sadly on this occasion, I wasn't doing it with a 99 ice cream cornet in my hand.

As you would probably expect, there have, over the last couple of years been many changes to our lives, and in some cases to the way that we do things around here. For some of us these changes were neither expected, sought after or welcomed. A little background may be useful here. For thirty years I was out doing a normal job, with all that would entail, doing my bit to support our family and that was that. Yes, I would help out at home, a little here, a little there, but in the main, our home was looked after by Wendy, and she does a great job too, or maybe I should say did!

Since the previous summer Wendy, as you know, had been setting up and establishing her new Teashop. Business had very quickly spiralled and was doing really well, but the resulting fallout from this is that it leaves her with so little time to do much else. As a result of this vastly reduced available time, I have had to step up to the plate and take on responsibility for much of the domestics, and as I'm sure you can imagine, I was really excited about that I can tell you!

Apparently, things are a little quieter for me during the winter months and so, I was doing my best to keep our home shipshape. I get involved in all those marvelous jobs that so often in the past I would have taken for granted and shied away from whenever possible. You know the sorts of jobs I mean, like doing the washing, although I did know how the washer worked, doing even more of the ironing, hoovering, dusting, changing beds, washing up, tidying rooms, cleaning the bathroom, the loo, the list is endless. I must say though, that I am still one for getting the washing in that tumble drier whenever possible, but this has been the case all along. In the past, I would get my orders, when Wendy was heading out somewhere, "When the washing has finished, please can you get it out on the line!" she'd say, and off she'd pop, wherever she was going. So, as ever I would endeavour to cut out the middle man and get it straight into the drier and only then, once finished, I would get the basket full of washing out beside the washing line, so when Wendy returned, she would see it there and automatically presume that I had just been gathering up the newly wind tossed items off the line, after they'd been blowing in the breeze for the previous couple of hours. I know, it's just down right lazy!

One of the tasks which I've found to be the biggest drain on my skills is making the tea each day. I didn't expect that these women would have lasted this long putting up with my cooking, but they have. They put their orders in and I do my best to oblige, turning out a meal to be proud of, although I can never recall getting much option in the past, I just got what I was given, but there you go. Beyond the obligatory beans on toast, most things have been a struggle, but I'm trying my best to become acquainted with an array of recipe books and the 'Good Food Guide' online, which has turned out to be a real boon. Up to now, the most common complaint I have received has been, "Why do we always have to have army surplus-sized portions?" In my defence, I am trying to get to grips with the portion control, honestly! Getting so involved in the domestics has really opened up my eyes to a whole new world. I used to think that I was quite domesticated, but I had never realised or appreciated quite how much there is to do, to keep a home clean, cooked for and comfy, but I certainly do now.

13 OUR FIRST TIMERS LEAD THE WAY

I can't quite remember what I was doing at the time, but all I can remember was hearing, in a very loud voice "Dad! Dad!, there's a pig leggin' it about out here!" I rushed through the house to the front door and lo and behold, Olivia, who had called me, wasn't kidding at all. 'Precious', one of our pigs was now heading straight for the front door. Maybe she fancied a warm by the fire, after all it was a very chilly day. I quickly bunged some shoes on and said to Olivia, "Just watch her for a minute and keep her occupied, while I get some food. What I expected her to do, to keep her occupied, I'll never know, but I ran into the barn, being sure that I closed all the doors behind me and literally in seconds, I was heading out through the doors at the other end with a bucket of feed in my hand.

As I came around the corner, Precious spotted me with the bucket, which she obviously recognised and came galloping across the lawn towards me outside the pig pen. Now, if I said that for a pig, Precious isn't a little lass at all and at a year old stands over waist high to me, you will understand that I didn't fancy getting in the way of this porker when she reached me, which didn't take many seconds at all. As I'm one for making things extra secure around here, when it comes to keeping animals where they should be, I sometimes do go a little over the top. What I do is tie the pigs' gate tightly shut with baling twine, just in case if they ever fancied having an impromptu wander, they couldn't. So, with the gate being tied up, as well as being bolted, I couldn't just easily let her in without cutting the string first and all the while, this little piggy was looking for afternoon tea. It's just as well that I keep my knife in my pocket and so moments later she was being welcomed back into the pen by Petal, her house mate. I ran around to the back of the pen to feed them so at least they would be occupied for a few minutes.

When Olivia had first called me, I knew exactly the reason Precious was out and how she had escaped. In reality I suppose it was my fault, as she had worked out that I had disconnected the battery from the electric fence, in order to charge it, and even though it had only been overnight, it was just long enough for the menace to suss out that there was a route out to Adventureland and it didn't mean getting a zap off the wire in the process. I fed the pigs some more grub and grabbed the recharged battery to reconnect things back up once again. Now, overnight the pigs had trampled the electric wire into the mud and so I had to hastily replace some of the wire, feed it through the connectors around the perimeter fence and get it all sorted to switch back on again. I could see that without the fence being switched on, she had tunneled her way out for a wander. After connecting everything up I ran back around the pen to check that the fence was working all the way around…..and for some reason it wasn't, oh flip! I hadn't switched it on. I ran back around to the front, switched it on and ran back, checked it again and still it wasn't working. I ran back around and in my haste hadn't connected up one small wire which I promptly did and ran back around the pen again. At last, thankfully it was working.

I was jiggered, up to my ears in mud and had received two electric shocks for my efforts, but hey, all's well that ends well! Over the following 24 hours we found out exactly the extent of Precious' roaming round the farm. She had been through the veg patch, all the way up to the Llama enclosure, over to see the cows, the sheep, and the hens and had wandered around our garden and even up to the front farm gate, which was open! In all the time that she was wandering, we had a busy Teashop service, yet nobody had noticed this extremely large lump of pork, who was out for a stroll, unless of course the customers had seen her, but presumed that it was just a normal day around these parts.

After recently getting the top field seeded with grass, I was quite pleased with myself and thought all-in-all that a good job had been done, and I could now sit back and watch it grow into that wonderful meadow that I sought after. Well that was before I had visitors arrive and suggest otherwise. Only a few days after the field was sown I noticed, as I walked up the green mile each morning, that as I got close to the field, a flock of pigeons would take to the air from that very same field. Not good news at all. Each day it looked like this gang of pigeons was growing and they were bringing more and more of their friends along to feed on my field. I found that I could whistle from well down the field and I could clear it completely, as a result, but that was never going to be a long term solution to keep them off the seed. So I needed yet another plan 'B'. Immediately I knew what I could do, I could make my very own 'Worzel Gummidge', so that's exactly what I did, well sort of.

I looked out an old pair of jeans that had seen better days, a lovely checked shirt, I'd not worn in years and a straw hat which was ideal for the look I was going for. I gathered together the bits I required, like my tools, some lengths of wood, nails, baling string and began to create my straw-filled friend. It wasn't long before he was almost complete, but there was a problem, he had no head. So by using an inside out animal feed bag I was able to make him a head, that fitted just right on his broad shoulders. After giving him a face and parking his hat on top he looked a right bobby dazzler and so soon enough I took a walk with him up to the top field. A few minutes later he was in position, proudly standing his ground in the centre and was all set to see off any marauding pigeons who dared to come near. Now it may just be me, but do you know, he did start off doing a cracking job. I saw no pigeons in there for days after he'd arrived and I'm up and down there many times each day. So I was hopeful that he could do the trick, but over the coming weeks the efficient job he started out doing, began to falter. Unfortunately it turned out that there were other factors involved with why the grass wasn't growing so well, including partridges that showed no fear, an abundance of rabbits, and no rain, which was clearly not going to benefit my newly seeded field at all. It did in fact take several months for the top field to become green and even then it was somehow more flowers than it was grass, but hey, I'm not one to be complaining and neither will the cows, they'll eat 'owt! It may just have turned out that I was given the wrong mix of seed all those weeks ago as it was wall-to-wall wild flowers and looked great, but it's not what I expected at all.

Thinking about what to feed the animals reminded me of when we first got Wendy's Jubilee hens back in 2012. As it happens, it wasn't long before I had to take our first trip with one of these hens to the vets and it just so happened to be Queenie. Well, how was I to know that straw was good for bedding, but hay wasn't. Back then, straw and hay were much the same thing, to me! I didn't know there was a difference. That was the day I found out that hens will often eat hay, but they wouldn't eat straw, as eating hay can block things up for them and they can become crop bound. Very quickly it was established that we had a decision to make, do we spend £57 for the vet to operate and remove the blockage, or not, bearing in mind she only cost us £12.00 to start with. Of course, they operated, she was one of our girls and that was that. All went well and when I went back to pick her up, there was a surprise awaiting us, she had laid her very first egg and by George it was a whopper!

From that moment on Queenie, was a firm family favourite. She had a super temperament and was great with the grandkids, loved getting picked up and always looked beautiful too! That is except for the time when she was struggling through moulting, and as well as losing most of her feathers, she would get everywhere sideways on, as for whatever reason, she was walking like a crab for days. Back when we lived in suburbia, we would come home many Sunday afternoons, after Church and find that she had taken herself and the other ladies for a stroll up the lane and they regularly needed retrieving from neighbours gardens. So, the day we launched ourselves out of the city into the country, was a momentous occasion not only for ourselves, but for other members of the family, including the dogs and the hens. By this time Wendy had hatched some hen's eggs in our incubator too and we had kept a couple of them to add to the flock. Queenie, was in her element out here, she was able to wander without fear of getting into much bother. If there was ever a boss around the farmyard, Queenie was that lady, keeping not only the hens in check, but would also sort out the ducks and dogs too. Then things all changed on the farm, that late spring morning, when I found that Queenie had died overnight, peacefully in her sleep. She hadn't been ill, there were no signs of distress, but it was just her time to go. She leaves behind her many wonderful memories and in all that time she hardly missed laying her daily egg. Now we just have to deal with Rita her sidekick, who spends her days wandering the farmyard like a little lost soul.

Talking of the farmyard, we decided that we would surprise our Shetland ponies with another of Wendy's bright ideas. In the small paddock they use during the winter months, they have a shelter behind the stables, but rarely use it. From time to time we may have popped out somewhere, away from the farm and then it starts raining or it gets dark and also because I'm a softie, I'm keen not to leave them outside. Well, we were talking about the situation one day and Wendy came up with a humdinger of an idea. Of course I could put the ponies inside their stable before going out, so they wouldn't get soaked or away before it gets dark, but because the stable door is taller than they are, this makes the stable pretty much dark, as soon as they go into it, even with the top door open. The ponies are only 31 inches tall and so they can't see anything over the stable door as it's a good 18 inches taller than them. That is, until we had a new stable door made, so when we go out, we can put the ponies safely inside, they can stay warm and dry and the bonus is, they can watch the world go by, with their heads over front of the door and they love it, so that's a great result all round.

At long last, the weather had begun warming up ever so slightly over the recent days and as a result, it had been nice being able to spend more time outdoors, especially when there weren't jobs to do. That includes in the evenings after it had started getting dark. It's at those times when I get to do one of my favourite things, which involves just standing and listening. That's when you get to hear so much more than when you are rushing about doing what you do during the day, and it's also when sounds become so much more alive. I suppose it helps having less background noise to deal with too. As I walk around and pause from time to time, I hear the sheep, who are now all lying down, gently chewing away their cares and I hear the lapwings playing in the darkness across the field. I hear the frogs at the water's edge, each calling to their mate in the night, then there's the rooks chattering away, high up in the silver birch, as they start settling down for the night. Then just before heading back into the house comes what sounds like a block of coarse sandpaper on a piece of rough Yorkshire board timber. That'll be the pigs then, as you can always bank on them having a good old scratch against the chestnut tree before bed!

Time seems to fly by, and before we knew it, it was time to bring some more weaners onto the farm, and so arranged with the breeder to buy another three gilts. I'd been down and chosen the ones I wanted, so it was just a case of turning up and collecting them. Once I'd got them into the back of the Landrover I trundled off home, excited to be introducing them to Precious and Petal, who had no clue that their peace was about to be shattered by three young whippersnappers! Surprisingly the young pigs calmed down as soon as we started to move and sat calmly all the way home, although that was all of ten minutes. As I drove, I was considering all the things that could go wrong, when we arrived back home and how I could eliminate any possibility of a mishap, or certainly how I could reduce the risk of something untoward happening. Very soon, I was back on the farm and reversed through the yard all the way up to the gate at the front of the pig pen. My first wish came true, as both Precious and Petal were sound asleep in their bed and hopefully they would stay that way whilst the new arrivals were offloaded. I had roped in our Naomi, to open the pen gate, very quietly, whilst I tried gently to lift each one in turn out the back of the Landrover. Trying to do it in silence was never going to happen really, was it?

As soon as I lifted each of the pigs out the back of the truck, they squealed for dear life and never mind the sleeping pigs being woken up, you could probably hear them on top of the Wolds. With a little haste, I was soon able to lift each of them into the pen before the porky snooze monsters had a chance to come and see what all the commotion was about. They soon made their introductions, but the little ones weren't bothered about all that getting-to-know-you stuff and just wanted to take advantage of all this new found space they had to run around in and explore. They were galloping around that field like pigs possessed, as fast as their little legs could take them and soon enough everything was looking well in pig world. I continued checking on them regularly throughout the day, but they had feed, water and shelter and a lovely cosy bed for the night, so I could do no more and decided to leave them in peace. Early the next morning, I made my way out to check on the pigs and serve up breakfast, but could only find one of the weaners. After a bit of detective work, I figured out what had happened overnight.

As it was their first night and they were all so excited about the new surroundings, they hadn't made their way into their new bed for the night, but had for some reason slept outside. As it turns out, two of them had managed to squeeze under a fence and had slept under an enormous pile of leaves on the other side, but unfortunately the chubbiest of the three wasn't able to get herself under the fence into the same bed as her sisters. She seemed fine, if not a little chilly and she soon seemed to warm up. As it happens we noticed over a period of a few days that the chubby little pig was very lethargic, a bit less chubby and wasn't as energetic as her sisters. So the next morning, she and I took a little trip to visit the vet to get her checked out. The vet explained that the pig was suffering from septicaemia, which explained the lethargy and her losing weight. Over the next month we did everything in our power to turn things around, including 3 courses of antibiotics, dozens of bottles of milk replacer and hours of TLC, but unfortunately we lost her, just as we thought the corner had been turned and she was coming out the other side. It was very sad, but again these are learning experiences which are all part of this adventure we find ourselves on.

Onward and upward we will press on and luckily, the sun rose the very next day. It started off like any other, up early, out quickly and it looked as though it wasn't going to rain, so that was good news. I was all organised, but on this day for whatever reason I decided that I would sort out and feed the animals in reverse order rather than follow my normal routine. Well as it turned out, it's a blummin' well good job that I did too. Well, it's not what you expect to find at that time in the morning at all, is it? To be greeted with a backside up in the air. As I walked across the field, I automatically surveyed across the field in front of me, to see if I could locate all three of the field's residents, Miguel and Marj the Llamas and Mac the Tup. I could immediately see Miguel, as he stands out on any day with his striking, regal looking, white head, against his brown body and then I spotted Marj, who is completely brown, as she lolloped out of the shadows and across the field to meet me.

That was only two of the three accounted for, so where was that little monkey we call Mac? As I reached the perimeter fence, I once again searched the field to see if I could see him and eventually I did, but the view I had of him wasn't at all what I expected. It appeared from where I was standing that he had found some tasty treat along the fence bottom and was bent down, on his front knees, with his rear in the air having a nibble. It must have been good, because when I called him over, he didn't make any attempt to come and see me, which is quite unusual. I walked around, through the gate and up towards him, to see if I could see just what was so interesting for him not to come over. It was only then as I got close to him, that I could see that he was in fact attached to the very bottom of the fence by his short and curly horn, which explained why his rear was in the air. And there was I thinking he didn't love me anymore! I had no clue as to how long he had been in that position, he may well have been tethered like that all night, but anyway, now I just had to release him and give him his freedom once more. That was easier said than done. He had somehow twisted and curled his horn through the stock netting fence and heaven knows how he'd done it. I had to turn not only his head, but his whole body in order to somehow work his horn free, so bit by bit I carefully freed him from each part of the fence and all the while he was making no attempt at all to help me. I came to the very last part which was stuck and with an almighty tug, the fence twanged as his horn was released and he was once again free to roam. For a brief moment I did expect the Llamas, who had been attentively watching on from the sidelines, to offer a round of applause, but unfortunately not. Mac immediately knew what was coming next, either that or he thought he would be in for a good telling off and so he galloped down to the other end of the field and stood where he does every morning as he awaited breakfast being served. I didn't even get a thank you! Sheep eh, who'd have 'em!

Back in October we started to consider, which of our ewes were going to be lambing this spring and obviously Mabel, who got a reprieve from the butchers last year, came up in conversation. Our biggest concern was that she was so small and we didn't want her getting into any trouble during the pregnancy or during the delivery, as a result of her size. After much discussion, we decided that we would try her with the rest of the ewes and keep a very close eye on her. On November 4th, I brought Mac the Tup down from the top field, daubed him up with raddle and let him loose on all these ewes. It's funny how things turn out, as he quickly started sniffing around several of the ewes, with his tongue going ten to the dozen, but then he spotted our Mabel across the field, who was just watching on from afar. Well, that was it, he forgot about the rest of the ewes for the day and promptly started to romance our Mabel. We walked away and left them in peace, awaiting spring to arrive and although we were concerned whether we had done the right thing with Mabel, with fingers crossed, we were hopeful that things would turn out just fine.

In the days leading up to Mabel's due date, we were watching her like a hawk. She was up and down like a yo-yo and with the weather getting ever so slightly warmer, that didn't help her as her coat is extra thick at the moment, in the weeks leading up to shearing. By the end of the week, I had started on my cycle of checks through the day and night, ensuring that the ewes were all in good shape as we awaited the commencement of Lambing 2017. Friday morning arrived, which was a day ahead of Mabel's due date and all had been well through the night, and so back to my bed I went for a little more kip, before jumping up again as my next alarm went off at 6am. I hurriedly got myself up and out and although I was greeted with a picture of serenity and calm across the sheep field, in the far corner was our Mabel who was still continuing with her unsettled up and down routine. I waded through the rest of the sheep, who looked at me funny, wondering where on earth breakfast was, but I had other things on my mind! As I got closer to her, I could see that her waters had just gone and she was now in full delivery. Within a few minutes she was laid down on the grass and pushing hard whilst the pain of each contraction was reflected across her chubby little face. In what seemed like only moments later, Mabel gave birth to her firstborn, a gimmer lamb, which was our first lamb of the year. She did so well and sailed through the delivery and she's been doing a fantastic job as a mother ever since. With the cutest little lamb you could ever wish to see, she thankfully, confirmed that we had definitely made the right decision all those months before, on November 4th.

As we started to approach Easter, things started to once again get busier. Firstly we were preparing for the Easter holidays, (not that we get one of course) but whilst the kids are off school, we get an influx of additional customers in the teashop and of course I run our animal tours around the farm, twice a day. Ahead of time, I have to make sure that everything looks good and is in place, before the increased numbers of visitors arrived. The sorts of things that I need to be on top of are like making sure the hand washing facilities are all stocked up, with plenty of soap and paper towels, any nettles are cleared from around the field perimeters, any hosepipes or other farm equipment that may be laid about is removed or put away safely, and the walkover disinfectant mat is topped up and ready for day one. Alongside all the pre-Easter preparations, we were continuing with our lambing too. On Sunday morning, in the early hours, Pip, one of our first timers had not one, but two lambs, which was a big surprise. Pip, if you recall was the first lamb we had on the farm back in 2014. She was very much unexpected and had been born very small too. We had held off putting her in with the Tup until last November, but much like Mabel, decided we would go with it, but monitor her progress carefully. Well after having so many concerns and then having twins, we wondered why we had been so worried about her, but that wasn't the full story. Back in 2014 when Pip was born, her mother stopped feeding here very soon after her birth and was then bottle fed by the family until she was weaned.

Anyway, back to her twin. After she had given birth to her twin lambs, things started off so well, she cleaned the two of them up wonderfully, and got them both feeding and just at the moment when we thought we could breathe that sigh of relief, we noticed that she had taken a sudden disliking to the little boy. She was mothering the gimmer lamb perfectly, but with the ram lamb, she would push him away each time he came near. He soon learned that there were other ways to get fed and so each time his mother was taken up feeding his sister, he would come from behind and sneak a feed at the same time. We were worried that we would lose him quickly as both of the lambs were very small and so tried many ways to get Pip to accept him, but without much success. As all our lambs are birthed out in the field, we tried to force the relationship somewhat, and we put Pip and her twins into a pen in the field corner, so they were all close together for a few days. Wendy made up a bottle several times a day to top the little one up and to ensure he didn't go backwards. The really frustrating part of this situation was knowing that Pip herself was rejected, by her mother a couple of days after she was born and then there we were witnessing a very similar situation and we really expected so much more of her.

Things improved very quickly, as the little ram lamb was a determined little soul and after only a few days Wendy stopped topping him up as he was continuing to thrive with his unorthodox method of feeding from his mother and that was always going to be the best way for him to progress. Over time, Pip began to tolerate him more and more, even if she wasn't allowing him to feed via the normal route, she had stopped giving him a hefty nudge to clear him off, which was a big leap forward in their relationship. Initially we believed that we had eleven ewes, which we thought were in lamb this year and I say believed because we don't have them scanned to check, but all eleven had been in with Mac the Tup and they all looked like they had been growing nicely. We were almost half way through and at that point we had four sets of twins and Mabel's single. We had never had so many twins before and looking at the size of Delilah, Baa Baa and Coco, we were hopeful of even more. It was a lovely sunny spring day and I had found a few moments to park myself on the fence corner to watch the pregnant ewes, to see if there was any movement in the delivery ward and to check that all was well. That's when I noticed something odd. Although 'Brock', Stanley's twin sister, was nice and chunky, to look at, she had appeared to have not 'bagged up', like the other ewes. This is when their udder grows and fills up with colostrum and milk, shortly ahead of giving birth. I wandered over to her and as she is very tame she came over to see me. I took hold of her and without giving her a chance to say no, I straddled over her, facing her tail end and promptly thrust my right hand underneath her back end to have a rummage and find out for myself if her udder was in fact growing or not. Sometimes, because they are very woolly in the spring, their udder can often be hidden and so I wanted to check that this wasn't in fact the case. Unfortunately, my initial thoughts were correct and there wasn't a sniff of an udder and so for whatever reason, 'Brock' wasn't in lamb after all. What a shame, because I'm sure she'd have made a great mother, well there's always next year.

On a very busy day on the farm, when I was up to my ears in mucking out the stables, I was contacted by one of the local branches of the 'Yorkshire Country Women's Association' asking if I would pay them a visit one evening to talk about our adventures here on the farm. So the agreed date arrived and after much planning, what with us in the middle of lambing too, I just needed to be all organised and have somebody able to watch the sheep in my absence. Off I went, with all that I needed, bearing in mind that I used to talk to and present to large groups of people, in my previous life, but over the last 3 years haven't done anything remotely similar, unless you count entertaining the animals.

I travelled the short distance to Bubwith, where the meeting was taking place, and sat quietly as they finished going through the concluding business of their meeting. It was nice to see what went on and what they were up to, which included everything from their day trips out, all the way through to giving assistance and aid to those members of the association who were ill or just needed the support of their friends. The business was completed and I quickly set myself up, and after a short introduction, I was ready for the off. With the use of technology and lots of photos, I was able to visually walk the ladies through the journey we had taken up to that point and hopefully gave them an insight into some of the experiences and challenges we had gone through over the previous 3 years. After almost an hour, I was all done. Well I say I was done, but that wasn't quite the truth as there was then a wonderful supper which needed wading through before I could leave. It would have just been so rude if I hadn't sampled almost every delight that had so lovingly been baked or prepared for the evening, and besides, I could call it research as we did of course have a teashop! I really enjoyed the evening, met some lovely people and as a result I was now looking forward to my next scheduled event, as I had been asked to talk at another YCWA meeting and a Women's Institute meeting a little while later.

It was now mid-April and after weeks of anticipation the swallows had returned to Long Meadow Farm. Over a period of four days, all 5 pairs of swallows were back. They were very quickly on with rebuilding and renovating their nests and with a bit of rain here and there it gave them plenty of mud to get the job done right. One of the nests needed a little more attention than the others, as a wren family had moved into it and had almost completed all the work they were doing to it, when the swallows arrived home, swiftly turfed them out and then started to make it look the way they wanted it to. Ultimately we ended up with 10 swallow nests in and around the farmyard which was the most we have seen since moving in.

I'd always thought that it was a great investment putting in post and rail fencing around the farm, but that was before we met our latest crop of lambs. Now I know that we have experienced issues with lambs going walkabout in previous years, but my goodness, from only a couple of weeks old the little monsters were already giving me the run around. I swear it must be in their genes, as two years ago, the main culprits were Daisy and Daffodil and surprise, surprise, this time around it's their lambs who have decided not behave themselves. Because the lambs are so small, they can easily go under or over the bottom two rails in the fencing, but when they get to the other side of the fence and see the grass isn't all that greener, they lose all memory of how to return to mum through the fence. The result is that they open their little mouths and bleat like good 'uns. Oh, how they moan, and more often than not it's been happening just after it's got dark. Now I'm the sort of fella who can't stand back and just listen to the lambs bleating and in most cases, it's just that they've lost mum in the field, but more recently it's been time after time that they've been stuck on the wrong side of the fence. I would firstly stand and watch for a few minutes to see if they get back through themselves, but when they don't, that's when I have to get involved. I realise that if I leave them to themselves, they'll get back eventually, but I just can't stand back and do nowt. With Daisy for example on one side of the fence and her renegade little ram nose to nose with her through the fence, I have to go and help them out. That 'helping them out', more often than not involves far more running around than I could do with, in the dark. On one night alone, for 40 minutes I attempted to have that same little ram returned to mum and in the end, after he had covered every blade of grass in the cow field, off I went to get my big fishing net, only to find them all playing happy families once more, on my return. I know, I'm stupid and I should learn to just leave them to it.

It wasn't long until lambing 2017 came to an end, with us having our last two ewes, Baa Baa and Coco, both giving birth to twins. In total we had 17 lambs with 12 being ram lambs and 5 being gimmers. It's the most successful year we've had to date, and Mac the ram had done a fine job. This year's influx are most certainly the cutest lambs we've ever had too. There are just so many different colours, from those who are completely dark brown, like their Dad, there's black ones, black ones with a white flash on their head or their ear, two white ones and lots of multi-coloured ones with a mix of greys, browns, white and black. Very soon after lambing, it was time for some of last year's lambs to move on. It's sad, but they've gone to live on a farm up in North Yorkshire and we have to be sensible with these things as we only have so much space around here, and the grass only goes so far. I would get some of them into the freezer, but living with these women, who "don't eat lamb", I have to do the next best thing and sell them on. The sheep weren't the only animals who were leaving us, as Max our visiting billy goat also left to go home. At the time it appeared that he had been busy whilst he'd been with us, as both of our goats, Stacey and Bambi, were growing wider by the week, but we didn't expect their kids to arrive until June.

We would also be bidding farewell to George and Mildred, two of our Aylesbury ducks. Why would you get rid of them? I hear you ask, well let me explain. We had four ducks on the farm, George and Mildred, and Frank and Betty, (as in Spencer) who happen to be the parents. Now for far too many weeks, George had been getting into bother with his father, several times a day and to say the least it was getting just a tad wearing. For some reason, George believed he had the right to do just as he wished, just when he liked, but of course Dad thought differently, especially when it involved George making amorous advances towards his mother! To make matters worse, Betty had been sitting on a nest full of eggs for several weeks, but George kept chasing her off the nest and so the eggs were all being wasted and broken in the turmoil which ensued. So, to bring peace once more to the farmyard and to give me a break from hurtling around the place like a bat out of hell, separating these scrapping ducks every half hour, we found another forever home for them to live and so they soon tootled off too.

As I've previously mentioned, we have two llamas, who we named Miguel and Marguerita (Marj). Mac the ram was living with them and that relationship appeared to be working fine, thank goodness, so that was a weight off my mind. The thing was though, that I'd been trying to get close to the llamas for months, not just for a cuddle you understand, but to better care for them, but for too long, without success. The time arrived when I just needed to be able to get Miguel's head collar off, as it was just starting to get a little tight. Prior to coming to the farm, they hadn't had much people contact at all and were in a shed with other Llamas and Alpacas, with the result being that they were very nervous. Over some weeks I got them feeding out of my hand and as they are very inquisitive, they would always come and see me when I walked by their paddock or if I went in to feed them, but it's when you try to stroke them or make any physical contact with them that I'd have the real problem. With the help of my Dad, I put my extensive joinery skills to use, and we built a small pen inside their enclosure, in order to get them into a smaller more manageable space to work with. That pen was soon increased in height, as they both tried to leap over the sides and I didn't want them to hurt themselves, but their leaping didn't relent and so back to the drawing board I went.

I did some research online for a llama trainer locally who may be able to help me out, or at least offer some advice, but unfortunately without success. I then found myself watching countless YouTube videos and reading lots of information on the internet, to see if there was a way of getting closer to them and at the same time attempting to calm them down. They are such beautiful animals and I was keen to have them tamed, for their sake as well as for mine, well with me being only a little fella, I wouldn't want to get squished to death, would I? Eventually, I came to a realisation that what I needed to do was man up. For far too long I had been afraid to get trampled by them, but all the excuses in the world wasn't going to get that head collar off, and so off I went to their paddock armed only with my rope. I decided that watching all those cowboy films wasn't only going to benefit me in catching sheep, as it had done before, but Llamas too. I was going to lasso Miguel, in order that I could get the job sorted, once and for all. I stood leaning against their fence for around twenty minutes, with both of the two llamas and Mac staring back at me motionless, wondering what the heck I was up to. It was then time for action, the time had come and there was now no turning back. I grabbed the rope, quickly made my best lasso, filled my back pockets with Llama food, and with a bucket load of courage I headed in to the Llama field.

Moments later, there I was, hanging on for dear life as Miguel the Llama began leaping around the paddock, with me at the other end of the rope. Now when I say leaping, I mean he was higher up in the air than me and that's all of five feet six and a half inches. He was throwing his head about, with all four of his feet off the ground, trying to rid himself of this rope which was now around the base of his neck. I pulled him closer and closer, dragging him towards me and then I quickly tied the rope to a fence post and continued pulling him towards me until he was close enough to unclip his head collar and then once again release him. I swear, I thought my heart was coming out of my chest, it was beating so hard. The job was done, his old head collar was off and now I just need to replace it with a new one, but as I went off in search of a darkened room to lie down in, I decided that little job could wait for another day! For a couple of weeks after that traumatic experience, he had clearly gone off me as he wouldn't come anywhere near, but over time he was back to his normal self and feeding once more out of my hand.

The weather was continuing to be nice to us, so we agreed it was time to be getting more of those seedlings out of the greenhouse and planted out in the fresh air, so Wendy and I set to, clearing any weeds that had appeared over recent weeks in the veg patch. Merrily busying away we were when I heard another of those ear piercing shrieks from Wendy, but do you know, I wasn't quite sure whether it was a shriek of delight or fright. Initially I shouted over to her but soon quickly made my way across to where she was, to find out what the problem was, and as I got closer I needed no explanation at all. We had been experiencing far too many bunny incidents around that time, with a rabbit hole opening up in the middle of the greenhouse and another in the carrot patch too, but this was taking things too far. Wendy had been digging away when she started to push the spade into the ground, when the earth gave way, caving in, right in front of her. She then found herself looking down in amazement at 7 sets of eyes all peering up at her from this newly opened up hole. What she had found was a rabbit burrow full of young rabbits. By the size of them, these young rabbits were clearly old enough to be starting to fend for themselves, but what were we to do now. They were all huddled together, hoping that somehow what was going on was just a dream, but it wasn't. One of them made a break for freedom and disappeared through the netting which surrounded the soon to be sweetcorn patch, but the other six just sat quietly, hoping to goodness we hadn't noticed them, but we had. We couldn't just leave them open to the elements and so whilst we thought about what to do we lifted each of them one by one safely into a large container. We did a bit of further excavation and found that there was a separate tunnel which ran up alongside this now open burrow and so we thought it best that we carefully put each of the young bunnies down this tunnel and hope that all would end well as a result. We set things up afterwards, placing some netting over the hole, so they could come and go as they wished and in the days following, we did see fresh footprints each day, so we think that all ended well in that part of Bunnyville.

It was just a single bark that woke me that morning. Scout the eldest of our three border terriers, as well as losing his hearing, has taken to alerting me that he needs to go and spend a penny. Unfortunately this so often happens at some unearthly hour, and even though my bed was calling me back for just another hour or so, I decided that I may as well just get up and on with life. The sun was already very bright and I was soon thinking about what jobs lay in store for the day. Soon enough I was excitedly stepping out the door, with that stupid grin on my face. In fact I think that I was singing too, well who wouldn't on such a beautiful day? Then it was decision time, footwear, what was it going to be today? I went down the lazy route and decided to wear my trainers, rather than go down the more energetic, lacing-up-my-boots route. As you do in these situations, my first foot went in, my left, followed by my second which was obviously my right. Now this was when my day suddenly took a very bad turn for the worse. Well it's not what you'd expect at 5 o'clock in the morning, or any time of the day for that matter. As my right foot slipped inside the training shoe, which happened so quickly, there was an almighty pop! Or maybe it was more of a crunch, but either way it was followed very quickly by a squelch. I needed no thinking time at all to understand exactly what had just happened. I had previously experienced a toad in the trainer many months before, but I was able to stop the squish ahead of time, but this time the speed of action meant that there was no baling out early on this occasion and this time it wasn't a toad!

Oh dear! I quickly pulled my foot out of the shoe and what beheld my eyes was not a pretty sight, not a pretty sight at all. Mr. Snail had seemingly made an error of judgement the night before and must have been attracted to the sweet smells which were exuding from my trainer and so had decided to take a closer look. Big mistake! He was now left with half of him and his house stuck to my heel and the rest of his remains were smeared across the inside of the shoe. I've said it before and I'll say it again...check your shoes Shaun, before you put them on each morning. Heaven knows what will be lying in wait next time, I dread to think.

Thinking back to when we were younger, much younger, I know was a right pain each time Wendy got anywhere near the end of every one of her pregnancies. I'm not the most patient of people and whilst out on the road, before the arrival of the mass-marketed mobile phones, I would have to find myself a payphone several times a day, to call her to check that all was well and to make sure she hadn't gone into labour. Well, the thing was, it was that time once again, as we reached towards the end of a number of pregnancies around the farm and I've got to say it was driving me bananas. Firstly our two pygmy goats seriously looked like they were going to explode and from my reckoning they should be due any day now, but as much as I'd like to, this impatient little soul can't choose either the day or the time that their kids are born. Alongside the goats of course we had Lyndsey and Flora, two of the highland cows whom we were still hoping were pregnant. I say hoping, because we didn't have them scanned to check and we don't have the vet in with his extra-long marigold to check either, we just let nature take its course.

In the previous two years, around the same time, I had spent far too long leaning against that fence, just staring, wondering, are they or are they not and on both occasions, we've ended up with no calves. This year though, things were different. They definitely looked like they were growing. Other heifers who were at the same party, with the same bull, had either had calves or were well on the way to having them, so all the signs were good. In a moment of desperation, I got the two of them into the race and had a rummage down below to see if they were starting to 'bag up', which is when their udder starts to more fully develop, ahead of giving birth. The only problem was, that it did feel as though there was a start of udders growing, in both cattle, but as I didn't have anything to compare it to, I wasn't sure whether they were on their way or not. In the end I just had to once again take a step back and leave things for nature to take its course.

14 AWAITING THE BIG DAY

The weather was now getting noticeably warmer and it was time once again, to get the sheep sheared. I had arranged for Mark, the shearer and his sister Jenny to come over and get the job sorted and they duly arrived at Long Meadow Farm…but they were early! I had been busy getting roped in to washing up in the Teashop kitchen and hadn't noticed that I had received calls and texts from Mark letting us know that they would be arriving early. "Give us two minutes" I shouted, as they stepped out of their van. I grabbed a bucket of feed and escorted the sheep through from where they were until we reached the field, where I had previously made a shearing pen in the corner. I had been saving this field to house the sheep after they had all been sheared and so the grass was wonderful, it was just what they were after. In fact they were so interested in this grass that they weren't much interested in the bucket of feed I was trying to tempt them with at all, it was that field full of new green grub they were after. Anyway, 25 minutes later, with Mark and Jenny's help, the ewes were all in the shearing pen and we were ready for action. Soon enough the fleeces were coming off and before they went back into the field, I would check each of their feet to ensure that were still in good nick and trim them up as required.

It wasn't long until they were all sheared and back onto pasture, they were loving life, but that didn't last long at all, as it soon started to rain. Well I'm not sure about other sheep, but mine don't mind any sort of weather…except rain, and without their woolly coats on, it was fast becoming a nightmare for the poor little dears. They all just stood there moaning a bucket load with their sad faces on until I moved them back into the field with the shelter and only then did my peace and quiet return. Who was it who said, "Let's get Shetlands, they're a really hardy breed, they'll cope in all weathers!"

The pregnancy problems continued around the farmyard, well into June and our Betty had been in a right mood all week! Generally she had been staying in the house and keeping herself to herself, but all of a sudden, like overnight, her mood just changed and it wasn't a pretty sight. I had obviously discussed her with Wendy and you'd think after living with females for over 33 years now, I'd understand them a little more, but apparently not. She's got awfully lazy of late too, spending much of her time just sitting on her rear, in her room, being antisocial. Can I confirm, that it's Betty who was being lazy and antisocial, not Wendy! So, there I was minding my own business, getting on with the things I needed to get on with, when I walked past their house. Betty, literally flew out of that front door like she was possessed, ranting at me about something or other. The thing was though, that I couldn't understand what she was saying….well as Betty's an Aylesbury duck, obviously I didn't have a clue what she was on about, did I? I can only put it down to her hormones being all over the place and getting bored rigid having to sit on that nest of eggs for most of the day, well I suppose I'd be the same too!

It was around that same time that I learned yet another lesson, never leave your newly collected eggs on view…. not even for a minute. I'd finished my morning rounds and everyone was fed and watered. I'd collected the hen's eggs and was all set to give them a wash, but decided to give them a quick hot water rinse and sit them in the sink, whilst I put the wheel barrow away. Big mistake! I then returned to wash them and in what can only have been a minute or so, they had disappeared, well almost. The resulting sight that welcomed me, from eleven eggs, was one broken shell and the remains of a single yolk. The rest had vanished, but the footprints gave the game away…rooks! They must have been watching me, thought Christmas had arrived early and seized their opportunity to grab a free breakfast. Although I wasn't a happy bunny at all, as you would imagine, I was impressed with the speed that they had executed their plan. That that didn't help me though, because I was now almost a dozen eggs down and my ears were about to start ringing from 'er indoors, for not having enough eggs for her baking. I couldn't lay them myself and so all I could do was to quickly get into the hen pen and somehow encourage the hens to lay more eggs. After a little bit of chat and a whole lot of singing, an hour or so later, they duly baled me out and I walked away with another half a dozen eggs. They got extra corn that night, I'll tell ya!

We have been lucky enough to have young tawny owls on the farm each year we have been here and this year was to be no different. Just as dusk was falling, we were blessed to have a real treat around the place. That's the time when the two newly fledged young tawnies came to life and it was such a joy to see. On many evenings we were able to walk quietly up to the tree they were in and stand right underneath the branch the birds were sitting on and look up at them. As they stared back, with what looked like saucer-sized eyes, blinking slowly as they do, they were I'm sure wondering, what on earth these clowns were doing staring up at them.

Back at Christmas time, Wendy, bought me a really fancy watch for Christmas. It would tell me what the weather was doing, it gave me the day's date, it relayed any messages I had received on my phone, it could play my musical choices which were also on my phone and unsurprisingly, I could even tell the time with it. But best of all, it has come into its own this week as it told me that I had covered over 5000 steps in just a couple of hours and that was just chasing flamin' runaway lambs, now that has to be a real boon!

The weather was continuing to be warm, well in fact it was unseasonably warm, like the hottest June since 1975, and so as a result we've had additional new challenges to deal with. Under normal circumstances I would check all of our water troughs and feeders each morning and again in the evening, but during the warmer weather that has to be increased. It's weird, but sometimes it's as though you just turn your back after topping up a feeder and the pigs for example empty a full cast iron water feeder in one go, but I wonder to myself, would they have in fact done that if I hadn't woken them up from their sunbathing snooze? I thought that in my wisdom, as it was so warm, that some of the animals may like a bit of a shower to cool them down. With the cows, it was only Monica and Flora who were keen on the shower, the other two ladies were having none of it and would just walk in the other direction when they saw me dragging the hosepipe towards the cow field. The pigs too love a good soaking, but you know that immediately they will go and roll in the mud, which doesn't half make a mess, but at the same time it does protect them from the sun. The ponies are another pair who like to get cooled down, but again they will, after getting hosed down, go and roll on their backs in the dirt, every single time, but they even do that after getting groomed each time too.

We have had a miraculous occurrence on the farm, only two nights before. It was on my final rounds in the evening, I was in the cow field just checking that all was well, particularly with our two, hopefully expectant cows, Lyndsey and Flora and willing the time away so that the calves we had hoped for so long would be born, and that's when the miracle happened. Each of our cows has their own character and personality. Monica at nineteen is the matriarch, the boss, she only has one speed setting, which is slow and loves a cuddle more than the others. Morag, her three year old calf often plays the moody teenager, taking advantage of her mother's good nature, but gets pushed around by the others, when Mum's not around. Lyndsey, is the quietest in nature, but has the biggest mouth, if that makes sense, as she can be a right moaner when she wants to be. She has the fanciest coat too with it being the thickest, and it also looks like someone has spent hours putting highlights into it too, which hasn't happened by the way, it's all natural. Finally we have our Flora, who beyond all the others is by far the most temperamental cow we have. In fact she is the archetypal moody cow.

Flora, more than the others is the one who isn't keen on a cuddle, won't stand still for grooming and is the only one of them to ever give me a kick. Well, anyway, things all changed that night, as I walked towards her to check all was well, for a change, she remained rooted to the spot. After reaching her she didn't immediately walk away from me, but just turned and gave me a look, a look which I thought that I'd seen before, not with her, but with some of the pregnant sheep. I gave her a stroke and very quickly I could feel that her yet-to-be born calf was having a party inside her and the look she gave me was one of...help! It may have been that it was only wind and not any calf movement at all, but time would tell. We had experienced similar behaviour many times with the sheep during their pregnancies and leading up to them giving birth, so we were hopeful that any birth with Flora wasn't far away. As it happened her good mood continued from then on, but alas her calf still wasn't making an appearance on the farm.

At the time we were awaiting not only calves being born, but we were also waiting on Stacey and Bambi the pygmy goats, delivering their kids, and Betty the duck was diligently sticking to her task of sitting on her nest of eggs, so they couldn't be far from hatching either. As much as I was looking forward to them all arriving, I just hoped that they wouldn't all appear at the same time. It was a sunny Thursday afternoon and it was time to give the cows some hay. I'd been holding off putting them into the newly grown top field until any calves arrived. So they were being left in the middle field until the big day. As a result, I've been topping them up every so often, obviously without encouraging them to be putting on too much weight, as I don't want them to struggle giving birth, by them having whopper calves. Anyway, whilst sorting them out, I could hear Bambi, one of our goats, bellowing away, down by the stables. Being heavily pregnant she had been moaning quite a bit over the previous few days and so it appeared that things were at last starting to move towards the new kids being born. She was getting steadily louder and louder, but I needed to let my ginger ladies out of their pen, before I headed back to the farmyard. Just moments later I was hurtling back down the green mile and even over the sound of the quad engine, I could hear her moaning. Brakes on, engine off, parking brake in place and off the quad I leapt, and through the two sets of gates, slamming them behind me and into the stable where Bambi was standing looking very pleased with herself. Dash! I'd missed it!

There she was busying away cleaning up her newborn kid, a girl, who incidentally was her complete double, with a black front end and a completely white back end. At the top of my voice I shouted for the troops to come and see what was going on and before I knew it an audience of admirers had congregated at the stable door to coo over this new kid on the block. Then, just when we thought that things were settling down, our Bambi, surprised us all and no more than twenty minutes after the first birth, she popped out her second kid and again it was a girl. Once again I lifted up my head and hollered… "twins!" and once again the troops all came running. This one was very different from the first and as much as the first looked like a double of her mother, the second looked exactly like Dad! Goodness me, that was a lot of excitement for one day, two girls born to Bambi and now we just had to wait for Stacey's baby to be born too and hopefully, that wouldn't be a long wait away.

Sure enough, we didn't have to wait long at all, as the very next day, Stacey, who happens to be Bambi's mother, started belly aching just after lunchtime and by five o'clock, she had also given birth to not one, but again two kids as well, but this time she had a boy and a girl. The boy looks just like his mother, but the little girl is something else. She had a striking white coat with several jet black spots dotted across her body, she was just beautiful, but then again I thought they all were! In the following days both mothers were doing a great job and I have to say, it never ceases to amaze me how instinctively these mothers know what they are doing. There were a few minor hiccups, with little ones attempting to feed from the wrong mother, but things settled down very quickly. After only twenty minutes the kids were up and about and in only a couple of days they were skipping and leaping about the goat pen, just like you would imagine kids to be. It was only a couple of days in and they were getting into mischief with a couple of them already squeezing their chubby little bodies under the gate to go exploring that big world out there. I could see for sure that we were going to be given the run around in the coming month. Ooh and I couldn't wait!

I'd been thinking for some time about moving the goats to another part of the farm, and at the same time my plan was to provide them with even more activities to keep them occupied so that hopefully they would not need to go wandering around the farm for additional entertainment. So the plan got underway. I shipped the hens out into a new enclosure, which then freed up their old house and pen for the goats to move into and when the kids were a couple of weeks old, they could make the trip down the field to their new home. I gathered up countless pieces of timber and after dumping them all in the new goat pen, I grabbed my tools and the bits I needed and set to building, what I thought was a really marvelous climbing frame for the goats. Mr. L, my old woodwork teacher would surely have been very proud. I even had enough bits left to make a lovely see-saw too, so I'm thinking they'll have plenty to keep themselves busy and hopefully out of mischief too. Well maybe!

After the previous week's goat fest on the farm, I had hoped things were settling down in the goat pen, but alas, that wasn't quite how things were turning out. Those little goats have got so much energy and if they're not sleeping, they're bouncing their way around the place, at breakneck speed. Other than coping with them burning off all this energy, we have had a bit of a situation to deal with. As part of my morning farmyard routine, my running order means that I take care of the ponies ahead of the goats. Well, as I was sorting out the ponies, one morning this week, I could hear clattering and banging going on in the next door stable. Each time there was a clatter, there was also a squeal immediately after. I went to investigate further and discovered that Bambi, the younger of the two mother goats was, for whatever reason, giving Stacey's little boy a hefty wallop, if he went anywhere near her. I had stern words with Bambi, on a couple of occasions, but my words fell on deaf ears and she just continued to be nasty towards him. He on the other hand was just attempting to stay out of her way and was rather subdued as a result of her actions. My plan has always been that I would move the goats to a larger pen when the kids were born, where I have built a climbing frame and see-saw for them and lots more space to keep them occupied. As a result of all this shenanigans, I decided to move Stacey and her twins up to the new pen early and then after a few days of settling in, I then moved Stacey and her two kids in as well. It wasn't long before happiness and harmony once again reigned in Goatville.

The births were coming thick and fast on the farm now, but before you get too excited, it wasn't my coos, we were still awaiting that big day for the ladies. It was Betty, the duck, who brought us the new babies. Over the space of 48 hours she had ten of her eggs hatch. Unfortunately one of the ducklings didn't make it, as she had problems and died, but the remaining nine were all healthy and full of energy. Which is just as well really, as Frank and Betty would march them around the farm from dawn till dusk, every day, without much time for a breath at all. As parents they are doing a great job and have learned from their experiences the previous year. She was very protective of these little yellow bundles of fluff and if I didn't give them a wide enough berth, then she would snap at my legs as I walked past them, just to warn me off. Both Frank and Betty had their own roles to play in the rearing of the ducklings, with Betty's job to see off any unwanted interest from us humans or other animals, and this then left Frank to sort out any misbehaviour from the young 'uns and it appeared to work a treat.

When Queenie the last of our original pet hens passed away, she left behind her Rita the very best friend a hen could ever have wished for. Now Rita had lived with her from being just days old and spent most of the hours in every day following her around the farmyard. They were most definitely like chalk and cheese, with Queenie being the complete lady, very well behaved and loving the attention from anyone who came to visit. Rita on the other hand was a total nightmare, well most of the time anyway. Nobody could get close enough to her to stroke her, she was the one who would be in the thick of any trouble in the farmyard, whether she should have been involved or not, and she was unsurprisingly always the last to get herself off to bed each evening. So why am I telling you this? Well, basically because after Queenies untimely death, Rita appeared to turn over a completely new leaf and it was as if there had been a complete transformation. If I didn't know better, I would have said that Queenie, upon her death bed had taken it upon herself to have a little word with Rita, to enlighten her as to the benefits of playing ball with these human folk that she lived amongst, as the result of doing so would bring countless blessings her way.

Before her good friend was even cold, Rita was like a new hen! Rather than charging around the place at great speed for most of the day, she had taken it upon herself to take her time with things and slow down, and very quickly she saw the benefits of doing so. Staff and visitors began to feed her, spend time with her and give her attention, which she had never experienced before. She soon realised that being nice to people paid dividends far more than pecking at people and being standoffish and antisocial. She is now a pleasure to have on the farm ,and I'm sure another benefit of her behavioural turnaround is that she is laying far more of her beautiful blue eggs than she had ever done before, which was great news for us. We hoped that this reformed Rita would continue in the same way going forward, and hoped that maybe she would have a word with a few of our other residents about their behaviour too, with the goats being first on that list.

After moving the goats into their new surroundings a couple of weeks previous, they very quickly settled in, but then decided that they would do a little renovating and remodeling around the place. Picture the scene, very tall, but over hanging white poplars line along the front side of their home with chestnuts and oaks along the back so they have plenty of shade for those far too few sunny days. They also had probably twenty bushes or trees in there also to break things up a little and add variety to their landscape…well at the time, that's what I thought. It appeared that Stacey and Bambi didn't agree with my thinking on that and promptly took it upon themselves to decimate every single one of the bushes and trees. Apparently my goats loved these bushes and trees as much as me, but I loved to look at them whereas they loved to eat them. Every single bush or tree had each of their branches systematically stripped of leaves from earth to my shoulder height, which was as far up as they could reach on their tip toes. Afterwards I pruned everything back, so at least it looked better and we hoped that it would put an end to their tree pruning days for the foreseeable future, but unfortunately that wasn't to be as they immediately began removing the bark from each tree in turn. As it happens, the tree stripping wasn't the only concern I had regarding the goats. For the last few weeks I have been witnessing far too much bullying going on around the farm in one way or another and I don't like it one bit.

Before Stacey and Bambi had their kids, life was sweet and the two of them, mother and daughter, got on great and that continued all the way through until the time that they both gave birth to their sets of twins. For whatever reason things all changed from that point in time and Bambi began to bully her mother. I'm not sure why it was happening, was it because she was jealous that Stacey's attention was taken elsewhere? Was it because she felt the need to be overprotective of her own two kids, or was it that she was just down right mean? I may never know the answers to those questions, but what I did know was that I wasn't not going to stand around and watch whilst the bullying went on, and that went for the other animals too. Yes, we primarily saw it going on with the goats, but it had been happening in the pig pen, the sheep field, the cow meadow and with the hens too.

With all this bullying going on around the place, it did take me back to when I was much younger and witnessed bullying as a child, whilst at school. Now as much as I've always been short in stature and back in those days I was definitely a 'ginger nut', I was not the one getting bullied. Why? Because I was never going to allow myself to be bullied. Back in those days I had a temperament which matched my hair colour and so, little or not I was always going to be standing up for myself. I recall on many occasions, that I would get involved in other people's battles, because I saw from the outside that somebody was being bullied and wasn't going to stand by and let it happen, if I could do something about it. All too often I couldn't do a great deal about it as I was half the size of the bullies, but nevertheless I tried, and was surprisingly successful on numerous occasions. That I suppose is the benefit of having a rather large gob and sounding mean, well maybe not the sounding mean part!

I can remember as a twentysomething, being out on a walk with our rescue dog 'Ziggy' and came across a gang of youths chasing two girls, who eventually caught up with them and soon began physically abusing these same two girls, laying into them. As was normally the case, I didn't think twice, well it's easy to talk yourself out of it if you think about it, isn't it? I shouted to Ziggy and we ran across the playing field where we were, in order to reach this unsavoury activity which was going on. I waded in, again without thinking much about it at all, until I had done enough that these two girls, now battered, bruised and crying could quickly get off home and leave this gang behind. It was at that point that I felt a whack around the back of my head and turned to see further youths had arrived on the scene, with one of them wielding a length of 2 by 4 timber which he was just swinging back to take a second strike at my bonce! Well, OK, maybe I did come off worst sometimes, whilst standing up against bullies, but whilst I have any sort of influence with bullies, I'll forever be using it, whether on the farm or off it!

The time was at last drawing near for our long awaited Highland calves to make an appearance at Long Meadow Farm. Lyndsey and Flora had been picked up at the end of July 2016 and had been away partying with the bull until early October that same year. We had left them away with the bull for that length of time to enable them to go through more than one cycle, which would increase their chances of being serviced by the bull during their stay, and therefore becoming pregnant. From my reckoning they could potentially give birth anytime realistically from early May 2017, but due to their size we didn't expect any movement until a little later in the summer. Since failing miserably on our first two attempts at calving, back in 2015 and 2016, I have chosen not to have them scanned and just decided to look out for the signs which would tell me that they were in calf and also as things progressed these signs would also show me that any forthcoming birth was imminent. As is in my nature, I commenced watching Lyndsey and Flora much more closely from the beginning of April to see if I could observe any of the signs which Pete Fletcher had told me to look out for. These signs obviously included an increase in their size, some growth on their udder and some changes going on around their rear end, which I needed to look out for. I had seen that they had both increased in size over the recent weeks and months and after marching all four of the cows through the race one by one, I was able to have a rummage down below to compare each of their udders to establish if Lyndsey and Flora were any larger than the norm. From my limited knowledge Flora definitely was, but I wasn't sure about Lyndsey. Well, as you could imagine, my hopes were raised. Unfortunately, shortly after the race rummaging I witnessed some mounting going on with Monica and Morag both mounting Lyndsey, which generally happens when a cow is in season. Well, that put paid to any calf springing forth from Lyndsey's belly any time soon and so it was down to my final hopes resting with our Flora. Now to say that I was resting a great deal of hope on Flora is an understatement to say the least. I have wanted to be around highland calves since being young. This was now our third attempt at making it happen and my patience was being tested to even greater heights than ever before.

After our disappointment with Lyndsey I pushed any doubts to the back of my mind and started to notice further changes with Flora which, to me all pointed towards a positive outcome in the days to come. As mentioned, Flora had up to this point always been the temperamental member of our Highland family, but out of the blue this all changed. I was able to walk up to her, several times a day and without any fuss she would lick my hand then stand there and allow me to stroke her face, her head and back and then let me feel her udder to see if there was any movement going on down below. Late in the evening when she was laid down I would go up to her and feel her sides, to see if I could feel movement inside and felt positive that the movement I was feeling, was definitely that of a growing calf inside her. With this noticeable change in her temperament and these further positive signs, it again bolstered my hopes even further for a magical outcome in the end. Time was now pressing on though and we were well into July, but with no calves yet making an appearance. Every day I was reading books and trawling the internet for signs of hope, which would tell me that calves were often born late. It soon got to the stage where I was now resting my hopes on a particular forum online where some breeders had experienced calves going beyond their due date by up to three weeks. Each morning I would rush out in the early hours, excitedly anticipating that today was going to be that day and I would find that little ginger teddy bear staggering around her mother's legs, but each day my hopes were dashed. Wendy and I were so excited as we waited for our calf to be born and as sad as it may seem, we would regularly take a drive across the Wolds and through Thixendale, just in order that we could pull over at the roadside and talk to the Highland cows with their newborn calves who were in the roadside pastures.

Very quickly the time came and went when I could justifiably extend the prospective due date any further than I already had and now needed to face up to the fact that sadly I wasn't going to witness the birth of a Highland calf any time soon on the farm. I was completely hacked off about it, but what could I do. It didn't matter that I was being asked several times a day if we had a calf yet, the outcome was the same. It made no difference that I had already named the calf, it made no difference that I'd been waiting for Doric for so long, now was just not to be our time. For the record, his or her name was going to be 'Doric' as Doric is the dialect from the North East of Scotland and particularly in and around Aberdeenshire. I left that part of the world as a three year old and so unfortunately left without picking up the local accent. By calling my calf Doric, I felt that it would be my way of marking my heritage and history further afield and my way of making some sort of a mark south of the border. Never mind, onward and upward, maybe next time, eh!

EPILOGUE

Without doubt, the most common question I get asked when I'm out and about and normally with a little jest is… "Are you still 'Living the Dream'? This question stems from my column of the same name, which I write in the Yorkshire Post. I sometimes think that people presume that in some way the novelty has worn off, or we have found things too difficult to contend with. We leapt into our adventure with our eyes wide open and I can confirm that our dream is most certainly very much alive and kicking. What I think is that we can all meander our way through life focusing on the negative, because in my view that takes less effort, but we all have it in our power to change things and make our own dreams become a reality! In our case, we made the decision to take our passion for the outdoors and our desire to make changes to simplify our life. We wanted to get out there and make it happen, whatever was thrown our way. When we leapt, we did so without a great deal of thought about how we were going to cope with the life changes we were about to experience. Yes, we can definitely say that we were a little naive, and from time to time we can definitely say that we wore rose tinted glasses. But the hard work was certainly expected, as were the long hours. Dealing with the changeable weather conditions and the frustrations of working with livestock were factors we hadn't realised would impact so heavily on so much that we've been involved in. We've experienced everything from frozen pipes in the winter, hypothermia during spring lambing, all the way through to not enough shade for the cattle in the summer and too much rain for the sheep in the autumn. The seasons have certainly challenged us in our journey so far, but like all of the challenges we've experienced, they have made us stronger. They have helped us appreciate more readily all that we have and the wonderful opportunity we have been afforded to live our dream. Good or bad, highs or lows, the experiences over the last few years have without doubt helped us become who we are today.

ACKNOWLEDGEMENTS

A big thank you to the many people who have assisted in so many ways to make this adventure less of a bumpy ride than it could've been, but special thanks go to Pete Fletcher, Rob Matthews, Mark and Jenny Dale, Lucy Oates, Simon Richardson, Matthew and Sarah Green, Steven and Emma Darley, The Layton Family, the 80+ people who held back the tide on Boxing Day 2015 and of course the man above, who has blessed us with all that we have.

Printed in Poland
by Amazon Fulfillment
Poland Sp. z o.o., Wrocław